T0378577

Educational Leadership for Social Justice and Improving High-Needs Schools

A volume in
International Research on School Leadership
David Gurr and Elizabeth T. Murakami, *Series Editors*

Educational Leadership for Social Justice and Improving High-Needs Schools

Findings from 10 Years of International Collaboration

edited by

Bruce G. Barnett
University of Texas at San Antonio

Philip A. Woods
University of Hertfordshire

INFORMATION AGE PUBLISHING, INC.
Charlotte, NC • www.infoagepub.com

Library of Congress Cataloging-in-Publication Data

A CIP record for this book is available from the Library of Congress
http://www.loc.gov

ISBN: 978-1-64802-372-9 (Paperback)
　　　 978-1-64802-373-6 (Hardcover)
　　　 978-1-64802-374-3 (E-Book)

Copyright © 2021 Information Age Publishing Inc.

All rights reserved. No part of this publication may be reproduced, stored in a
retrieval system, or transmitted, in any form or by any means, electronic, mechanical,
photocopying, microfilming, recording or otherwise, without written permission
from the publisher.

Printed in the United States of America

CONTENTS

Acknowledgments ix

PART I
HISTORY AND REFLECTION OF THE ISLDN

1 Introduction... 3
Bruce G. Barnett and Philip A. Woods

2 International Educational Leadership Projects............................... 13
David Gurr, Lawrie Drysdale, and Helen Goode

3 Socially Just School Leadership: Ten Years of Learning
From Each Other.. 31
Pamela S. Angelle and Michele Morrison

4 What Factors Help and Hinder the Work of Social Justice
Leaders? A Summary of Findings From the Social Justice
Leadership Strand.. 51
Deirdre Torrance, Ian Potter, Christine Forde, Pamela Angelle,
Helene Ärlestig, Christopher Branson, Annie Cheng, Fiona King,
Rachel McNae, Paul Miller, Michele Morrison, Katarina Norberg,
Elson Szeto, and Joe Travers

vi ▪ Contents

5 The International School Leadership Development Network's High-Needs Schools Strand: Ten Years of History............................ 73
Jami Royal Berry, Betty Alford, Mette L. Baran, Karen Bryant, Kristine Hipp, and Glady Van Harpen

6 Review of Methodological Approaches in Studies of High-Needs Schools Across Multinational Contexts................................. 93
Nathern S. A. Okilwa

PART II

CROSS-STRAND AND CROSS-COUNTRY COMPARISON

7 From the Mouths of Babes: Policy Recommendations From P–12 Students.. 115
Keneisha Harrington, Britt-Inger Keisu, Björn Ahlström, Parker M. Andreoli, and Hans W. Klar

8 Leading Successfully in High-Needs Contexts: Australian and New Zealand Cases 135
David Gurr, Lawrie Drysdale, Fiona Longmuir, Kieran McCrohan, Rachel McNae, Michele Morrison, and Sylvia Robertson

9 A Comparison of Social Justice Leadership Meaning and Praxis: The Interplay of Unique Social Cultural Contexts in Turkish, Palestinian, and Lebanese High-Needs Schools.......... 153
Khalid Arar, Deniz Örücü, and Julia Mahfouz

10 Economic, Cultural, Associational, and Critical Justice in Schools in Catalonia, Spain and Baja California, Mexico: A Pilot Study 173
Brian Corrales-Maytorena, Claudia Navarro-Corona, Charles Slater, Patricia Silva, Serafín Antúnez, and Michael E. Lopez

11 Social Justice Leadership in High-Need Contexts: Strategies From Principals in Spain, Mexico, and the United States 201
Cristina Moral, Elizabeth Murakami, and Celina Arcadia-Torres

12 Leadership for Sustained School Improvement in a High-Need School in Nepal and in Southern California: Vital Practices and Processes in Fostering Learning.............................. 221
Chetanath Gautam, Rosario Ambriz, and Betty Alford

Contents ▪ **vii**

13 Social Justice Imperatives for Leaders in High-Needs
Schools: Research From ISLDN Studies and Issues
for Future Consideration 241
Stephen Jacobson and Paul Miller

14 What Have We Learned About Social Justice Leadership
in Struggling and Underserved Schools and Communities? 259
Philip A. Woods and Bruce G. Barnett

About the Editors 283

ACKNOWLEDGMENTS

There are many people who have made possible the work of the International School Leadership Development Network (ISLDN) over the past 10 years. We acknowledge the British Educational Leadership Management and Administration Society (BELMAS) and the University Council Educational Administration (UCEA) for their support and recognition of the project; the teams of international researchers who have designed, conducted, and analyzed the research and worked in cooperation with each other; and all the school leaders and others who have given of their time to participate in the research and who commit their professional lives to the advancement of social justice in education.

Educational Leadership for Social Justice and Improving High-Needs Schools, page ix
Copyright © 2021 by Information Age Publishing
All rights of reproduction in any form reserved.

PART I

HISTORY AND REFLECTION OF THE ISLDN

CHAPTER 1

INTRODUCTION

Bruce G. Barnett
University of Texas at San Antonio

Philip A. Woods
University of Hertfordshire

This book acknowledges the realization that school leadership matters. Numerous studies and reports verify the important roles that principals, head teachers, and directors play in developing a school environment conducive to students' academic and social emotional learning, teachers' growth and development, and parental engagement (Day, Gu, & Sammons, 2016; Leithwood, 2012; Organization for Economic Co-operation and Development, 2016; Robinson, Lloyd, & Rowe, 2008). Although studies of school leadership have long been the purview of English-speaking Western cultures, increasing attention is being devoted to understanding school leadership practices in other developed and developing nations around the world (Arlestig, Day, & Johansson, 2016; Day & Gurr, 2014; Hallinger & Walker, 2017; Hernandez & Murakami, 2016; Ylimaki & Jacobson, 2011).

As educators and policy makers seek to understand global educational policies and practices, regional and international networks of nations, nongovernmental organizations, and multi-national companies have emerged

---

Educational Leadership for Social Justice and Improving High-Needs Schools, pages 3–12
Copyright © 2021 by Information Age Publishing
All rights of reproduction in any form reserved.

(Pashiardis, 2008). In particular, the field of educational leadership preparation and development is becoming more engaged in international collaboration (Lumby, Crow, & Pashiardis, 2008). Walker and Townsend (2010) revealed successful cross-national partnerships: (a) congregate a small group of "like-minded energetic people" who are able to locate funding, create a vision, and establish political support; (b) rely on linkages with existing professional networks; (c) embrace and encourage diversity; (d) establish high-profile events in different locations; and (e) promote activities, events, and products that support colleagues from different countries who otherwise would not be able to participate.

Guided by these principles of effective cross-national partnerships, in 2008 members of two professional educational leadership professional organizations, the British Educational Leadership, Management, and Administration Society (BELMAS) and the University Council for Educational Administration (UCEA), began discussions about establishing an international comparative research project. As a result of these conversations, the International School Leadership Development Network (ISLDN) was launched in 2010. Two research strands of the ISLDN have emerged: (1) leadership for social justice and (b) leadership in high-need schools. The network consists of researchers from over 20 countries conducting empirical research on leadership for social justice and leadership in high-need schools. The project's website (https://isldn.weebly.com) describes each of these strands and the research team members conducting studies around the globe.

To commemorate the 10-year anniversary of the ISLDN, this book is a compilation of the work conducted by network scholars. Other international research consortia have emerged in the 21st century; however, the ISLDN is the second longest operating project after the International Successful School Principalship Project (ISSPP), which began in 2001. Since its creation, ISLDN scholars have delivered papers at a variety of international conferences and shared findings in research publications, including books (Angelle, 2017; Murakami, Gurr, & Notman, 2019) and special issues of journals (Bryant, Cheng, & Notman, 2014; Gurr & Drysdale, 2018).

Until now, however, the dissemination of ISLDN research has occurred separately for each strand. Therefore, the purpose of this book is to document the history of the ISLDN and to provide descriptions and reflections of the project's research findings, methodologies, and collaborative processes across the two strands. This volume captures studies of school leaders from 19 countries representing six continents—Africa, Asia, Australia and Oceania, Europe, North America, and South America. The authors examine important external and internal contextual factors influencing schools in different cultural settings, provide insights about the values and practices of social justice leaders working in high-need school settings, and critically examine the ISLDN's current body of work and suggest how future research can address the project's gaps and oversights.

At the suggestion of the network members, the editors (each representing one of the sponsoring professional organizations) developed a call for proposals that was distributed to all members of the ISLDN. This book reflects members' collective insights and contributions, many of whom have been involved from the beginning of the project. Part I reports important historical information by examining the development of the network, synthesizing the methodological approaches utilized, and summarizing key findings from the two strands. Part II expands the existing ISLDN research by reporting empirical findings across both strands in multiple international settings. Finally, the concluding chapter synthesizes the findings and insights of the contributing authors, the significance of the project in the educational leadership landscape, and promising future research directions for the network.

PART I: HISTORY AND REFLECTION OF THE ISLDN

These chapters recount the evolution of this consortium as one of a growing number of international research projects focusing on school leadership. Detailed accounts of the formation of and findings from each research strand are reported as well as a methodological analysis of these studies. Several chapters examine promising future lines of inquiry to expand our knowledge base of school leadership in different cultural contexts, especially where social justice leaders work in high-need settings.

Chapter 2 positions the ISLDN project within an array of other 21st century international educational leadership research projects. David Gurr, Lawrie Drysdale, and Helen Goode compare and contrast the ISLDN with six other international research projects: (1) International Successful School Principalship Project, (2) International Study of the Preparation of Principals, (3) Leadership for Learning, (4) 7 System Leadership Study, (5) Asia Leadership Roundtable, and (6) World School Leadership Study. The scope, scale, contribution, and impact of these six international research consortia are presented. Their conclusions raise important issues about the logistical and methodological challenges facing international research teams, including how to involve new members, sustain activities without funding or sponsorship, create context-sensitive research protocols, and compare results across studies. They provide a thoughtful critique of how the ISLDN project can broaden its impact on our knowledge base by providing more reliable cross-national comparisons, increasing the dissemination of the network's findings, and developing quantitative research designs.

6 ■ B. G. BARNETT and P. A. WOODS

Chapter 3 by Pamela Angelle and Michelle Morrison documents the research journey of the social justice leadership research strand, including the initial team building and "growing pains"; its exploration of researcher positionality; and the formulation of research focus and methods, data collection, and interpretive framework. The work of the research network is also analyzed through the perspective of the Community of Practice (CoP) theory and lessons considered from this analysis. The authors highlight key research findings from the social justice leadership studies and suggest avenues for moving this research forward. They suggest developing quantitative methods and expanding participation to include more researchers in developing and non-Anglophone countries, thereby incorporating broader perspectives of social justice leadership that expose and potentially mitigate the Eurocentric analytical bias.

In Chapter 4, Deirdre Torrance and her colleagues synthesize the findings concerning social justice leadership from eight national education systems—England, Jamaica, Hong Kong, New Zealand, Republic of Ireland, Scotland, Sweden, and the United States. They draw from case study data gathered in those countries through policy analyses and field visits. Macro (national) and meso (school and local authority) factors that assist or hinder the practice of social justice leadership are identified. Their analysis finds that the headteachers studied have a significant understanding of the specific factors that shape their social justice practice, as well as an ability to recognize and create opportunities to develop the understandings and practices of others within the school community. Important support factors identified by the headteachers at the micro level include engagement with professional networks, both within the school and with peers and colleagues within the wider system. Building networks and collaborative practice were identified as important strategies, not only in promoting a social justice agenda, but also in sustaining social justice leaders themselves. A key finding is that essential to social justice leadership is a realization that the work has an inherent political nature and requires skilled mediating within and between the macro and meso levels of the system.

Jami Berry, a founding member of the ISLDN, and her colleagues provide a historical overview of the high-need schools strand of the project in Chapter 5. They begin by describing the important foundational elements of this work by clarifying the research team's definition of high-need schools, guiding research questions, and research protocols. They also review the findings from a series of high-need school studies conducted from 2014–2019 across four continents. Their analysis reveals several themes emerging from this cross-national comparison, including how principals create caring cultures and supportive communities, set high expectations for student and teacher performance, distribute leadership and encourage collective responsibility for student learning, understand the school and community context, and adapt their leadership to meet local needs. They conclude by sharing the voices of the high-need schools research team members, revealing their reasons for participating in the project, personal and professional growth, insights about leadership from an international perspective, and future ways to expand and strengthen the ISLDN.

Chapter 6 by Nathern Okilwa provides an in-depth examination of the research methodology used in studies conducted by members of the high-need schools strand. In taking stock of this work, he uses Hallinger's (2013) conceptual framework for conducting reviews of leadership studies to capture the research questions, participants, locations, data collection procedures, and analysis strategies employed in 18 studies of leaders in high-need schools. His analysis reveals several trends in this corpus of work, including the exclusive use of qualitative methods examining leadership, student learning, and school and community contexts; a tendency to focus on female elementary school principals' perceptions as well as the perspectives of teachers and parents; and the preponderance of sites in the United States (50%), with additional studies conducted in Australia, Belize, Brazil, Mexico, Nepal, and New Zealand. The chapter raises important questions about conducting cross-study reviews of this nature and suggests future lines of inquiry for the ISLDN, such as using mixed method designs, conducting longitudinal studies, and increasing the representation of non-Western contexts.

PART II: CROSS-STRAND AND CROSS-COUNTRY COMPARISON

This section presents the first concentrated effort of ISLDN researchers across the two strands to collaboratively conduct empirical studies or analyze previous studies using social justice and high-need schools perspectives. These studies provide a clearer understanding of the intersection of the values and actions of social justice leaders, especially those leading impoverished and struggling high-need schools. These narratives capture portraits of the values, practices, and policies of school leaders from Africa (Mozambique), Asia (Israel, Lebanon, Nepal, Turkey), Australia and Oceania (Australia, New Zealand), Europe (England, Spain, Sweden), and North America (Belize, Jamaica, Mexico, United States).

Chapter 7 by Keneisha Harrington and her colleagues critically examines students' perspectives of school-level policies intended to improve the learning environments of a high-needs elementary school in the United States and an upper secondary school in Sweden focused on gender equity and diversity. Using critical policy analysis as a framework, the authors focus on what school leaders can learn from students' voices during school

8 ■ B. G. BARNETT and P. A. WOODS

improvement and social justice-oriented reforms in their schools. At the U.S. elementary school, students were found to experience and understand policy at the school level through physical, social emotional, instructional, and relational changes in their environment. Their perspectives reveal the importance of issues such as cultivating physically safe and emotionally secure learning environments, student engagement, and a school climate that values teamwork and kindness. The findings from the Swedish school concerning how the school seeks to foster social justice through gender equality and diversity work demonstrate the consequences of not considering student perspectives. Designed without students' input, the school's activities led to feelings of detachment and disengagement and social justice being seen as "on the side"; students felt instead that social justice needed to be integrated into their teaching and learning experiences.

Using Leithwood's (2012) school leadership framework, Chapter 8 reports David Gurr and his colleagues' examination of ISLDN studies of social justice leadership and leadership in high-need schools in Australia and New Zealand. They begin by providing important contextual background about the educational systems in these two countries before describing how early childhood, primary, and secondary school leaders in these two countries strive to set directions, develop people, redesign the organization, and improve programs. Their analysis reveals specific instances and examples of these school leaders' strong sense of service and clear vision for their schools, strategies for recruiting talented teachers and developing leadership teams, commitment to developing programs and practices to reengage disenfranchised community members and to overcome crises faced by their communities, and innovations aimed at improving instructional practices and programs. The authors provide several conclusions about the commonalities found across these studies and future directions of the ISLDN aimed at broadening the research lens to examine the personal and professional development of these leaders using life histories and narrative research strategies.

In Chapter 9, Khalid Arar, Deniz Örücü, and Julia Mahfouz examine the meanings and praxis of social justice leadership of school principals in three high-need schools in the Middle East. The cases are drawn from Turkey, the divided city of Jerusalem, and Lebanon, and narrative analysis is used in examining the data. The leadership of two of the principals involves their struggles with the dominant groups in their community; the third principal represents the ethnic majority in his context. Different forms of contested terrains and educational ideologies, and the wider political, social, and economic elements in their particular contexts, shape their work as social justice leaders. However, there are similarities between the three school leaders. In their pursuit of promoting social justice, they all take risks and develop an acumen for dealing with the inner dynamics of their communities. Despite their different cultural and social contexts, all three have similar social justice visions and employ similar strategies to promote this vision. These strategies include role modeling, building communities both in the school and outside the school, and demonstrating an ethic of care and empathy for all students.

Chapter 10 by Brian Corrales-Maytorena and his colleagues reports a study of social justice leadership in high-need schools in Mexico and Spain. The investigation proceeds from the view that there is a need to broaden the perspective from English-speaking countries to include understandings of social justice in Latin America. The study aims to understand to what extent the directors of schools in Catalonia, Spain and Baja California, Mexico perceive their schools to be socially just by analyzing the barriers that hinder the promotion of impartiality, respect, participation, and critical reflection on society. Directors perceived that school policy was based on fairness and respect, parents were treated with respect, and management practices were characterized by fairness and respect. They perceived that most social justice problems predominantly emanated from society. They saw obstacles emanating from regulations and policies outside of the school and from family contexts affecting parents' participation in the school. The chapter also acknowledges that school leadership development in Spain may need more emphasis on developing a critical, social justice leadership perspective.

Chapter 11 by Cristina Moral, Elizabeth Murakami, and Celina Torres-Arcadia examines how social justice school leaders in two Spanish-speaking (Mexico and Spain) and an English-speaking country (United States) deal with socio-political issues that aggravate discriminatory practices for historically and socially excluded students, particularly indigenous populations, migrants, and involuntarily placed families. Their cross-case comparison of these principals reveals how they balance macro-contextual factors (societal, professional, political, economic) with their personal context (values, empathy, responsibility). After describing the societal and cultural values underlying the three countries, the authors provide concrete examples of the social justice leadership actions these school leaders employ to address students' academic and social-emotional needs and their strategies for developing learning opportunities for parents, families, and the local community. Their analysis underscores the importance of school leaders possessing "contextual intelligence" as the means for assimilating their past and current events in order to create a preferred future for underprivileged students and families.

In Chapter 12, Chetanath Gautam, Rosario Ambriz, and Betty Alford compare and contrast a high-need school in Nepal and Southern California where school principals are striving to turn around their students' academic performance. Similar to the other chapters in Part II, important contextual information is provided about the broader educational context affecting

Nepalese and California schools and their communities. Despite stark differences in the contextual factors affecting these two schools, the findings reveal both principals worked tirelessly to build a foundation of trust with students in order to initiate and sustain community engagement, built a collaborative culture for learning and improvement, and increased student learning. Examples reveal how principals identified specific academic goals (learning English, becoming literate), devised collaborative strategies for teachers and parental engagement, and were vigilant in addressing students' social-emotional needs during the school turnaround process.

Chapter 13 reviews findings from Stephen Jacobson and Paul Miller's past ISLDN studies, as well as others they have conducted, to reveal practical implications for school leaders seeking to promote social justice in high-need schools, regardless of national context. The chapter draws on studies of high-need schools in six very different national contexts: Belize, Jamaica, England, Mozambique, New Zealand, and the United States, with specific (although not exclusive) attention paid to those national studies the authors conducted as part of the ISLDN. The authors' analysis identifies four imperatives for social justice leaders, especially in high-need schools and communities: (a) improve the academic performance of all the school's children, (b) reconnect the school with its students' parents and the larger school community, (c) create future economic opportunities for students, parents, and the community, and (d) provide for succession planning and sustainability. Examples from research conducted in high-need schools spanning these different cultural contexts are presented to illuminate these imperatives.

The concluding chapter by the co-editors, Philip Woods and Bruce Barnett, examines the emerging trends and patterns about social justice leadership and leadership in high-need schools revealed by the ISLDN consortium members. Using two conceptual frameworks, their analysis captures the structural factors, personal beliefs and values, and change management strategies characterizing school leaders' efforts to influence students' academic and social emotional learning outcomes by confronting issues of inequity, racism, and lack of opportunity their students experience. Similar to what has been reported in many other studies of school leadership, effective social justice leaders are adept at understanding how the political, social, cultural, and institutional contexts hinder and help their activism to improve the life chances of these underprivileged students. The chapter also synthesizes how future ISLDN studies can broaden the impact, visibility, and scope of our understanding of social justice leadership in different cultural contexts. They conclude by highlighting the realities of conducting collaborative international research projects, noting the challenges ISLDN members experienced as well as the factors that helped them overcome these obstacles.

Collectively, these chapters clarify the ISLDN's purpose and capture the guiding research questions, methods employed, and findings that have resulted in the first 10 years of the project. The book also expands the network's knowledge base by having members of the two strands join together to conduct new empirical studies or examine previous studies using the lenses of social justice leadership and high-need schools leadership. Finally, by acknowledging the benefits and challenges of conducting unfunded cross-national research, the authors provide insights and precautions for other educational scholars and practitioners striving to establish and sustain an international research consortium.

REFERENCES

Angelle, P. S. (Ed.). (2017). *A global perspective of social justice leadership for school principals.* Charlotte, NC: Information Age.

Arlestig, H., Day, C., & Johansson, O. (Eds.). (2016). *A decade of research on school principals, studies in educational leadership.* Dordrecht, The Netherlands: Springer.

Bryant, M., Cheng, A., & Notman, R. (Eds.). (2014). Exploring high need and social justice leadership in schools around the globe. *Management in Education, 28*(3), 77–120.

Day, C., Gu, Q., & Sammons, P. (2016). The impact of leadership on student outcomes: How successful school leaders use transformational and instructional strategies to make a difference. *Educational Administration Quarterly, 52*(2) 221–258.

Day, C., & Gurr, D. (Eds.). (2014). *Leading schools successfully. Stories from the field.* London, England: Routledge.

Gurr, D., & Drysdale, L. (Eds.). (2018). Leading high needs schools: Findings from the International School Leadership Development Network. *International Studies in Educational Administration, 46*(1), 147–156.

Hallinger, P. (2013). A conceptual framework for systematic reviews of research in educational leadership and management. *Journal of Educational Administration, 51*(2), 126–149.

Hallinger, P., & Walker, A. (2017). Leading learning in Asia–Emerging empirical insights from five societies. *Journal of Educational Administration, 55*(2), 130–146.

Hernandez, F., & Murakami, E. (2016). *Brown-eyed leaders of the sun: A portrait of Latina/o educational leaders.* Charlotte, NC: Information Age.

Leithwood, K. (2012). The four essential components of the leader's repertoire. In K. Leithwood & K. S. Louis (Eds.), *Linking leadership to learning* (pp. 57–67). San Francisco, CA: Jossey-Bass.

Lumby, J., Crow, G., & Pashiardis, P. (Eds.). (2008). *International handbook on the preparation and development of school leaders.* New York, NY: Routledge.

Murakami, E., Gurr, D., & Notman, R. (Eds.). (2019). *Leadership, culture and school success in high-need schools.* Charlotte, NC: Information Age.

Organization for Economic Co-operation and Development. (2016). *School leadership for learning: Insights from Talis 2013.* Paris, France: Author.

Pashiardis, P. (2008). *The dark side of the moon: Being locally responsive to global issues.* Keynote presentation at the Commonwealth Council for Educational Administration and Management Conference, Durbin, South Africa.

Robinson, V. M. J., Lloyd, C. A., & Rowe, K. J. (2008). The impact of leadership on student outcomes: An analysis of the differential effects of leadership types. *Educational Administration Quarterly, 44*(5), 635–674.

Walker, A., & Townsend, A. (2010). On school management–International Council on School Effectiveness and Improvement, Commonwealth Council on Educational Administration and Management. In P. Peterson, E. Baker, & B. McGaw (Eds.), *International encyclopedia of education* (pp. 681–697). Oxford, England: Elsevier.

Ylimaki, R. M., & Jacobson S. L. (Eds.). (2011). *US and cross-national policies, practices, and preparation.* New York, NY: Springer.

CHAPTER 2

INTERNATIONAL EDUCATIONAL LEADERSHIP PROJECTS

David Gurr
University of Melbourne

Lawrie Drysdale
University of Melbourne

Helen Goode
University of Melbourne

The aim of this chapter is to explore the International School Leadership Development Network (ISLDN) in a wider context of international school leadership research endeavors. The ISLDN is one of a limited number of large and sustained multi-national, collaborative research projects. Its value and status need to be recognized through exploring its significance, scope, scale, contribution, and its impact on research in comparison with other large international multi-national collaborative projects. In this chapter, we will identify gaps and future directions for the ISLDN as well as reflect

---

Educational Leadership for Social Justice and Improving High-Needs Schools, pages 13–29
Copyright © 2021 by Information Age Publishing
All rights of reproduction in any form reserved.

13

14 ▪ D. GURR, L. DRYSDALE, and H. GOODE

on being involved in international projects and provide some guidance to those considering this type of research.

Firstly, we identify the ISLDN as one of seven similar international projects. In order to see how the ISLDN is positioned, we will describe the seven international projects as a point of comparison. This will help inform how it compares in scope, scale, contribution, and impact. We have written about four of these previously (Gurr, Drysdale, & Goode, 2020) and add another three to help demonstrate similarities and differences.

We will describe each project in order to outline the nature, scope, and impact and to amplify the similarities and differences. The seven international educational leadership projects are: International School Leadership Development (ISLDN); International Successful School Principalship Project (ISSPP); International Study of the Preparation of Principals (ISPP); Leadership for Learning (LfL); 7 System Leadership Study (SLS); Asia Leadership Roundtable (ALR); and World School Leadership Study (WSLS). We can add to the descriptions of most of the projects, and adopt an insider view as participant observers in five of seven projects. All three authors are active members in the ISLDN, ISSPP, and ALR and two authors are involved in the SLS and WSLS projects.

INTERNATIONAL SCHOOL LEADERSHIP DEVELOPMENT NETWORK

Much of the description of the ISLDN is outlined in other chapters in the book (see Chapters 5 and 6 in Part I). In order to compare the ISLDN with other international educational leadership projects and see how it is positioned, we will describe the key features of the project. The ISLDN was established in 2010 as a result of collaboration between British Educational Leadership, Management, and Administration Society (BELMAS) and University Council for Educational Administration (UCEA; Angelle, 2017a). In 2011, the project divided into two strands to meet the needs of researchers who had expressed interest in the program: educational leadership in high needs schools and social justice leadership. The common thread between the two strands is the context in which they are set, that is, challenging circumstances. Schools in high need situations and issues of social justice tend to be in low socio-economic areas. The project website (https://isldn. weebly.com) identifies 44 international scholars and 28 in the social justice strand. The two strands have generally operated autonomously. Each group has developed their own methodological approach and set their own agendas. Currently, the two strands meet as a large group at the annual conferences of UCEA and BELMAS to share experiences, ideas, methodological approaches, and findings.

High-Needs Schools Strand

The purpose of the international work of the High-Needs School Strand (HNS) was to determine various qualities of leadership critical to leading high-needs schools focusing on the following three areas: learning, leadership, and context (Baran & Berry, 2015).

In defining high needs, researchers were requested to provide an operational definition of high-needs schools within the context of the school studied; however, as a guide, high-needs schools shared one or more of the following characteristics: (a) a high percentage of individuals from families with incomes below the poverty line; (b) a high percentage of school teachers not teaching in the content area for which they were qualified; (c) high teacher/principal turnover; (d) high percentage of non-native language speakers; (e) high percentage of historically/socially excluded groups; (f) high percentage of indigenous groups; (g) high percentage of students with learning difficulties; (h) lack of infrastructure; and (i) high needs based on an event such as a natural disaster.

The research questions were:

1. *Focus on learning:* What fosters student learning in high-needs schools?
2. *Focus on leadership:* How do principals and other school leaders enhance individual and organizational performance in high-needs schools?
3. *Focus on context:* How do internal and external school contexts impact individual and organizational performance in high-needs schools?

The members of the high-needs research strand agreed to adopt a qualitative methods approach and conducted multi-perspective case studies. From the outset, protocols were discussed and refined over time. However, it was not until 2015 that the final set of protocols were forwarded to members and terms and research guidelines defined (Baran & Berry, 2015).

The publication record of the ISLDN has been moderate. Despite the recent finalizing of the protocols, several members had conducted small scale, case study research to empirically explore high-needs leadership and either published these or presented their findings at UCEA or BELMAS. For example, members regularly presented at international community building symposia at UCEA from 2015–2019. The group conducted several sessions at the New Zealand Educational Administration and Leadership Society (NZEALS) Conference in 2016. Several members collaborated to publish a special issue of case studies using the protocols in *International Studies in Educational Administration* (Gurr & Drysdale, 2018).

16 ▪ D. GURR, L. DRYSDALE, and H. GOODE

Gurr, Murakami, and Notman (2019) summarized 19 high-need cases from an edited book (Murakami, Gurr, & Notman, 2019) and observed that one of the most striking aspects across the cases was how the school leaders adapted their interventions or practices to suit the context; the principals demonstrated contextually responsive leadership, and there was a reciprocal relationship between leadership and context. Principals understood that context operated at various levels, such as within school, local, district, state, national, and international levels.

Another finding was that successful principals demonstrated personal qualities that enabled them to lead more effectively; for example, they had skill sets that helped them deal with conflict, harness support and resources, align people with school directions, and develop and implement key improvement strategies (Gurr & Drysdale, 2018)

Social Justice Leadership Strand

The members of the social justice strand explored social justice leaders in different countries and settings to determine how the principals formed their views, understood social justice within their own context, and initiated and implemented a social justice agenda. Social Justice principals were defined as those who were "committed to reducing inequalities" and making "this aim a high priority in leadership practice" (Angelle, 2017b, p. 308).

The specific research questions were:

1. How do social justice leaders make sense of "social justice"?
2. What do social justice leaders do?
3. What factors help and hinder the work of social justice leaders?
4. How did social justice leaders learn to become social justice leaders?

The social justice strand members claim that their defining feature is a "network of researchers, guided by the same research questions, adopting a common methodological approach, and undertaking work in a diverse range of international contexts" (https://isldn.weebly.com/social-justice.html).

The social justice strand also adopted a qualitative case studies approach, but rather than being multi-perspective, the strand has focused on a single principal in either a primary or secondary setting. The team used a snowball sampling approach where research participants identified other participants for further research. In selection, the principal self-identified as a "social justice leader" (phrased appropriately for different contexts). To participate in the project, researchers had to agree to complete certain activities (described as "three tickets") which included: an interview with a principal using the project selection and interview protocols; linking of the interview with a macro, meso, and micro social justice framework created by the project; and providing a researcher positionality statement, which was a reflective statement on their personal philosophy and views regarding the work of social justice.

Focusing the work of social justice leaders on reducing inequalities has added a different dimension to principal effectiveness because success is based on the central issue of addressing inequality. In their synthesis of the papers in the *Research in Educational Administration and Leadership* special issue, King and Robinson (2017) described values, self-awareness of values, and relationships as central to understanding social justice leaders. The principals had a strong sense of personal identity shaped by their values, education, and life experiences. The guiding values of the principals covered the areas of social, personal, and professional values. They had a strong sense of mission and moral purpose. For these leaders, social justice went beyond rhetoric. They took an active stance by recognizing injustice among groups, acquiring necessary resources, redistributing resources, and providing opportunities for the marginalized. In terms of their qualities, they were persuasive and influential, proactive rather than reactive, highly visible in their schools, and acted as role models.

INTERNATIONAL SUCCESSFUL SCHOOL PRINCIPALSHIP PROJECT

The ISSPP is the oldest and longest running of the international research projects. Initiated in 2001 with the collaboration of academics from eight countries (Australia, Canada, China, Denmark, England, Norway, Sweden, and the United States), the aim was to explore the characteristics and practices of successful school principals. Throughout the project's time, academics representing other countries either applied or were invited to participate. Currently, academics from over twenty countries are involved which evidences the scale of the project. A more detailed outline of the project is available at the website (https://www.uv.uio.no/ils/english/research/projects/isspp/).

Several important distinctive aspects of the project demonstrate the dynamics of international comparative research projects. Firstly, project topics changed over time and the project divided into streams. While this project initially focused on the successful principal leadership, several of the country representatives moved to the topic of sustainability by returning to their case study schools. More recently, new topics emerged, and researchers divided into several strands, including exploring principals in underperforming schools in favorable and unfavorable contexts; principal identity; leadership for teacher quality; school governance; and the role of middle leaders.

Secondly, a set of protocols were developed in order to provide consistency among researchers so that findings could be compared. The project used qualitative methods using multi-perspective case studies. Currently, protocols are being updated to match changing topics. An attempt to use a common quantitative survey between countries proved to be unworkable in most countries.

Thirdly, research was able to be conducted in a range of contexts within countries, including rural, urban, low and high socio-economic settings, and primary and secondary schools. This allowed researchers to investigate leadership in diverse contexts.

Fourthly, the project was able to widely publish its finding from different countries, which is some indication of impact and contribution to the field (Arlestig, Day, & Johansson, 2016; Day & Gurr, 2014; Day & Leithwood, 2007; Drysdale, 2011; Moos, Johansson, & Day, 2011; Gu & Johannson, 2013). There are more than 20 countries represented by active research groups, with more than 150 case studies conducted and more than 200 papers, book chapters, and books published.

This project demonstrates how scholars from diverse backgrounds can successfully come together to engage in large, multi-country research collaborative research, and, in the case of the ISSPP, how this collaboration was enhanced through sustained interactivity, emotional literacy, commitment, resilience, and acceptance of diversity (Day & Gurr, 2018).

In summary, the project has identified key characteristics and behaviors of successful school leaders such as personal values, character traits, skills, and cognitive styles that are antecedents to successful leadership. These include characteristics of both heroic and post heroic stereotypes (Drysdale, Bennett, Murakami, Johansson, & Gurr, 2014). The research has demonstrated how leadership contributes to sustaining success over time. Finally, the research shows how successful leaders can overcome contextual constraints to achieve desired results.

INTERNATIONAL STUDY OF THE PREPARATION OF PRINCIPALS

The ISPP was established as a network of international researches to explore: "How can principal preparation programs be useful to novice principals?" The ISPP has a project website at http://www.ucalgary.ca/ispp/. This project was in response to the limited research on novice principals. The major research was conducted between 2004–2009, although the project continues at a lesser scale. The researchers investigated novice principals from 15 countries and across five continents. The project used mixed methods and was conducted over three stages: comparing the current offerings in principal preparation programs; conducting case studies; and developing a survey instrument gathering information related to the challenges faced by early career principals. The case studies used individual interviews and focus groups examining novices' experiences, support, and challenges. The survey collected data on their experiences and appropriateness of the preparation programs (Clarke, Wildy, & Styles, 2011; Webber & Scott, 2013; Wildy & Clarke, 2008).

While researchers tended to report their own country experience, there was an attempt to conduct cross-cultural comparisons. For example, Webber and Scott (2013) and Wildy and Clarke (2008) each developed a principal preparation framework which was used to compare principal preparation programs in selected countries—Australia, Turkey, Canada, Kenya, and South Africa (Slater, Garduno, & Mentz, 2018).

An important outcome of the ISPP was to show that despite cultural and economic differences between the countries in the study, there were more similarities than differences in the challenges faced by new principals. Another significant ISPP outcome was that only four of the countries in the study had formal preparation programs for principals (Canada, United States, England, and Scotland).

What the ISPP project was able to show was that for novice principals, there were numerous personal, organizational, and system barriers that impacted and challenged them personally. Context emerged once again as a significant factor, particularly in regard to available resources and support, and remoteness. Finally, the study found that preparation programs did not provide adequate skills development. Overall, the key recommendation of the project was that systems needed to provide formal preparation programs that were focused on the needs of beginning principals, especially for those in remote locations.

LEADERSHIP FOR LEARNING

The Leadership for Learning (LfL) project emanated from Cambridge University and was established in 2001. It involved collaboration between seven countries (Australia, Austria, Denmark, England, Greece, Norway, and the United States) and eight research groups (two were in the United States). The project was supported by a philanthropic group, the Carpe Vitam Foundation, with the agenda to challenge existing educational policy (MacBeath, Frost, Swaffield, & Waterhouse, 2003). The project involved a longitudinal study that comprised researchers and critical friends working with three schools from each country. The central research questions were:

- What is understood by learning in different contexts?
- What is understood by leadership?
- What are the links between leadership and learning?

Selection of the schools was through professional contacts and invitations to schools. Each school had a critical friend who was a researcher, and who at various times would work closely with the school as a supportive critic, and then, as the schools developed, more distantly as a researcher.

Whilst there are several important publications of this project (e.g., MacBeath & Dempster, 2008; MacBeath, Dempster, Frost, Johnson, & Swaffield, 2018), the core focus has been on the development and championing of a LfL model to stimulate debate, further research, and, most importantly, challenge dominant policy discourses.

The model is bounded by four common framing values: leadership for learning, democratic values, critical friendship, and moral purpose. At the base of the model, leadership and learning are bookended by activity and agency to emphasize that "leading and learning are necessary forms of activity, enacted by those with a strong sense of their own human agency" (MacBeath et al., 2018, p. 42). The tiers represent the pervasiveness of the project's view of leadership—found in students, teachers, senior managers, and communities of learners to use the project terms. In essence, the project believes leadership should be viewed as an activity that can be exercised by anyone, and learning applies to all. The leadership actions are guided by five principles at the top of the model: focusing on learning, sharing leadership, engaging in dialogue, sharing accountability, and creating favorable learning conditions. The principles are fully described in chapter three of MacBeath et al. (2018).

7 SYSTEM LEADERSHIP STUDY

The 7 System Leadership Study (7SLS) is an example of an international project that has a different purpose and scope compared with the previous projects. First, it is an empirically focused project involving seven countries and led by Alma Harris and Michelle Jones during their time working in Malaysia. The research project focused on the systematic comparative analysis of leadership development and leadership practice in differentially performing education systems. The countries included Australia, China (Hong Kong), England, Indonesia, Malaysia, Singapore, and Russia. It was a three-year study funded by the University of Malaya. The objectives were to explore how leadership programs were designed to meet the needs of schools in different systems; identify how school leaders responded to leadership programs; and reveal how the programs impacted on practice. The project also was aimed at contributing to theory building of the relationship between leadership development and school–system performance.

To achieve these objectives, the project proceeded in several ways. A survey was constructed that was used across the seven countries. This was based on Kouzes and Posner's (2012) Leadership Practices Inventory (LPI). In addition, some countries used multisite qualitative case studies involving semi-structured interviews. Country policy and practice contexts were described and literature associated with comparative education, and human and social capital were used to inform the project. There have been several reports of this project, notably a special issue of the *Asia Pacific Journal of Education* (Harris & Jones, 2015), synthesis/conclusion papers such as Harris and Jones (2015, 2017, 2018), Harris, Jones, and Adams (2016), and other papers (e.g., Adam, Harris & Jones, 2017).

The eight articles in the special issue were a mixture of empirical, analytical, and conceptual articles, because, as Harris and Jones (2015) described, each country was at a different stage in the data collection process. In synthesizing the somewhat disparate collection of papers, Harris and Jones (2015) concluded that the broader contexts surrounding schools is crucial for understanding performance, and that the interaction between culture and context in the area of policy making is vitally important for understanding how similar policies, such as the use of standards and standardization, can be interpreted differently and lead to different practice outcomes. "Collectively, the articles highlight how context matters and, indeed, how it has always mattered to those at the sharp end of policy delivery" (Harris & Jones, 2015, p. 316).

In the most recent summary of this project, Harris and Jones (2018) concluded that: all systems were investing in leadership programs; all systems have, or were planning to introduce, leadership standards; context was shown to impact on leadership practice; and, the influence of culture on policy implementation was a significant factor influencing school and system performance.

ASIA LEADERSHIP ROUNDTABLE

The Asia Leadership Roundtable (ALR) is an academic collective of educational leadership researchers in the Asia Pacific area organized by the Asia Pacific Centre for Leadership and Change (APCLC) of The Education University of Hong Kong (or Hong Kong Institute of Education as it was known). It was initiated by Phil Hallinger and Allan Walker in 2010 (https://www.eduhk.hk/apclc/roundtable2010/). The initial meeting was intended as a means of enhancing collaboration in research and development in the areas of educational leadership and change. Participants were drawn from universities and training institutions in the Asia Pacific region

22 ▪ D. GURR, L. DRYSDALE, and H. GOODE

(Hong Kong, China, Thailand, Taiwan, Singapore, Vietnam, and Malaysia) as well as from global partners of the APCLC. The ALR meetings have always been by invitation only and participation has been limited to between 50–60 people. The organizers saw this as a capacity-building exercise for regional participants. Global scholars were invited to support this by discussing current research needs, the latest research trends, and future directions for educational leadership research in the Asia Pacific area. Each year different Asia Pacific countries hosted the round table. Global scholars included invitees from Australia, Austria, Chile, England, Germany, Israel, Malaysia, Netherlands, Norway, Scotland, South Africa, Sweden, Switzerland, Turkey, United Kingdom, and the United States.

An important outcome of the ALR was a recognition of the overall scarcity of quality empirical research in East Asia. As a result, a project within the ALR was initiated to research Instructional Leadership in East Asia (ILEA) involving the seven regional countries. The project required them to conduct a literature review in their country, case studies using qualitative methods, and local validation of research instruments for large-scale research. Two special publications demonstrated the success of this strategy: *Journal of Educational Administration* (Walker & Hallinger, 2015) and *Journal of Educational Administration* (Hallinger & Walker, 2017). The 2015 special issue published the literature reviews and the 2017 special issue reported case studies. The country scholars used a common protocol for their case studies. Hallinger and Walker (2017) reported findings that showed that compared with U.S. research on instructional leadership, ILEA countries were more directive, less collaborative, and less involved in curriculum coordination; however, school leaders were more involved in classroom observation, more highly visible, and emphasized school harmony.

The success of the ALR can be measured beyond the growth in publications. For example, at the 2010 conference, all keynote speakers were from non-Asia Pacific countries and the provocateur sessions were led by guests from non-Asia Pacific countries. At the 2019 conference, all keynotes were presented by representatives of the Asia Pacific region as were the panel discussions and group activities. Furthermore, at the 2019 conference, 20 of the 25 conference papers submitted were from academics from universities in the Asia Pacific region. As noted earlier, the original intention for the establishment of this network was to enhance collaboration in research. This intention, too, was achieved. Each conference had a theme which then informed the discussions and working groups. As the ALR network evolved, country reports outlining accomplishments, models developed to inform research and practices, and ongoing challenges within each country's context began to inform the basis of discussion groups and working parties. In this way, the ALR promoted opportunities for sharing and for developing locally relevant research. For example, at 2017 ALR, the Taiwanese group noted that whilst they had borrowed a Western framework for their research, it had been extended and contextualized to the Taiwanese context.

WORLD SCHOOL LEADERSHIP STUDY

An emerging international collaborative project that has the potential to inform practice spanning many countries is the World School Leadership Study (WSLS). The project is coordinated by Stephen Huber and his team from Switzerland (Huber, Skedsmo, Tian, & Schwander, 2017). The project was formally proposed in 2016, although its genesis was much earlier, at least from 2011 when discussions were held at the ALR in Bangkok. For example, earlier research on school leadership professional learning (Huber, 2011) and a self-assessment inventory for aspiring principals (Huber & Hiltmann, 2011) informed the current project.

The project was a response to a lack of international comparative studies on leadership practices in terms of preferences, strain, behavior, and performance on the one hand, and on working conditions, professional health, and resilience on the other hand. The WSLS aims to gain empirical insights into how school leaders' functions, practices, and work conditions affect their health in general and resilience.

The WSLS research focuses on six specific areas of school leader work: resources and demands; values and professional understandings; practices; person-job-organization-system fit; school quality and its development; and health resilience and well-being.

The overall project is a mixed methods study. Quantitative data are collected via an online survey and an end-of-day log, whilst qualitative data are collected via documents, interviews, and case studies. To serve both national research interests and to provide international comparisons, the research design incorporates a compulsory common core of data collection that all the participant countries apply, with the option for country-specific data collection elements to suit local needs. The mandatory component includes a country report (document analysis and expert interviews) and an online survey (the online survey has a common core plus scope for country-specific additions). The optional section of the study includes case studies of school leaders, and/or interviews with stakeholders, and an end-of-day log to capture a sense of the work of school leaders (Huber et al., 2016).

At the time of writing this chapter, country reports were being prepared, and the survey has been trialed and is being rolled-out for country use in 2020 and beyond. Researchers from over 30 countries have indicated their support for the project and agreed to participate. Countries represented in the project include: Australia, Austria, Chile, China, Cyprus, England, Germany, Hong Kong (HKSAR), Malaysia, Mexico, New Zealand, Norway,

24 ■ D. GURR, L. DRYSDALE, and H. GOODE

Singapore, South Africa, Spain, Sweden, Switzerland, Thailand, and the United States. While there are high expectations surrounding the projects, findings are still to be published.

DISCUSSION

In terms of status and positioning, the ISLDN ranks second to the ISSPP in terms of scope and scale. The ISDLN is celebrating its 10th anniversary while the ISSPP is in its 20th year. The impact and contribution of the ISLDN is more limited as evidenced by the number of publications compared with the ISSPP. The ISSPP members set early targets and the project was largely driven by the need to deliver products (publications). Compared with the other international projects, the ISLDN compares favorably, but the challenge is to produce more and target "A" grade journals in order to demonstrate greater impact. Presentations at international conferences have been consistent, with the UCEA and BELMAS as the preferred conferences, although members have presented widely at conferences such as American Educational Research Association (AERA), European Conference on Educational Research (ECER), New Zealand Educational Administration and Leadership Society (NZEALS), Australian Association of Educational Research (AAER), and the Commonwealth Council for Educational Administration and Management (CCEAM). Like most of the international networks in this chapter, the challenge is to have the project voice heard and recognized.

Noting again that this is the 10th year for ISLDN, the question of longevity needs to be addressed. How long can a project maintain its energy, enthusiasm, and commitment? Most projects lack a key sponsor to help support the project. Only the ALR and LfL have had their projects financially supported. Members of the ISLDN have had to rely on their institution for support, apply for grants, or self-fund. This puts an extra burden on members to attend conferences and meetings. The ISSPP split into strands in order to cater for the expanded membership as new countries joined and sustained interest. Once a goal was achieved new goals emerged; however, the danger with several strands is that projects can become fragmented. The ISLDN created two strands very early, mainly because of the specific interests of members, and potential challenges of managing and coordinating a large group. With very large groups, coordination and coherence are more of a challenge. Introducing new members also presents a challenge for starting points in the project and playing "catch-up" with the older members. New strands offer the opportunity for new members to join the network at different times and select a strand that suits their needs and interest; however, with a large diversity of strands there is a danger that the original charter of the network can be undermined and lost.

Research protocols are an essential feature for international groups. The social justice group established protocols early, whereas the high-needs group took until 2015 to publish their protocols. This delayed research for the high-needs group, although some members followed the ISSPP protocols in order to get going with their research.

Qualitative methods are the choice of most international networks in educational leadership. Both strands of the ISLDN used case study methods, yet interestingly, the high-needs group adopted multi-perspective case studies, while the social justice stand used a single interview with the principal. It could be argued that while both groups operate under the same ISLDN banner, they are separate and discrete projects. Whether this dilutes the project in terms of coherence, resources and publishable findings is an open question. In terms of recognition, using case study as a methodology has limitations due to the complexity of the findings and how this complexity can be conveyed succinctly. Large-scale quantitative methods appear to have more credibility among the academic community, tertiary institutions, and policy makers. Yet, quantitative methods require expertise that may be problematic with the current group of ISLDN scholars. More recent projects like the WSLS have been designed from the beginning with mixed methods to collect data and support their findings, and the ISSPP continues to explore the use of teacher surveys to enhance the case studies.

An opportunity and challenge for the ISLDN is to compare the findings across projects to identify trends and gaps. This is not easy because the projects are complex in that they explore leadership in a range of contexts and through research that produces rich and detailed findings. Contexts vary across and within countries. The sites can be early childhood centers, elementary or secondary schools, and located in rural and urban environments. Often political, technical, social, and economic forces impact the schools. The education systems can be very different. Different language, ethnic, and cultural backgrounds make for leadership complexity. The length of the various projects, the qualitative nature of much of the research, and the wide range of publications highlight the challenge in identifying trends and common findings.

In their early chapter, Gurr et al. (2020) highlighted how international projects like these bring the interplay of leadership and context into focus. All the international projects recognize that leadership practice is not context free. The ISLDN assumes from the start that school leaders are working in challenging circumstances. The social justice strand starts with the proposition that social justice principals work to decrease inequality as priority. High-needs principals are situated in challenging internal and/or external environments. What appears to be common in all the projects is that successful leaders understand the contexts surrounding their schools, can respond appropriately to these, and can even influence context; there is also evidence for a reciprocal relationship between leadership and context. School leaders are not captured by their environment, but work within it to achieve their goals. Sometimes they see opportunities in their environment and provide innovative solutions. In other cases, leaders are able to influence the context to derive benefits for the school community.

Another general finding was that common frameworks of leadership practice were supported in most of the projects. Most apparent was that the ISLDN and ISSPP offered evidence to support the four-element leadership framework of Leithwood and colleagues (e.g., Day et al., 2010; Leithwood, Day, Sammons, Harris, & Hopkins, 2006). This framework helped to explain the leadership work of principals across diverse contexts. It does not mean that the principals were all acting in the same manner, but rather that broad categories of practice can help to understand what successful principals do, which leads to the final observation.

The projects acknowledge that leaders adopt different strategies and approaches in leading. They use a range of interventions that are supported by a skill set that complements their personal qualities and characteristics. There is no one style or set of qualities; however, there are personal qualities that appear to be antecedents for successful leadership in a range of contexts. The projects acknowledge the complexity of leadership, but strive to gain a better understanding to enhance the theory and practice of school leadership.

CONCLUSIONS

We have entered an exciting era of international collaborative educational leadership research projects and the establishment of long term and extensive international networks, with new projects appearing such as the recently formed International Study of Teacher Leadership (https://sites.google.com/mtroyal.ca/istl). The ISLDN and the other international research projects have each explored and investigated similar research questions and used common protocols. The challenge is to consolidate the findings so that researchers can make more valid and reliable cross-country comparisons. For example, the projects have identified contextual differences between countries, regions, rural and urban, and low and high socio-economics factors, but often these findings offer little guidance for practice. The next step is to make more nuanced observations, analysis, and interpretation of the data to fine-tune our conclusions. These projects show that there is significant progress in international collaboration, but the challenge remains for current and future research networks to go deeper in the comparisons made so that we paint a more definitive picture of educational leadership across nations and sectors that contribute to the

International Educational Leadership Projects ▪ **27**

work of educational leaders. The ISLDN will need to extend its reach by increasing its publications and set more challenging targets for members. The network leaders will need to provide training and encouragement to move in the direction of more quantitative research to capture sponsorship and influence policy and practice. The ISLDN will also need to provide more comparative cross country analyses, which may highlight contextual difference. As it stands, the ISLDN can be proud of its achievement over the past 10 years and brace itself to a challenging future.

REFERENCES

Adams, D., Harris, A., & Jones, M. S. (2017). Exploring teachers' and parents' perceptions on social inclusion practices in Malaysia. *Pertanika Journal of Social Sciences and Humanities, 25*(4), 1721–1738.

Angelle, P. S. (Ed.). (2017a). *A global perspective of social justice leadership for school principals.* Charlotte, NC: Information Age.

Angelle, P. S. (2017b). Moving forward. In P. S. Angelle (Ed.), *A global perspective of social justice leadership for school principals* (pp. 303–320). Charlotte, NC: Information Age.

Arlestig, H., Day, C., & Johansson, O. (Eds.). (2016). *A decade of research on school principals. Studies in educational leadership.* Dordrecht, The Netherlands: Springer.

Baran, M. L., & Berry, J. R. (2015). *The international school leadership development network (ISLDN) High needs schools group research protocol and members' guide.* ISLDN and UCEA/BELMAS.

Clarke, S., Wildy, H., & Styles, I. (2011). Fit for purpose? Western Australian insights into the efficacy of principal preparation. *Journal of Educational Administration, 49*(2), 166–178.

Day, C., & Gurr, D. (Eds.). (2014). *Leading schools successfully. Stories from the field.* London, England: Routledge Press.

Day, C., & Gurr, D. (2018). International networks as sites for research on successful school leadership. In C. Lochmiller (Ed.), *Complementary research methods in educational leadership and policy studies* (pp. 341–357). Cham, Switzerland: Palgrave MacMillan.

Day, C., & Leithwood, K. (2007). Building and sustaining successful principalship. In C. Day & K. Leithwood (Eds.), *Successful principal leadership in times of change* (pp. 171–188). Dordrecht, The Netherlands: Springer.

Day, C., Sammons, P., Hopkins, D., Harris, A., Leithwood, K., Gu, Q., & Brown, E. (2010). *10 strong claims about successful school leadership.* Nottingham, England: National College for Leadership of Schools and Children's Services.

Drysdale, L. (2011). Evidence from the new cases in International Successful School Principals Project (ISSPP). *Leadership and Policy in Schools, 10*(4), 444–455.

Drysdale, L., Bennett J., Murakami, E., Johansson, O., & Gurr, D. (2014). Heroic leadership in Australia, Sweden, and the United States. *International Journal of Educational Management, 28*(7), 785–797.

28 ▪ D. GURR, L. DRYSDALE, and H. GOODE

Gu, Q., & Johannson, O. (2013). Sustaining school performance: School contexts matter. *International Journal Leadership in Education, 16*(3), 301–326.

Gurr, D., & Drysdale, L. (2018). Leading high need schools: Findings from the International School Leadership Development Network. *International Studies in Educational Administration, 46*(1), 147–156.

Gurr, D., Drysdale, L., & Goode, H. (2020). Global research on principal leadership. In R. Papa (Ed.), *The oxford research encyclopedia of educational administration.* Oxford University Press. https://doi.org/10.1093/acrefore/978019026 4093.013.714

Gurr, D., Murakami, E., & Notman, R. (2019). Making world connections: Educational leadership in high-need schools. In E. Murakami, D. Gurr, & R. Notman (Eds.), *Leadership, culture and school success in high-need schools* (pp. 185–194). Charlotte, NC: Information Age.

Hallinger, P., & Walker, A. (2017). Leading learning in Asia–Emerging empirical insights from five societies. *Journal of Educational Administration, 55*(2), 130–146.

Harris, A., & Jones, M. S. (2015). Transforming education systems: Comparative and critical perspectives on school leadership. *Asia Pacific Journal of Education, 35*(3), 311–318.

Harris, A., & Jones, M. (2017). Leading educational change and improvement at scale: Some inconvenient truths about educational reform. *International Journal of Leadership in Education, 20*(5), 1–10.

Harris, A., & Jones, M. (2018). Why context matters: A comparative perspective on education reform and policy implementation. *Educational Research for Policy and Practice, 17,* 195–207.

Harris, A., Jones, M., & Adams, D. (2016). Qualified to lead? A comparative, contextual and cultural view of educational policy borrowing. *Educational Research, 58*(2), 166–178.

Huber, S. G. (2011). The impact of professional development: A theoretical model for empirical research, evaluation, planning and conducting training and development programmes. *Professional Development in Education, 37*(5), 837–853.

Huber, S. G., & Hiltmann, M. (2011). Competence Profile School Management (CPSM): An inventory for the self-assessment of school leadership. *Education Assessment Evaluation and Accountability, 23*(1), 65–88.

Huber, S. G., Skedsmo, G., Tian, M., & Schwander, M. (2017). *World School Leadership Study (WSLS) research and monitoring of school leaders' profession: Design brief, facts-sheet.* Zug, Switzerland: International Research Consortium, Institute for the Management and Economics of Education (IBB) at the University of Teacher Education.

Huber, S. G., Skedsmo, G., Tulowitzki, P., Schwander, M., Robinson, V. M., & Spillane, J. P. (2016). *World school leadership study: Concept and design.* Paper presented at the American Educational Research Association Annual Conference, Washington, DC.

King, F., & Robinson, K. (2017). Making sense of it all: Values, relationships and a way forward. *Research in Educational Administration and Leadership, 2*(1), 128–138.

Kouzes, J. M., & Posner, B. Z. (2012). *The leadership challenge: How to make extraordinary things happen in organizations* (5th ed.). San Francisco, CA: Jossey-Bass.

International Educational Leadership Projects ▪ **29**

Leithwood, K., Day, C., Sammons, P., Harris, A., & Hopkins, D. (2006). *Seven strong claims about successful school leadership.* Nottingham, England: National College of School Leadership.

MacBeath, J., & Dempster, N. (Eds.). (2008). *Connecting leadership for learning: Principles for practice.* Abingdon, England: Routledge.

MacBeath, J., Dempster, N., Frost, D., Johnson, G., & Swaffield, S. (Eds.). (2018). *Strengthening the connections between leadership and learning.* Abingdon, England: Routledge.

MacBeath, J., Frost, D., Swaffield, S., & Waterhouse, J. (2003). *Making the connections: The story of a seven country odyssey in search of a practical theory.* Cambridge, England: University of Cambridge, Faculty of Education.

Moos, L., Johansson, O., & Day, C. (2011). *How school principals sustain success over time: International perspectives.* Dordrecht, The Netherlands: Springer.

Murakami, E., Gurr, D., & Notman, R. (Eds.). (2019). *Leadership, culture and school success in high-need schools.* Charlotte, NC: Information Age.

Slater, C., Garduno, J. M. G., & Mentz, K. (2018). Frameworks for principal preparation and leadership development: Contributions of the International Study of Principal Preparation (ISPP). *Management in Education, 20*(10), 1–9.

Walker, A., & Hallinger, P. (2015). A synthesis of reviews of research on principal leadership in East Asia. *Journal of Educational Administration, 53*(4), 554–570.

Webber, C. F., & Scott, S. (2013). Principles for principal preparation. In C. L. Slater & S. Nelson (Eds.), *Understanding the principalship: An international guide to principal preparation* (pp. 73–100). Bingley, England: Emerald.

Wildy, H., & Clarke, S. (2008). Principals on L-plates: Rear view mirror reflections. *Journal of Educational Administration, 46*(6), 727–738.

CHAPTER 3

SOCIALLY JUST SCHOOL LEADERSHIP

Ten Years of Learning From Each Other

Pamela S. Angelle
The University of Tennessee

Michele Morrison
The University of Waikato, NZ

As the story is told, the idea for the International School Leadership Development Network (ISLDN) began as a casual conversation at the 2009 British Educational Leadership, Management, and Administration Society (BELMAS) meeting in Sheffield, England. The cross-country collaborative research project on educational leadership was formalized through a memorandum of understanding between BELMAS and the University Council of Educational Administration (UCEA), where both organizations pledged support for the project. The call for researchers was met with positive response, so much so that two self-selected strands of research resulted in a high-needs schools (HNS) research team and a social justice leadership (SJL) research team.

Educational Leadership for Social Justice and Improving High-Needs Schools, pages 31–50
Copyright © 2021 by Information Age Publishing
All rights of reproduction in any form reserved.

31

32 ▪ P. S. ANGELLE and M. MORRISON

This chapter documents the research journey of the SJL research strand. We first detail the development of the project from initial team building, including the exploration of researcher positionality, to the formulation of research focus and methods, data collection, and interpretive framework. Next, we highlight the scholarship and key research findings that have emanated from this project. We then reflect on the "growing pains" that accompanied our formation as a research network and potential avenues for moving SJL research forward. Finally, we consider the utility of community of practice (CoP) theory (Lave & Wenger, 1991; Wenger, 1998, 2010) as a retrospective sensemaking heuristic and the lessons that might be learned from this.

DEVELOPMENT OF THE PROJECT

Building a Team and Constructing a Project

Initial meetings of the SJL research team took place at the annual meetings of UCEA and BELMAS. At international team building sessions, an open invitation was issued to attendees interested in collaborating on IS-LDN research and subsequently disseminated via collegial and professional networks. The opportunity to extend research horizons (both relational and empirical), enlarge global data sets, undertake wide-ranging comparative study, and broaden collective insight generated considerable excitement. While "an increasingly inter-connected policy and practice world" (Day & Gurr, 2018, p. 341) enables, if not demands, international research collaborations, these are a relatively recent phenomenon across the educational landscape. As such, many of us found ourselves entering new territory, a "fourth age in research" (Adams, 2013, p. 557) that transcends individual, institutional, and national research configurations. It soon became apparent that working across borders, cultures, and institutional arrangements, in intermittent and often asynchronous time, with associated issues of identity, performance, and ownership, would add complexity to team building (Anderson & Steneck, 2011; Griffin et al., 2013; Parker & Kingori, 2016).

One of the first discussion items centred on membership of the network. It was agreed that researchers would evidence their initial commitment to the SJL research strand by uploading three documents in a shared online repository: a statement of researcher positionality, a description of education provision in the country/ies researched, and a case study commensurate with the research protocol. The three "tickets" signified membership of the research community, enabling access to the data repository, attendance at bespoke research meetings, and collaborative presentation and publication opportunities.

From a planning perspective, we soon discovered the limitations of pre-conference sessions and videoconferencing in generating and sustaining research momentum. With funding support provided by BELMAS and UCEA, 3-day bespoke research meetings were held in Atlanta, Georgia (IS-LDN Social Justice Strand, 2014); Gosport, England, UK (2015); Hamilton/Dunedin, New Zealand (2016), and Lleida, Spain (2018). Consolidation of group protocols and design of the conceptual framework were primary outcomes of the inaugural meeting, with collaborative publication plans and development of the quantitative tool emerging subsequently.

In addition to bespoke meetings affording the concentrated time and space in which to move the project forward, deliberate location in different parts of the world helped equalize travel expenses. More importantly, however, opportunities to visit schools, converse with practitioners, and experience local culture added richness to discussion. In New Zealand, for example, we visited Whakarewarewa, a Māori village in which indigenous Tūhourangi Ngāti Wāhiao inhabitants shared aspects of culture, history, and the geothermal environment shaping their settlement for almost 700 years. Although fleeting, authentic cultural experiences such as these served a dual purpose, breathing life and meaning into static images and text, and providing a useful point of reference when reflecting on the extent to which indigenous and other cultures infused the daily activities of students and staff in the schools visited.

Project Methods

Our objective in developing this research project was to conduct a global study under one design and one protocol. Arguably fraught within national confines, the onto-epistemological challenge of framing SJL and its pursuit internationally proved an even more complex undertaking. Language assumed huge importance as we sought to define SJL and construct research questions in an open and inclusive manner.

Agreeing a definition of SJL was both foundational to our study and more difficult than anticipated (see also, Berkovich, 2014; Theoharis, 2007). While Americans looked to race as the predominant construct in such a definition, the United Kingdom looked to class differences and New Zealand to culture. Colleagues from Sweden had particular difficulties as social justice called to mind the justice system of courts and law, rather than practices dealing with marginalized students. It quickly became apparent that a complex definition would not only fail to encapsulate the totality of diverse researcher understandings and secure consensus; it would also require considerable translation in practice. Conversely, a simple and succinct articulation of a social justice leader would provide an inclusive

34 ▪ P. S. ANGELLE and M. MORRISON

beginning point, make greater sense to potential participants, and open possibilities of listening. Ultimately, the group agreed upon: *A principal/ headteacher who is committed to reducing inequalities and makes this aim a high priority in their leadership practice.*

Discussion ensued regarding research questions, with focus and language the main sources of contention. Our task was to construct questions that would address issues of social justice as it was practiced in a world of many cultures and myriad ways of schooling. At the same time, we were anxious not to privilege Western, predominantly Anglophile and Anglo-American values and constructs in a manner that excluded other ways of knowing and participating. The SJL research team thus decided on the following research questions:

> How do social justice leaders *make sense* of "social justice"?
> What do social justice leaders *do*?
> What factors *help and hinder* the work of social justice leaders?
> How did social justice leaders *learn* to become social justice leaders?

Following from these questions, the agreed upon research design, utilizing a constructivist worldview and an exploratory approach, was a qualitative study. We realized that interviewing a sample of 1–5 school leaders in each country imposed limitations of sample size. However, at this point in the project, we were more interested in sacrificing breadth of perceptions about social justice for a deeper exploration of principal agency and practices for social justice. In this way, we could better understand the nuanced work of individuals in specific contexts across countries.

A protocol, agreed upon by all team members, included both initial questions for a first interview and follow-up questions for a second interview conducted six months to a year later with the goal of understanding each leader's unfolding social justice rhetoric and the extent to which this shaped their actual practice. All team members agreed to the common design, use of the interview protocol, purposive and snowball site/participant selection based on recommendation and self-identification as social justice leaders, and thematic analysis using the interpretive contextual framework. This uniformity in research design and implementation in 14 different countries enhanced the trustworthiness of cross-national findings, thereby distinguishing ISLDN SJL research from temporally and methodologically diverse studies in single sites.

Positionality

While we gathered data in schools across the world, we also began to consider individual researcher positionality regarding social justice and the manner in which personal experience and prejudices (including the preconceived ideas alluded to in the previous section) shape notions of what social justice is and how leaders pursue it. Recognizing that the term "social justice" is used "by both the political right and political left to mean quite different things" (Angelle, Morrison, & Stevenson, 2015, pp. 98–99), our initial motivation was for transparency and trustworthiness in our data analysis and findings. However, this reflexive exercise quickly became a source of learning from and about each other.

In the process of examining our positionality for this research topic, we delved into issues of equality vs. equity, the value of inclusion, student voice, and who we meant when we referred to marginalization. We each wrote a position statement and shared our personal values and beliefs about social justice and marginalized children. More than a simple SJL strand membership prerequisite, these narratives of lived experience and meaning-making highlighted the conceptual pluralism arising from researchers' intersubjective engagement in the world. Consistent with the social constructivist epistemology (Berger & Luckmann, 1967) underpinning the vision for our research, statements of positionality provided richness of understanding, not only of our research but also of our research colleagues.

At the time of initial analysis in 2014, 33 positionality statements from scholars in 14 countries were examined. In his analysis, Slater (2017) identified common themes across the positionality statements, including equal opportunity for all children, marginalization, and inclusion. As Slater (2017) notes, while the statements represented 14 countries from around the world, the language surrounding social justice was remarkably similar. Focusing on students, researchers shared that we must be the voice for students (China), serve students so they may live life fully (Costa Rica), place value on diversity (Israel), and maintain high yet realistic expectations for the "disadvantaged" or "less able" child (Scotland). Positionality on social justice centered on equity to gain equality (USA), fighting injustice for marginalized children (New Zealand), reducing unjust democratic conditions (Turkey), and remaining aware of the dangers of low expectations (England; Slater, 2017). Slater's (2017) work highlighted for the research team common drivers underpinning our collective efforts. This served an important reminder to hold individual positions less tightly and strengthened our resolve to advocate for marginalized children, however defined.

The Interpretive Framework

Awareness of positionality reinforced for the research team the uniquely personal and political nature of leadership for social justice. This cannot be divorced from the social, cultural, political and historical milieu in which we are situated and the diverse contexts in which agency is enacted. Meaningful analysis of principals' lived experiences in a single school site, in multiple sites within national borders, and across national borders therefore rested on our ability to grapple with and somehow distill multiple conceptions of context. This realization prompted the iterative design of an interpretive framework that would support consistent, coherent analysis of first phase interview data and form the basis for a grounded theory of socially just leadership (see Morrison, 2017a, for a detailed description of this process).

The common conceptual framework developed by the ISLDN social justice research network identified elements of context that shape leadership practice at the micro (personal), meso (institutional), and macro (national) level. The 2013 framework prototype (see Figure 3.1) had antecedents in earlier research calling for more sophisticated awareness of context (Dimmock, Stevenson, Bignold, Shah, & Middlewood, 2005). Introducing the framework to network members, Stevenson (personal communication, 16 April, 2013) drew attention to the school in the middle of the diagram, nested within a set of "micro" factors which were, in turn, nested within a set of "macro" factors.

These initial macro–micro elements were subsequently recast with different titles, and the school leader, rather than the institutional setting, positioned at the center (Stevenson, 2013b—see Figure 3.2). To the immediate

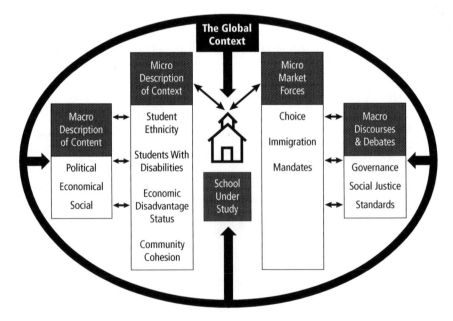

Figure 3.1 Framework for macro/micro examination of school context. *Source:* Stevenson, 2013a.

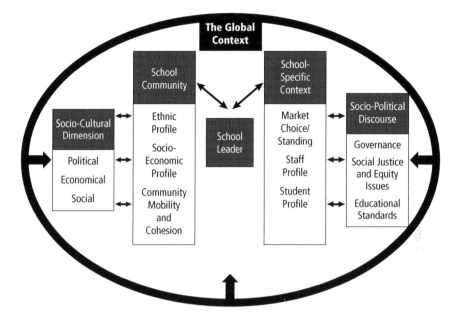

Figure 3.2 ISLDN framework V1. *Source:* Stevenson, 2013b.

right, were school specific factors such as student and staff profile (ethnicity, gender, age, mobility) and school reputation, beyond which were sociopolitical discourses shaping educational governance, qualifications and standards, and equity issues. To the immediate left, were community demographics, features that may or may not be mirrored within the school setting, and generic political, social, and economic influences at a national level. Situating the individual school leader at the center precipitated review of the original macro–micro nesting, with the micro-level representing the principal, the meso-level representing institutional or school-wide factors, and the macro-level retaining a societal and national policy focus.

Researchers who applied the first iteration of the ISLDN framework (Stevenson, 2013b) to Phase 1 data concurred that it served a useful purpose in unifying analysis and "keeping researchers on the same page." Further, the mapping of interview and country data revealed particularities of context that helped explain why policy mandated at national level was enacted in various ways at the school level, and why the global flow of education policies and discourses was diluted or enhanced by national interests. From a leadership perspective, framework mapping also assisted the identification of spaces in which determined school leaders could leverage shift. This aligned with Bourdieu's (2000) contention that change occurs in niches at the limits of fields. As poet and composer Leonard Cohen remarked in Anthem (1992), "There is a crack in everything. That's where the light gets in."

Somewhat ironically, personal factors driving the leader at the center, upon whose agency it was later identified that initiatives and interventions often depended, were omitted from the first iteration of the framework. This crucial oversight dominated framework critique during the inaugural research meeting in Atlanta, Georgia, 2014. As a consequence, the central element was expanded to include school leaders' personal and career biographies; defining events and influences attuning them to social justice issues; personal characteristics, motivations, and emotions that sustain them in their leadership endeavors; and paradigms in which they locate preferred discourses of SJL. Meso and macro level factors were supplemented with student voice, the school's institutional history (including rituals and artefacts), vision and mission, cultural dimensions, and regional/national education policy. The addition of the chronological or time dimension (see Figure 3.3) highlighted the ongoing pursuit of social justice and heightened perceptions of fluidity within the framework.

The conceptual framework served as a useful heuristic for examining the "idiosyncratic mix of external environmental conditions, internal organization dynamics, and leaders' prior experiences/backgrounds that together constitute fluid, relational leadership environments" (Morrison, 2017a, p. 60). It alerted researchers and leaders to the importance of context and the nuances of this shifting phenomenon, to factors that enabled and constrained leadership endeavors, and the potential for shift. The manner in which principals experience leadership enactment in context could only be surmised from the framework, however, and so it was the rich accounts of situated practice that formed the foundation for much of our scholarship.

SCHOLARSHIP

Ten years of SJL research has generated numerous publications, including journal articles (Angelle, Arlestig, & Norberg, 2015; Arar, Beycioglu, & Oplatka, 2016; Arar & Oplatka, 2016; Forde & Torrance, 2017; Morrison, McNae, & Branson, 2015; Richardson & Sauers, 2014; Silva et al., 2017; Slater, Potter, Torres, & Briceno, 2014; Szeto, 2014; Torrance & Forde, 2015); book chapters (Angelle et al., 2016; Arar, Ogden, & Beycioglu, 2019; Beycioglu & Ogden, 2017; Branson, Morrison, & McNae, 2016; Jones, Angelle, & Lohman-Hancock, 2019; King, Forde, Razzaq, & Torrance; 2019; King & Travers, 2017; McNae, 2017; Miller, Roofe, & Garcia-Carmona, 2019; Morrison, 2017b; Potter, 2017; Robinson, 2017; Slater et al., 2019; Szeto & Cheng, 2017; Torres-Arcadia, Murakami, & Moral, 2019); ISLDN compilations (Angelle, 2017a; Angelle & Torrance, 2019; Richardson & Sauers, 2014); and multiple presentations in conference venues throughout the world. This prolific scholarship, a selection of which is referenced above,

Socially Just School Leadership ▪ 39

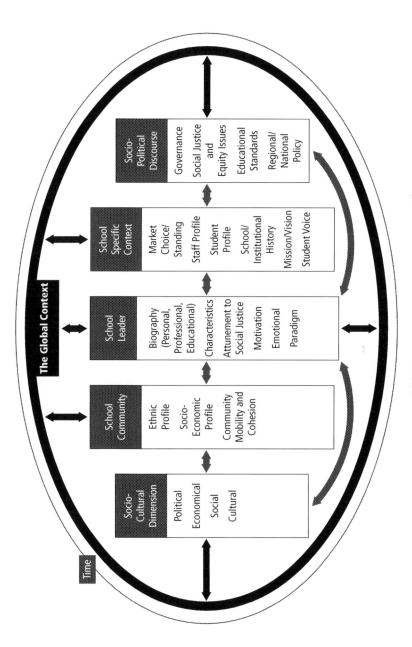

Figure 3.3 A micro/meso/macro contextual frame for social justice leadership in schools (V2). *Source*: ISLDN social justice strand, 2014.

has contributed to the social justice literature, opened dialogue among academics and school leaders, and added to the knowledge base of both scholars and practitioners internationally.

Integral to SJL research findings thus far is the importance of context to the practice of SJL. While the activism of the principal in maintaining a focus on the child has been routinely documented in many studies (McKenzie et al., 2008), concerted focus on context as a central rather than peripheral determinant of practice distinguishes our work. As such, it addresses Berkovich's (2014) call for socio-ecological perspectives that transcend a narrow "focus on actions by individuals and schools in an isolated manner, and [more properly recognises] the interdependence between social subsystems and levels" (p. 283; see also King & Travers, 2017).

Findings from the SJL studies have pointed to the importance of context as a key contribution to the literature writ large. The myriad contexts in which we examined what social justice leaders do, how these leaders make sense of social justice, and how the leaders learned to work for social justice produced findings that were remarkably similar; that is, despite the differences in the focus for social justice, the context in which social justice was practiced framed how the principal worked for marginalized children. As previously noted, while the focus of social justice ranged from issues of class (United Kingdom) to race (United States) to religion (Israel) and included countries with social democratic leadership (Sweden) to bureaucratic one-party states (China), the values and beliefs of the principals regarding marginalized children were analogous. The contextual examination of what helped and hindered the work of social justice in schools revealed the differences in each principal's practice.

Systemic inequities in resource distribution meant poverty was a recurring theme in the majority of participant countries, however determination of the children most impoverished by discriminatory policies and processes, and thus particularly deserving of educators' attention, varied according to practice settings. In the United States, for example, a focus on racial disparity was particularly evident in discussions of achievement and policy (Beycioglu & Ogden, 2017), whereas educational provision for poor, migrant, and special educational needs (SEN) students in charitable "rooftop" schools preoccupied one Hong Kong principal (Szeto, 2014), and a student deprivation index held Welsh school leaders accountable for reducing the educational impact of material and social barriers to opportunity (Jones, 2017).

In cases where researchers and principals were enculturated in the same national policy discourses, perceptions of greatest need were broadly similar. The macro policy context of the countries where the research has taken place therefore remains an essential component to consider when examining social justice. Indeed, in several studies the macro-context both

Socially Just School Leadership ▪ **41**

provided support and inserted barriers to the practice of social justice leaders. Whilst the national context exerts considerable power, international comparative studies have nonetheless emphasized that the behavior and decision-making of principals is influenced by the local context in which these decisions are made. As Osborn (2004) reminds us, Michael Sadler noted long ago that "in studying foreign systems of education we should not forget that the things outside the schools matter even more than the things inside the schools, and govern and interpret the things inside" (p. 266). Addressing social justice concerns thus demands both intra- and extra-institutional activism on the part of school leaders.

GROWING PAINS

As the ISLDN SJL strand research project has evolved, we have experienced learning from each other as well as practicing patience with each other. Crossing national boundaries for research collaboration presented barriers that included understanding language, university ethics requirements, school operations, cultural understandings, and funding. Thus, discussions about schooling in individual countries were as important as data analysis. Examples of challenges we faced as a research team follow.

Though all team members spoke English, language presented a potential problem; that is, the language of schooling, acronyms, structure, governance, and curriculum were all areas that needed to be defined, with examples, to foster understanding. Terms common to individual countries, such as sixth form, middle schools, free schools, charter schools, academies, walking principals, head teachers, school boards, and boards of governors, had to be clearly understood as we attempted to understand education in countries other than our own. We quickly realized that assumptions about schooling led to confusion and that honest and patient discussions were needed to understand, agree, and move forward.

Our goal was to examine how principals across the world not only understood social justice but how they practiced social justice. We wanted to glean how the socially just leader learned to hold these values and the influential background experiences that led them to prioritize the needs of marginalized children. This also became a subject of debate for the research team since the focus of social justice generally differed from country to country.

As we sought to learn about the language and practice of schooling in countries other than our own, we agreed that the best way to understand was to observe. While fleeting, visits to schools, dialogue with groups of school leaders, and immersion in local culture formed an integral part of annual research meetings. These encounters simultaneously reinforced the common humanity and moral purpose driving this research, surfaced and disrupted comfortable ways of knowing, enlivened the data in our shared repository, and enabled a subtlety in comparison that eluded those who did not experience firsthand the richness and diversity of contexts that others inhabit.

Simple understandings in-country were not at all simple to researchers unfamiliar with ways of being in cultures other than their own. The incalculable value of school visits brought firsthand knowledge of local customs, insider observations of regional culture, and opportunities to visit with students and teachers in classrooms to gain deeper understandings of experiences of learning. While visiting schools in Lleida, Spain, many of us were bemused by the arrival of students, accompanied by their parents, to school in mid-afternoon. This observation taught us the custom of siesta and the ways in which this supports students in their learning. The cultural experience of a Māori powhiri (welcoming ceremony) at a Bay of Plenty high school allowed us to participate in a unique and revered indigenous ritual. Time spent at a public school in Gosport, England, followed by a tour of a private school in the same town, afforded an inside glimpse into the fragile balance of class differences. The significance of school visits was recalled time and again as we furthered our research and grew our appreciation of education across the world.

Moving Forward

The SJL strand of the ISLDN research project has generated unique scholarship, new understandings of schooling and leadership for social justice, cross-national friendships, and global recognition for rigorous and meaningful research. As we move forward to the next 10 years of the project, we must consider what we have learned and how we might harness that learning into a deeper comprehension of SJL.

The rich, in-depth qualitative interviews conducted during the first phase of the project document the particularities of circumstance and nuances of practice shared by the principals whom we interviewed. While sample sizes were small, disallowing generalization within and across national borders, these accounts of lived experience provide crucial insight into the macro, meso and micro determinants shaping the policy-practice interface. Furthermore, a common research design and shared lexicon, together with ease of technology, enabled us to compare findings in different parts of the world.

As Hantrais (1999) suggests, the value of comparative case studies lies in the opportunity to observe the same phenomenon in a variety of national contexts, with a view to identifying and explaining similarities and differences. This is a far from straightforward exercise, however. Comparative studies have been criticized, both for a lack of methodological rigor (Osborn, 2004) and for ignoring multiple and diverse facets of culture in

Socially Just School Leadership ▪ **43**

addressing findings, opting instead to "average" societal culture (Cheong, 2000). The ISLDN SJL research team has endeavored to avoid these pitfalls by employing the same methodology and data gathering instruments, along with cultural immersion through country and school visits, and coming together as a team to explore data across cases to generate findings on an international basis.

We see three major avenues in which to advance our work. The first entails extending the qualitative data repository to include additional cases in countries already represented, thereby enabling a more representative national picture. The second involves expanding the network to include more researchers in developing and non-Anglophone countries, thereby eliciting broader perspectives of SJL that expose and potentially mitigate Eurocentric analytical bias. The third employs a quantitative tool to assess the relative weighting of factors supporting and impeding SJL, thereby enhancing the potential for generalizability within and across countries.

With regard to the latter, interview transcripts related to Research Question 3 (What factors *help and hinder* the work of social justice leaders?) were coded in 2016. These codes were placed in a code map (Anfara, Brown, & Magione, 2002) from which pattern variables were gleaned and quantification took place. The objective of quantifying the qualitative data was to construct items for a survey intended to measure the weight of issues which supported and acted as barriers to the work of social justice. As Angelle (2017b) noted:

> The significance of investigating the question of influences on decision making leads to issues that are both within the control of the principal (that is, administrative behavior, school culture, staff variables, and perceptions of the school) as well as issues beyond the control of the principal (that is, national policy, financial capital, politics, and student life issues). (p. 313)

Arising from initial survey item construction (for a more detailed description, see Angelle, 2017b), the final Social Justice—Behaviors and Supports (SJ-BAS) instrument was tested and validated through an online Delphi method. The SJ-BAS includes 24 items on perceptions of support for social justice practices ($\alpha = 0.965$) and 19 items on perceptions of barriers to social justice practices ($\alpha = 0.923$). Exploratory factor analysis found four support component factors, comprising School Culture and Practices ($\alpha = 0.918$), Resources ($\alpha = 0.928$), Communication, Collaboration and Guidance ($\alpha = 0.940$), and Parental and Community Support ($\alpha = 0.940$) and four barrier component factors comprising School Culture ($\alpha = 0.863$), Resources and Policy ($\alpha = 0.875$), Perceptions ($\alpha = 0.862$), Student Family Situation ($\alpha = 0.888$).

To address the concern with generalizability in the Phase 1 qualitative study, the SJ-BAS is currently being administered to a wider sample across the project team members' countries. The quantitative second phase of the ISLDN SJL study will allow for generalizing across countries. In this way, the project team will begin to draw cross-country conclusions regarding socially just leadership practices across the globe, and develop a grounded theory of social justice in schools.

A COMMUNITY OF PRACTICE? LESSONS LEARNED

A 10 year retrospective such as this invites consideration of the extent to which the SJL strand constitutes a CoP. In the 25 years since its inception, the term "community of practice" (Lave & Wenger, 1991; Wenger, 1998) has become common parlance, "reified to the point where aggregates of people in a research context are just presumed to be a community of practice" (King, 2019, p. 15). Wenger (1998), however, identifies three crucial disciplines that together distinguish a CoP from other social communities and networks: *domain, community,* and *practice.* Domain refers to the human endeavor or real life problem that commands and orients people's attention, participation and commitment, in this case, the nature of socially just school leadership. Community refers to members who spontaneously and collectively invest in joint activities and "thinking together" (Pyrko, Dörfler, & Eden, 2017), and practice to the discursive interactions and repertoire of resources emerging from ongoing domain engagement. To the three original disciplines, Wenger (2010) adds a fourth: the discipline of convening, whereby a member/members of the community take responsibility for organizing, nurturing, and overseeing the resourcing of the communal interactional space.

From an instrumental perspective, Wenger (2010) perceives a CoP as a learning partnership in which "capability is anchored in a mutual recognition and engagement" (p. 12). Communities of practice take diverse forms, varying in size, composition (homogeneous and heterogeneous, core and peripheral), location (local and global) and modes of interaction (face to face and virtual). In order to verify, empirically, whether a CoP actually exists, Wenger (1998) outlines a set of defining features including "sustained mutual relationships (harmonious or conflictual)" and "shared ways of engaging" that reflect an "absence of introductory preambles, as if conversations and interactions were merely the continuation of an ongoing process" (p. 125). Arising from this process are "mutually defining identities; the ability to assess the appropriateness of actions and products; specific tools, representations, and other artefacts; and a shared discourse that reflects a certain perspective on the world" (pp. 125–126).

Applying these criteria to our research endeavors over the past decade, it appears that the SJL strand of the ISLDN does, for the most part, reflect a

Socially Just School Leadership ▪ **45**

growing CoP. From spontaneous origins in 2008, the network has grown to include 35 members in 14 countries, the majority of whom are researchers. On occasion, principals participating in social justice research have accompanied us to bespoke research meetings, thereby contributing to evolving frameworks and understandings of comparative and situated practice.

Over time, membership has both assumed an upward trajectory as researchers in new sites have joined the network and fluctuated as the priorities of those involved have shifted. In a CoP, it is the strength of individual commitment to domain initiatives, rather than institutional directives, which determines the nature and duration of participation. Wenger (1998, 2010) comments that communities of practice will likely contain core and peripheral members and this has certainly been the case in the SJL research strand. A core group of researchers has attended every bespoke research meeting, whilst others have participated intermittently as circumstances have allowed, or confined involvement to empirical research and dissemination activities.

While communities of practice involve minimal formalization, the coming together of researchers from different cultural worlds posed unique challenges, as elucidated earlier in this chapter. Cultivating a fluid, diverse and geographically dispersed research network required ongoing investment in relationships, initiation of strategic conversation, negotiation of conflict, coordination of physical and virtual meetings, communication of practice decisions, and liaison and editorship of numerous conference and publishing undertakings. Variable attendance and extended periods between meetings meant that "introductory preambles" (Wenger, 1998) could not be dispensed with entirely. Although minimal in number, these verbal and written communications served an important function in welcoming new members and bridging research conversations. This leads us to suggest that an absence of introductory preambles is more likely characteristic of local communities of practice whose work is of an intense short-term duration, than an international research network such as ours. Indeed, Wenger (1998) concedes that distance does not prevent global communities of practice but can hinder them.

In most other respects, the SJL strand clearly reflects CoP dimensions. The discipline of convening has been jointly undertaken by Pamela Angelle (US) and Ian Potter (UK) who oversee SJL network administration, communication, and strategy. Leadership of the core group has, in large part, facilitated the development of a common lexicon, research protocol, and conceptual framework that guide SJL data collection and analysis in multiple and diverse research sites across the globe. These artefacts have been instrumental in maintaining fidelity to shared discourse and inquiry. Mutually defining identities have emerged through the ongoing "layering of events of participation and reification" (Wenger, 1998, p. 151) and our methodological journey reflects a developing ability to assess the appropriateness of tools and artefacts.

Although communities of practice seemingly offer huge potential for new knowledge creation, they are not limitation free. Wenger, McDermott, and Snyder (2002) identify membership exclusivity, the hoarding of knowledge, clique formation, and limitation of innovation as inherent risks. We would argue that the absence of commercial imperatives, reliance on multiple researchers in multiple sites for practice insights, and commitment to sharing this knowledge with diverse audiences means that a research CoP such as ours, minimizes the likelihood of the first three dangers becoming manifest.

We remain mindful, however, of Wenger's (2010) caution that "remaining on a learning edge takes a delicate balancing act between honoring the history of the practice and shaking free from it" (p. 182). Development of a quantitative tool during the second phase of this research has to some extent assuaged methodological concerns expressed by initial participants, some of whom disappeared from the research periphery. In addition, recent collaboration with colleagues working in the HNS strand (for example, McNae, Morrison, & Notman, 2017; Gurr et al., 2021, Chapter 8, this volume) has opened new avenues for thinking together, within and across CoP boundaries. In this way, we hope to embrace new perspectives and avoid the insularity of "groupthink" (Janis, 1972).

CONCLUDING THOUGHTS

Reflecting on the past decade, as we have just done, has alerted us to the irony that being steeped in social learning theory is one thing and intentional cultivation of a CoP, from the outset, quite another. This has been our experience, however. The SJL strand has evolved in an organic manner, responding to challenges, such as clarity around data access and use, in well-intentioned ways, not all of which have been preemptive in nature. Professional commitment and goodwill continue to form the bedrock of domain, community and practice involvement, something that deliberate attention to CoP principles during formative and subsequent stages would undoubtedly enhance (Wilson-Mah & Walinga, 2017). This highlights the importance of interactions, processes, and structures that build group identity, unite members in a common discourse, enhance analytical rigor, and sustain momentum. We would argue that attention to these aspects of being as a research CoP will more likely generate research that is iterative, creative, and worthwhile.

REFERENCES

Adams, J. (2013). The fourth age of research. *Nature, 47*, 557–560.

Anderson, M. S., & Steneck, N. H. (Eds.). (2011). *International research collaborations: Much to be gained, many ways to get in trouble.* New York, NY: Routledge.

Anfara, V. A., Jr., Brown, K. M., & Mangione, T. L. (2002). Qualitative analysis on stage: Making the research process more public. *Educational Researcher, 31*(7), 28–38.

Angelle, P. S. (Ed.). (2017a). *A global perspective of social justice leadership for school principals.* Charlotte, NC: Information Age.

Angelle, P. S. (2017b). Moving forward. In P. S. Angelle (Ed.), *A global perspective of social justice leadership for school principals* (pp. 303–319). Charlotte, NC: Information Age.

Angelle, P. S., Arlestig, H., & Norberg, K. (2015). The practice of socially just leadership: Contextual differences in US and Swedish principals. *International Studies in Educational Administration, 43*(2), 21–37.

Angelle, P. S., Morrison, M., & Stevenson, H. (2015). 'Doing' social justice leadership: Connecting the macro and micro contexts of schooling. In D. Anderson & J. Ryan (Eds.), *Working (with/out) the system: Educational leadership, micropolitics and social justice* (pp. 95–116). Charlotte, NC: Information Age.

Angelle, P. S., & Torrance, D. (Eds.). (2019). *Cultures of social justice leadership: An intercultural context of schools.* Cham, Switzerland: Palgrave Macmillan.

Arar, K., Beycioglu, K., & Oplatka, I. (2016). A cross-cultural of educational leadership for social justice in Israel and Turkey: Meanings, actions and contexts. *Compare: A Journal of Comparative and International Education, 47*(2), 1–15.

Arar, K., & Oplatka, I. (2016). Making sense of social justice in education: Jewish and Arab leaders' perspectives in Israel. *Management in Education, 30*(2), 66–73. https://doi.org/10.1177/0892020616631409

Arar, K., Ogden, S., & Beycioglu, K. (2019). Social justice leadership, perceptions and praxis: A cross-cultural comparison of Palestinian, Haitian and Turkish principals. In P. S. Angelle & D. Torrance (Eds.), *Cultures of social justice leadership: An intercultural context of schools* (pp. 43–66). Cham, Switzerland: Palgrave Macmillan.

Berger, P., & Luckmann, T. (1967). *The social construction of reality: A treatise in the sociology of knowledge.* London, England: Penguin.

Berkovich, I. (2014). A socio-ecological framework of social justice leadership in education. *Journal of Educational Administration, 52*(3), 282–309. https://doi.org/10.1108/JEA-12-2012-0131

Beycioglu, K., & Ogden, S. (2017). Social justice beliefs and behaviours: A cross-cultural look at Turkish and U. S. principals. In P. S. Angelle (Ed.), *A global perspective of social justice leadership for school principals* (pp. 111–126). Charlotte, NC: Information Age.

Bourdieu, P. (2000). *Pascalian meditations* (R. Nice, trans.). Stanford, CA: Stanford University Press.

Branson, C., Morrison, M., & McNae, R. (2015). In search of seamless education. In S. Gross & J. Shapiro (Eds.), *Democratic ethical educational leadership: Reclaiming school reform* (pp. 138–143). New York, NY: Routledge.

48 ▪ P. S. ANGELLE and M. MORRISON

Cheong Y. C. (2000). Cultural factors in educational effectiveness: A framework for comparative research. *School Leadership & Management, 20*(2), 207–225.

Cohen, L. (1992). Anthem. *On The future* [vinyl]. New York, NY: Columbia Records.

Day, C., & Gurr, D. (2018). International network as sites for research on successful school leadership. In C. R. Lochmiller (Ed.), *Complementary research methods for educational leadership and policy studies* (pp. 341–357). Cham, Switzerland: Palgrave Macmillan.

Dimmock, C., Stevenson, H., Bignold, B., Shah, S., & Middlewood, D. (2005). *Effective leadership in multi-ethnic schools: School community perspectives and their leadership implications. Project Report.* Nottingham, England: National College of School Leadership.

Forde, C., & Torrance, D. (2017). Social justice leaders: Critical moments in headteachers'/principals' development. *Research in Educational Administration and Leadership, 2*(1), 29–52.

Griffin, G., Bränström-Öhman, A., & Kalman, H. (Eds.) (2013). *The emotional politics of research collaboration.* New York, NY: Routledge.

Hantrais, L. (1999). Contextualization in cross-national comparative research. *International Journal of Social Research Methodology, 2*(2), 93–108.

ISLDN Social Justice Strand. (2014, February, 14–16). *A Micro/Meso/Macro contextual frame for social justice leadership in schools (V2).* Paper presented at the annual meeting of the International School Leadership Development Network, Atlanta, GA.

Janis, I. L. (1972). *Victims of groupthink.* Boston, MA: Houghton Mifflin.

Jones, K. (2017). Social justice leadership: A Welsh perspective. In P. S. Angelle (Ed.), *A global perspective of social justice leadership for school principals* (pp. 127–146). Charlotte, NC: Information Age.

Jones, K., Angelle, P. S., & Lohman-Hancock, C. (2019). Local implementation of national policy: Social justice perspectives from the USA, India, and Wales. In P. S. Angelle & D. Torrance (Eds.), *Cultures of social justice leadership: An intercultural context of schools* (pp. 169–194). Cham, Switzerland: Palgrave Macmillan.

King, B. W. (2019). *Communities of practice in applied language research: A critical introduction.* New York, NY: Routledge.

King, F., Forde, C., Razzaq, J., & Torrance, D. (2019). Systems of education governance and cultures of justice in Ireland, Scotland and Pakistan. In P. S. Angelle & D. Torrance (Eds.), *Cultures of social justice leadership: An intercultural context of schools* (pp. 67–92). Cham, Switzerland: Palgrave Macmillan.

King, F., & Travers, J. (2017). Social justice leadership through the lens of ecological systems theory. In P. S. Angelle (Ed.), *A global perspective of social justice leadership for school principals* (pp. 147–166). Charlotte, NC: Information Age.

Lave, J., & Wenger, E. (1991). *Situated learning: Legitimate peripheral participation.* New York, NY: Cambridge University Press.

McKenzie, K. B., Christman, D. E., Hernandez, F., Fierro, E., Capper, C. A., Dantley, M., Gonzalez, M. L., Cambron-McCabe, N., & Scheurich, J. J. (2008). From the field: A proposal for educating leaders for social justice. *Educational Administration Quarterly, 44*(1), 111–138.

McNae, R. (2017). School leaders making sense of the "self" with[in] social justice: Embodied influences from lived experiences. In P. S. Angelle (Ed.), *A global perspective of social justice leadership for school principals* (pp. 251–270). Charlotte, NC: Information Age.

McNae, R., Morrison, M., & Notman, R. (2017). *Educational leadership in Aotearoa New Zealand: Issues of context and social justice.* Wellington, New Zealand: NZCER Press.

Miller, P. W., Roofe, C., & Garcia-Carmona, M. (2019). School leadership, curriculum diversity, social justice and critical perspectives in education. In P. S. Angelle & D. Torrance (Eds.), *Cultures of social justice leadership: An intercultural context of schools* (pp. 93–120). Cham, Switzerland: Palgrave Macmillan.

Morrison, M. (2017a). Conceiving context: The origins and development of the theoretical framework. In P. S. Angelle (Ed.), *A global perspective of social justice leadership for school principals* (pp. 43–64). Charlotte, NC: Information Age.

Morrison, M. (2017b). "I wasn't really a decile 10 person": Deliberate enactment of social justice leadership in a high needs context. In R. McNae, M. Morrison, & R. Notman (Eds.), *Educational leadership in Aotearoa New Zealand: Issues of context and social justice* (pp. 73–87). Wellington, New Zealand: NZCER Press.

Morrison, M., McNae, R., & Branson, C. M. (2015). Multiple hues: New Zealand school leaders' perceptions of social justice. *Journal of Educational Leadership, Policy, and Practice, 30*(1), 4–16.

Osborn, M. (2004). New methodologies for comparative research? Establishing "constants" and "contexts" in educational experience. *Oxford Review of Education, 30*(2), 265–285.

Parker, M., & Kingori, P. (2016). Good and bad research collaborations: Researchers' views on science and ethics in global health research. *PLos ONE, 11*(10), 1–19. doi:10.1371/journal.pone.0163579

Potter, I. (2017). Change in context and identity: The case of an English school leader. In P. S. Angelle (Ed.), *A global perspective of social justice leadership for school principals* (pp. 231–250). Charlotte, NC: Information Age.

Pyrko, I., Dörfler, V., & Eden, C. (2017). Thinking together: What makes communities of practice work? *Human Relations, 70*(4), 389–409. https://doi.org/10.1177/0018726716661040

Richardson, J. W., & Sauers, N. J. (2014). Social justice in India: Perspectives from school leaders in diverse contexts. *Management in Education, 28*(3), 106–109.

Robinson, K. K. (2017). Retracing the steps of the journey: A literature review of social justice leadership from a global context. In P. S. Angelle (Ed.), *A global perspective of social justice leadership for school principals* (pp. 21–42). Charlotte, NC: Information Age.

Silva, P., Slater, C.L., Lopez Gorosave, G., Cerdas, V., Torres, N., Antunez, S., & Briceno, F. (2017). Educational leadership for social justice in Costa Rica, Mexico, and Spain. *Journal of Educational Administration, 55*(3), 316–333.

Slater, C. (2017). Social justice beliefs and the positionality of researchers. In P. S. Angelle (Ed.), *A global perspective of social justice leadership for school principals* (pp. 3–20). Charlotte, NC: Information Age.

Slater, C., Potter, I., Torres, N., & Briceno, F. (2014). Understanding social justice leadership: An international exploration of the perspectives of two school leaders in Costa Rica and England. *Management in Education, 28*(3), 110–115.

50 ■ P. S. ANGELLE and M. MORRISON

Slater, C. L., Silva, P., Lopez Gorosave, G., Morrison, M., Antúnez, S., Maytorena, B. M. C., & McNae, R. (2019). Leadership for social justice in schools in Mexico, New Zealand, and Spain. In P. S. Angelle & D. Torrance (Eds.). *Cultures of social justice leadership: An intercultural context of schools* (pp. 121–146). Cham, Switzerland: Palgrave Macmillan.

Stevenson, H. (2013a). *Framework for macro-micro examination of school context.* Retrieved from https://isldn.files.wordpress.com/2013/04/framework-4-15-13.pdf

Stevenson, H. (2013b). *ISLDN Framework v1.* Retrieved from https://isldn.files.wordpress.com/2012/11/isldn-framework-v1.pdf

Szeto, E. (2014). From recipient to contributor: The story of a social justice leader in a Hong Kong primary school. *Management in Education, 28*(3), 116–119.

Szeto, E., & Cheng, A. Y. N. (2017). Voices of school leaders for social justice in education across the world: A Hong Kong Case Report. In P. S. Angelle (Ed.), *A global perspective of social justice leadership for school principals* (pp. 209–230). Charlotte, NC: Information Age.

Theoharis, G. (2007). Social justice educational leaders and resistance: Toward a theory of social justice leadership. *Educational Administration Quarterly, 43*(2), 221–228.

Torrance, D., & Forde, C. (2015). To what extent can headteachers be held to account in the practice of social justice leadership? *Journal of Educational Leadership, Policy, and Practice, 30*(1), 79–91.

Torres-Arcadia, C., Murakami, E. T., & Moral, C. (2019). Leadership for social justice: Intercultural studies in Mexico, Untied States of American, and Spain. In P. S. Angelle & D. Torrance (Eds.). *Cultures of social justice leadership: An intercultural context of schools* (pp.147–168). Cham, Switzerland: Palgrave Macmillan.

Wenger, E. (1998). *Communities of practice: Learning, meaning, and identity.* Cambridge, England: Cambridge University Press.

Wenger, E. (2010). Communities of practice and social learning systems: The career of a concept. In C. Blackmore (Ed.), *Social learning systems and communities of practice* (pp. 179–198). London, England: Springer.

Wenger, E., McDermott, R., & Snyder, W. (2002). *Cultivating communities of practice.* Boston, MA: Harvard Business School Press.

Wilson-Mah, R., & Walinga, J. (2017). The people in the room: Convening interdisciplinary communities of practice in an institution of higher education. Papers on postsecondary learning and teaching: *Proceedings of the University of Calgary Conference on Learning and Teaching, 2,* 24–33.

CHAPTER 4

WHAT FACTORS HELP AND HINDER THE WORK OF SOCIAL JUSTICE LEADERS?

A Summary of Findings From the Social Justice Leadership Strand

Deirdre Torrance
University of Glasgow, Scotland

Fiona King
Dublin City University
Republic of Ireland

Ian Potter
Gosport and Fareham
Multi-Academy Trust, England

Rachel McNae
University of Waikato, New Zealand

Christine Forde
University of Glasgow, Scotland

Paul Miller
Educational Equite Services, England

Pamela Angelle
University of Tennessee

Michele Morrison
University of Waikato, New Zealand

Helene Ärlestig
Umeå University, Sweden

Katarina Norberg
Umeå University, Sweden

Christopher Branson
Australian Catholic University
Australia

Elson Szeto
Education University of Hong Kong,
Hong Kong

Annie Cheng (posthumously)
Education University
of Hong Kong, Hong Kong

Joe Travers
Dublin City University,
Republic of Ireland

Educational Leadership for Social Justice and Improving High-Needs Schools, pages 51–71
Copyright © 2021 by Information Age Publishing
All rights of reproduction in any form reserved.

51

52 ▪ D. TORRANCE et al.

Increasing emphasis has been placed on both leadership and social justice within educational theory, policy, and practice at a global level as part of a movement to improve the quality of education (King, Forde, Razzaq, & Torrance, 2019). Leadership is positioned as highly influential on social justice practices within schools, influencing pupil outcomes particularly for marginalized students. Social justice leadership (Bogotch & Shields, 2014) has emerged as a concept within the literature and policy discourse, used to describe the work of school leaders working to enhance the educational experience of all learners (Torrance & Forde, 2017), in an effort to reduce inequalities in education systems (King & Travers, 2017, p. 147). Whilst definitions of social justice and leadership are often lacking (Miller, Hill-Berry, Hylton-Fraser, & Powell, 2019), a helpful frame for the exploration of social justice leadership across different international contexts is provided by Shields and Mohan (2008):

> Our concept of social justice is one that identifies issues of power and inequity in schools and society and that challenges personal and systemic abuses of power as well as alienating and marginalizing beliefs, values, and practices. (p. 291)

Social justice leadership is inherently a political process (Cribb & Gewirtz, 2005) with head teachers/principals engaged in challenging injustice, mediating, negotiating, and selecting courses of action. Head teachers play a key role in such endeavors and yet, to date, little is understood about the practice of social justice leadership (Ryan, 2010). Arguably, head teachers have authority to empower others and to change practices. However, whilst individual head teachers can exercise a values-based commitment to social justice at the micro level (school leader) in their own practice, and in developing the practice of the schools they lead, the extent of their influence is supported and/ or constrained by the meso level (school, school context, school community) and macro level (country-wide, education system) and of society as a whole.

This chapter brings together the findings from eight education systems—England, Jamaica, Hong Kong, New Zealand, Republic of Ireland, Scotland, Sweden, and the United States—selected from over 20 countries contributing to the International School Leadership Development Network (ISLDN). A number of factors that help and hinder the practice of leadership for social justice are identified at meso (school and local authority) and macro (national) levels. Key themes emerging from interview data are presented to exemplify those factors from the head teachers' (micro) perspectives of practice realities.

THE INTERNATIONAL SCHOOL LEADER DEVELOPMENT NETWORK PROJECT

The ISLDN is a network of researchers and practitioners collaboratively sponsored by BELMAS (The British Educational Leadership, Management,

What Factors Help and Hinder the Work of Social Justice Leaders? ▪ **53**

and Administration Society) and UCEA (University Council for Educational Administration; Angelle, 2017; Young, 2017). In 2010, BELMAS and UCEA launched the ISLDN comparative studies project, examining the preparation and development of school leaders. The ISLDN has since evolved to form two strands: (a) preparing and developing leaders who advocate for social justice and (b) preparing and developing leaders for high-need, low-performing schools (Torrance & Angelle, 2019).

The ISLDN has worked together for a decade, collecting data from interviews with head teachers/principals in more than 20 countries. This chapter draws from the work of the ISLDN social justice strand using data generated from eight educational systems listed previously. Each country joined the ISLDN at a different point in time. A brief sense of that history follows, to explain the project as undertaken in those countries.

England

Membership of the network included researchers based in England from its beginning because the BELMAS lead role for the social justice leadership strand was with ISLDN cofounder Howard Stevenson. This was taken on by Ian Potter in 2015, co-coordinating the strand's group with Pam Angelle. Ian is a practicing school leader, a member of the Council of BELMAS and hosted the 2015 ISLDN meeting in Gosport, England, which was attended by researchers from across the United Kingdom and internationally. England-based members of the network have collected data from school leaders in both England and overseas, as well as contributing to publications and papers at conferences throughout the world.

Jamaica

Jamaica's membership of the ISLDN commenced in February 2014 through the Institute for Educational Administration and Leadership-Jamaica (IEAL-J). Paul Miller has represented the IEAL-J/Jamaica at ISLDN events since and has collaborated with ISLDN members. In particular, at the Annual BELMAS conference held in the United Kingdom and in 2017, at the UCEA conference in Denver, Colorado, USA. Paul Miller's introduction of the IEAL-J to the ISLDN, and the continued engagement of the IEAL-J and Paul in the network has also led to UCEA (in 2016) and BELMAS (in 2019) formalizing their relationship with the IEAL-J, through the signing of separate Memorandums of Understanding.

54 ▪ D. TORRANCE et al.

Hong Kong

The Hong Kong research on leadership for social justice was initiated in 2013. The team focused first on the micro and meso levels, and then on the macro level, specifically on political change. Analysis included the ways social justice leaders were prepared for their role and for practice within diverse school settings (Szeto & Cheng, 2018). In this longitudinal project, the social justice principals first struggled to survive in the face of permanent closure, then had to adapt to increasingly diverse student populations.

New Zealand

New Zealand joined ISLDN in late 2012 and remains an active network partner. University of Waikato researchers Christopher Branson, Michele Morrison, and Rachel McNae conducted multiple case studies during 2013–2015, findings from which feature in five edited books, a special New Zealand journal issue and numerous conference presentations. As New Zealand research team leader, Michele played an integral role in the development of the conceptual framework at the inaugural Atlanta research meeting in 2014, and hosted the third ISLDN meeting in Hamilton, New Zealand in 2016.

Republic of Ireland

The Republic of Ireland has been represented in this network from the 2009 BELMAS conference meeting by Bernie Grummell from Maynooth University. Fiona King from Dublin City University Institute of Education (DCU IoE) joined the network in July 2014 following conversations with Bernie Grummell, Howard Stevenson (BELMAS lead of ISLDN at that time) and Pam Angelle (one of the coordinators of the social justice strand). Joe Travers (DCU IoE) subsequently joined the network in October 2014 and both have conducted Irish case studies.

Scotland

The involvement of Scotland in the network was born out of a 2013 conference discussion between Howard Stevenson, who at that time had the BELMAS lead role for the ISLDN network, and Deirdre Torrance, then at University of Edinburgh. At a later meeting in Edinburgh with Howard, a colleague from the General Teaching Council for Scotland (GTCS) and the then Chair of the Scottish Educational Leadership, Management, and Administrative Society (SELMAS), Deirdre agreed to join the network and to conduct Scottish case studies. In 2014, Christine Forde, University of Glasgow joined the Scottish team, conducting further Scottish case studies.

Sweden

The Swedish team consists of Katarina Norberg and Helene Ärlestig, at the Centre for Principal Development, Umeå University, who joined the network when it started in 2010. The Swedish case study, based on interviews with two principals in ethnic multicultural schools, has been presented at conferences and published in a comparative study together with Pam Angelle's U.S. case. The Swedish team has also attended ISLDN network meetings and worked with projects that have benefited from knowledge and collaboration from both the social justice and high-needs strands.

United States

Researchers from the United States have been active in ISLDN since its inception in 2010. The U.S. representative, along with two representatives from England, has supported the convening of ISLDN meetings held in Atlanta, Georgia, and Gosport, England, United Kingdom. United States representatives have also served as co-leaders in ISLDN discussions at BELMAS and UCEA conferences. Throughout the last 10 years, additional researchers from the United States have joined the U.S. contingent, increasing the number of U.S. case studies.

DEVELOPMENT OF ISLDN PROJECT OUTCOMES

As is discussed in Torrance and Angelle (2019), the ISLDN research project drew from the work of Cribb and Gewirtz (2005) as a basis for understanding social justice, as well as from the work of Lee (2010), particularly her micro-political toolkit highlighting the significance of organizational context. Members of the ISLDN social justice leadership strand have created a continually developing framework within which individual cases of school leadership can be situated, with factors identified to help illuminate the context within which school leaders work. Originally drawing on the work of Dimmock, Stevenson, Bignold, Shah, and Middlewood (2005), locating schools in a local (micro) context within the national (macro) context, the ISLDN project has developed that framework further (Morrison, 2017), to

56 ▪ D. TORRANCE et al.

enable the exploration of the school leader (micro) factors, school (meso) context factors and country-wide (macro) context factors. The time dimension was added in recognition that "micro, meso, and macro contexts are continually in flux" (Morrison, 2017, p. 60) and so conceptions of social justice need to be fluid and open to change, responsive to "time, place and political context" (Hajisoteriou & Angelides, 2014, p. 897).

Accordingly, in 2014, the ISLDN research network moved into Phase 3 of its data generation and analysis, to which the data analyzed for this chapter relates. To further support the project's collaborative outputs, the original version of the network's framework for the macro–micro examination of school context was further developed as shown in Figure 4.1.

This refinement of the framework supports the analysis of key data for this chapter, with its focus on the macro and meso level, and how the head teacher micro level responds. The micro level constitutes the *school leader*, the leader's background, defining events and influences which have conscientized (raised their awareness of important social or political issues) or attuned them to social justice issues, personal characteristics, motivation, emotions, and the paradigm in which they lead—critical, liberal, libertarian, and so on. The meso level constitutes the *school-specific context* and *school community*, such as demography, geography, and social, political, and economic factors prevailing in the community locally to the school. The macro level includes the *socio-cultural dimension* and *socio-political discourse* that shape education policy, governance and funding.

METHODS

The work of the social justice leadership strand of the ISLDN has been guided by two overarching research questions that remain tentative but can be expressed as:

- "What is *social justice leadership*" and "What does it look like when we see it?"
- "How can an international and comparative methodology enhance our understanding of what social justice leadership means in different national contexts?"

Within the parameters of those two questions, a set of four provisional research questions were formulated to provide a structure to frame the interview protocol used with each case study head teacher. The semi structured interview protocol included both initial questions for a first interview and follow-up questions for a second interview. This chapter draws together the

What Factors Help and Hinder the Work of Social Justice Leaders? ■ 57

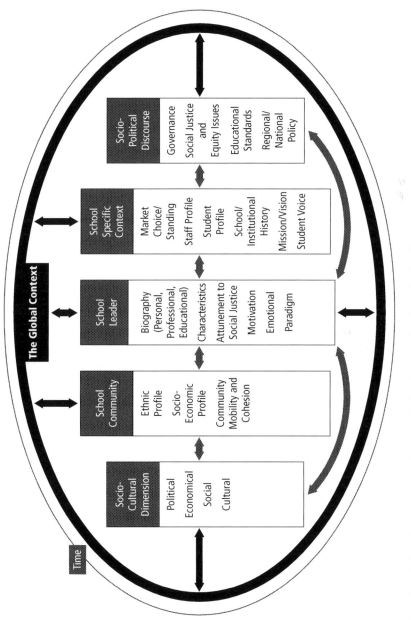

Figure 4.1 The ISLDN macro-micro framework for the examination of school context.

findings related to the third research question, exploring factors that help and hinder the work of social justice leaders.

The project methods developed by the ISLDN have enabled network members to utilize one research design and protocol. More detailed accounts of these aspects can be found in other chapters of this book. Essentially, ISLDN members collect both documentary data and data from interviews with head teachers/principals. Both educational policy discourses around leadership and social justice (Angelle, Morrison, & Stevenson, 2015; Torrance & Forde, 2015), as well as system-level data are drawn from. Key contextual information and data from contrasting international contexts are highlighted. In so doing, consideration is given to the extent to which policy rhetoric and practice realities are aligned in the practice of social justice leadership.

This chapter draws from case study data gathered through policy analyses and field visits in the eight education systems. Data is drawn from to investigate the development and practice of school leaders who work to promote social justice and fairness, actively tackling issues related to [in] equity and diversity. The mapping of the macro policy context for the eight countries (as shown in Table 4.1) formed an important starting point for the development of the case studies within each educational system. An analysis of the head teacher (micro level), alongside significant contextual factors (meso level) of each case study school (as shown in Table 4.2), enabled the expeditious contextualization of each individual school, as well as a comparison of contextual factors across the schools and educational systems (macro level).

SOCIAL JUSTICE POLICY CONTEXT

One of the critical issues emerging from the analysis of the ISLDN data is the importance of the context of the school leader (Angelle & Torrance, 2019; Torrance & Angelle, 2019). One way of looking at context would be to consider the meso level including the community that the school serves. However, this would not necessarily take into account issues related to the macro level including policy, regulation, governance, and funding. Further, the context of a school is shaped by wider macro social and political influences: culture, politics, traditions, and, specifically, the culture and history of public education within a particular system. Moreover, as education becomes the driver for [inter]national economic development and recovery (Miller, 2016), a common policy theme across education jurisdictions is the need to improve student achievement and outcomes to bring greater equality. However, evidence shows the opposite to be true (OECD, 2012) with improving student achievement and outcomes not bringing about equality. As such, head teachers "cannot be divorced from the social, cultural, political,

What Factors Help and Hinder the Work of Social Justice Leaders? ▪ **59**

and historical milieu in which they are situated and narrated" (Morrison, 2017, p. 44). The macro level of policy development and governance is set within a wider global context.

Table 4.1 presents the significant aspects of the macro policy context and this analysis formed an important starting point for the development of the case studies within each educational system.

TABLE 4.1	Social Justice Policy Context
England	A confused policy landscape with emphasis on outcomes for all, additional funding attached to pupils from lower socioeconomic backgrounds and promotion of parental choice within dominant market ideology, driving competition between schools and holding head teachers to account.
Jamaica	An emerging theme in social policy with "improving school attendance" an explicit goal and implicit reference to social justice in draft legislation, teaching standards, and national development plan/Vision 2030 document. 2005 educational policy anchor: Every child can learn, every child must learn.
Hong Kong	Policy on Whole School Approach to Integrated Education—although no explicit social justice leadership policy. In recent political discourse, principals' morality and integrity regarding social justice leadership are questioned by unjust and politically biased groups lacking understandings of social justice. The challenge to social justice leadership is system-wide in education.
New Zealand	Legislative commitment to indigenous Māori (1840 Treaty of Waitangi); however, disparities persist. Ongoing attempts to enhance inclusion and equity, alongside more recent emphasis on market ideology and competition creating systemic tensions.
Republic of Ireland	Emerging systemic tensions with primary schools privately owned but publicly funded; 90% managed by the Catholic Church. A social justice focus is on enhanced literacy and numeracy outcomes linked to self-evaluation, with additional funding for schools in areas of socioeconomic disadvantage. Little evidence of understanding social justice in broader socioecological contexts. Additional pressure on school principals and initiative overload within a tight financial climate.
Scotland	Ingrained within cultural heritage and a long-established policy commitment to all pupils, translated into the values of the Scottish parliament, national curriculum, quality assurance, professional values and head teacher accountability. However, an entrenched attainment gap exists which has become the focus of the current government.
Sweden	Strong social democratic values; a well-funded welfare state. Schools as key sites for developing a diverse society. Education Act and curricula promote equivalent and equitable education for all, adapted at local levels to meet pupil needs. Recent systemic tensions: increased migration without commensurate specialist resources; marketization and social segregation.
United States	Since World War II, education policy emphasized provision of equal educational opportunity for all and accountability for the educational outcomes for all. However, how those twin policies are enacted with an emphasis on testing, can place them at odds with each other and hinder the ability of principals to work for social justice.

60 ▪ D. TORRANCE et al.

While there are some common threads across different systems—for example, policies concerning addressing the needs of all pupils—what this means in practice is shaped by the wider policy context including the historical context of an educational system.

There are variations in the way in which policy is developed, the degree to which there is reference and concern for issues of social justice and equality in educational policy and the degree of conformity demanded of schools/school leaders. Even in more liberal cultures, head teachers have to negotiate their ways through the historical context of an educational system, notably where there are issues of colonialism and the position of indigenous populations, for example in New Zealand and Jamaica. In other systems, increasing diversity in long established systems has become significant. Ownership of the schools and the communities they served historically are both important contextual issues in long established systems—for example in Scotland, Ireland, and Sweden where there is an increasing diversity of pupil populations. Balancing policy demands with the evolving needs of their school is the critical task of social justice leaders.

Table 4.2 illustrates the way in which a variety of contextual factors combine with characteristics of the school, to create particular circumstances for a social justice leader. Table 4.2 also illustrates the variation across these case study schools in links between schools and governments through governance and funding whether local or central, and links to local community bodies including parent groups. School variables included: urban, suburban, or rural locations; the economic status of the local community that the school serves; the sector and size of the school; the positionality of the head teacher, for example, in terms of gender, ethnicity, social class background. However, arguably, what is most significant across these different contexts, are the specific issues related to the school, arising from its location, the communities it serves, and the emphases of educational policy. Such meso and macro factors are now explored in relation to factors that help and hinder the practice of social justice leadership.

SUPPORTS IDENTIFIED: MACRO LEVEL SUPPORTS

A range of factors that were supportive to the school leaders in advancing social justice were identified at the macro level—both formal and informal—by the case study school leaders (Table 4.3). Legislation, educational policy, and indeed wider social policy were noted as significant supports in helping to legitimate the focus on issues of inequality and social justice. Further, funding targeted around issues of marginalization, exclusion, and underachievement was also identified as a vital tool in shaping school

What Factors Help and Hinder the Work of Social Justice Leaders? ▪ **61**

TABLE 4.2 The Case Study Head Teachers (micro) and School Contextual Factors (meso)

		Gender	Experience	School	School Roll	Pupil Population	Challenges
England	HT*1	F	2nd headship	Coastal 11–16 comprehensive school; forced into Academy Sponsorship	<500	Predominantly White working class	Highly challenging circumstances
	HT 2	F	3rd headship	City 11–18 comprehensive school	>2,000	Ethnically diverse	Urban challenges
Hong Kong	HT 1	F	1st headship	City primary school, sponsored by a religious organization (ages 6–12)	Low intake crisis	Affluent community	Facing potential closure
	HT 2	M	1st headship	Peninsula primary school, sponsored by a local charitable organization (ages 6–12)	Low intake crisis	Mixed community	Facing potential closure
Jamaica	HT 1	F	1st headship	Rural and remote location; No running water or electricity (ages 7–12)	250 approx	90% parents small scale farmers	Poor to average socioeconomic background
New Zealand	HT 1	F	1st headship	Urban coastal state intermediate school (Year 7–8)	<500 [rising roll]	52% NZ European; 36% NZ Māori	Diverse socioeconomic backgrounds
	HT 2	M	2nd headship	Urban state primary school (Year 1–6)	<400 [rising roll]	85% Māori pupils; 13% NZ European	Most socioeconomic deprived backgrounds
Republic of Ireland	HT 1	F	1st headship	Outer city primary school, run by an independent non-government organization	<500 [rising roll]	90% Irish students	Area of rapid population growth
	HT 2	M	2nd headship	Inner city docklands Catholic senior boys primary school (ages 7–13)	<100 [falling roll]	95% "Irish students"; Very high SEN %	Significant socioeconomic disadvantage and drug issues

(continued)

TABLE 4.2 The Case Study Head Teachers (micro) and School Contextual Factors (meso) (Continued)

		Gender	Experience	School	School Roll	Pupil Population	Challenges
Scotland	HT 1	F	4th headship	Rural state funded infant school (ages 3–8)	< 400 [rising roll]	99% White	Mixed socioeconomic community
	HT 2	M	1st headship	Urban state funded secondary school (ages 11–18)	> 600	96% White	Mixed socioeconomic community
Sweden	HT 1	F	1st headship	Inner city independent compulsory school (ages 6–15)	< 200	99% minority; 1% White	Dramatic increase in immigration levels
	HT 2	M	1st headship	Inner city independent secondary school (ages 16–18)	< 600	45% minority; 55% White	Dramatic increase in immigration levels
United States	HT 1	M	1st headship	Rural town Year 9–12 school	> 300	11.5% minority; 88.5% White	61% of pupils living in poverty
	HT 2	M	2nd headship	Urban Year 9–12 school	> 1,100	58% minority; 62% White	66% of pupils living in poverty

Note: * The head teacher/principal of each school.

What Factors Help and Hinder the Work of Social Justice Leaders? ▪ **63**

TABLE 4.3	Macro Level Supports Identified by School Leaders
England	Autonomy to deploy resources; faith influences and some other agencies
Jamaica	Government grants and subsidies; perceived purposes of education
Hong Kong	Increased enrollment of high tariff pupils creating greater diversity; additional targeted government funding
New Zealand	Professional networks; favorable external review; engagement with Ministry of Education initiatives
Republic of Ireland	Legislation; wider societal issues providing a focus for discussion; national policy on school self-evaluation; national literacy and numeracy strategy; national program for delivering equality of opportunities
Scotland	Legislation; revised professional standards; national government priorities; supportive national initiatives used to push boundaries of established practice and challenge social injustice
Sweden	National steering documents (Education Act, curricula, policy documents); the National Principal Training Program; in-service programs
United States	Additional targeted government funding used specifically for increasing student achievement

developments. Another significant source of support included opportunities for professional learning for the teachers which enabled them to understand the wider policy context and issues of inequality and social justice. However, there is significant variation across the eight education systems.

BARRIERS IDENTIFIED: MACRO LEVEL BARRIERS

While legislation and policy can be regarded as providing head teachers with support in their practice of social justice leadership, they can also embody limiting factors providing little opportunity and recognition for the significant issues of inequality and marginalization evident in a particular school context. A narrowing of the policy agenda, with an increased focus on performance and attainment, accompanied by often impossible targets, can skew school efforts in working towards challenging inequalities and discrimination. Wider social issues such as the marginalization of specific groups, poverty, the minority status of the communities the school serves, all severely limit the impact of any strategies a school might initiate. Similarly, the funding of schools can present a limiting factor, not only from a lack of resources but also where funding is tied to specific initiatives and centrally dictated initiatives and outcomes which may not address the priorities of the school. Macro level barriers are summarized in Table 4.4.

64 ■ D. TORRANCE et al.

TABLE 4.4	Macro Level Barriers Identified by School Leaders
England	Political interference, bureaucracy around inter-agency working, skewed inspection framework (HT1), unrealistic social care policy (HT2)
Jamaica	Poverty and its impact on attendance; insufficient resourcing through inadequate Ministry of Education grants
Hong Kong	Societal change, e.g., low birth rate, academic banding of schools with parental choice; unequal allocation of resources and different funding sources
New Zealand	Poverty, transience, truancy, racism and social division, Ministry of Education regional resourcing decisions, the nature of intermediate schooling/roll turnover, distracting external accountabilities
Republic of Ireland	Wider social issues, societal inequalities that impede efforts to view education as a route out of poverty, perceived low expectations in some schools, lack of joined up thinking
Scotland	Government initiatives "going in waves," the narrowing perspective of Her Majesty's Inspectorate of Education, a cultural/parental view of "good kids and bad kids"
Sweden	No macro level barriers since policy documents support the work of social justice leaders: "As a principal you can lead in the direction you chose to lead"
United States	A focus on deficits, lack of funding to implement mandates, policies can be too narrow with a "focus on the end result in a lot of cases, rather than the whole child"

SUPPORTS IDENTIFIED: MESO LEVEL SUPPORTS

The meso level relates to local government, the school-specific context, local community, and local policy. Here, the culture within the school was identified as an important source of support for the development of social justice practices. In particular, the skill and commitment of staff to further the aims of social justice and ensure equitable outcomes for all pupils was key. Collaborative practices in the development of professional networks were also considered an important element of support (see Table 4.5).

BARRIERS IDENTIFIED: MESO LEVEL BARRIERS

As with the macro level, those factors that could provide support in the development of social justice leadership, could also pose significant barriers in achieving these aims at the meso level. The role, attitudes, and practice of teachers was highly significant in creating barriers to progress and change, particularly where there were issues of morale and personnel challenges. Additional identified issues related to teachers' capacity and

What Factors Help and Hinder the Work of Social Justice Leaders? ▪ **65**

TABLE 4.5	Meso Level Supports Identified by School Leaders
England	Peer support of other school leaders (HT1), Local Government support (HT2), teachers that "get it"
Jamaica	Community support and perspective on the purpose of education; continuing professional development (CPD) for teachers
Hong Kong	Building staff capacity, team approach to curriculum and pedagogic development, community resources
New Zealand	Supportive and capable staff, conducive culture with shared moral purpose and core values, length of time in headship, resource levels, community networks, collaborative multi-agency interventions
Republic of Ireland	Staff; conducive school culture with shared moral purpose and core values, resources and school building, working collaboratively, community networks
Scotland	Staff supportive of and committed to social justice practices, specific local government priorities
Sweden	Capable staff with conducive attitudes, role models of other school leaders, support from and shared responsibility with the municipality's school board, steering documents, a collaborative endeavor
United States	Conducive school culture providing supportive structure and high expectations, collaborative approaches

capability, along with a limited view of wider sociopolitical developments, which also limited opportunities for change and development. Such barriers partly relate to the limitations and/or lack of commitment of some teachers in a school to meet the needs of all pupils. Table 4.6 also highlights the way in which the immediate context of the school, as well as parental expectations, can curtail social justice leadership whether due to a limited support of education, or limited aspirations, or the experience of marginalization in these communities.

SUMMARY AND DISCUSSION OF COMMON THEMES

From the analysis of the case study data, it is clear that social justice leadership is contextualized. For example, maintaining a focus on improving outcomes for all pupils emerged as a dominant theme, contextualized differently within each education system and in particular in relation to how explicit social justice expectations are in macro level policies. In Hong Kong, policy focuses on a *Whole School Approach to Integrated Education*, with an absence of explicit national policy for social justice leadership. In Sweden, policy documents support the work of social justice leaders within an education system founded upon strong social democratic national values, perceiving schools as key sites for developing a diverse society.

66 ▪ D. TORRANCE et al.

TABLE 4.6	Meso Level Barriers Identified by School Leaders
England	Teachers who do not get it and are non-inclusive, family politics, teacher recruitment (HT1), other headteachers (HT2), influences of other agencies, including some faith leaders (HT2)
Jamaica	Teachers who pay more attention to well-off students, teachers who form cliques instead of focusing on sharing good practice
Hong Kong	Low staff morale, parental expectations, very limited resources, lack of multicultural and inclusive education
New Zealand	Personnel issues, erosion of relational trust, school governance arrangements, isolation of principal's role, emotional labor and stress levels, lack of access to specialist counseling support, deficit thinking
Republic of Ireland	Teachers who are passing through and not committed to meeting pupils' needs or to building social justice cultures and practices, low expectations and low standards for achievement and behavior, perceptions of parents
Scotland	Teachers' capacity, capability, limited world view, curriculum pressures, perceptions of parents and local government members, diminishing local government resources and personnel, school catchment areas and private education
Sweden	Teachers' competence, large school size potentially limiting involvement with individual pupils who have additional support needs
United States	Teachers whose vision is not aligned towards academic growth for all pupils, lack of time to practice care for both pupils and teachers, to address each situation individually, lack of support from district level

A number of significant factors that help or hinder head teachers in this enterprise have been identified. A broadly similar range of formal and informal supports were identified by the case study school leaders, at both the macro and meso levels. The importance at the meso level of the culture and values of the school is a strong similarity. Head teachers support and enhance social justice by prioritizing social justice leadership development. Across the eight systems, there is variation in the degree of head teacher autonomy within constrained budgets and level of centralized control. Barriers affecting all systems relate to the impact of wider socioeconomic contexts and the impact on children's progress.

Equally, the absence of key supports could pose significant barriers. The head teacher's (micro level) activist stance and practices is key in mediating the terrain, identifying and harnessing factors that help, limiting the impact of factors that hinder their work as social justice leaders. Social justice leaders capitalized on any legislation and national policy commitment to social justice, translating this into their school's context, legitimizing their actions in building social justice cultures and school practices. National mandates with flexibility in their local interpretation were found to be supportive of their efforts as well as targeted funding, with autonomy to deploy resources and strategies in local contexts. Teachers were identified as being key in such efforts and as such, the head teachers worked diligently to build a shared culture based on understood values, with both long-serving staff and staff they recruited. In that regard, they actively supported the professional development of all staff.

The head teachers in this study are involved in political activism (Cribb & Gewirtz, 2005), negotiating macro policy expectations through the meso level of the school context, utilizing their agency for positive change (King & Travers, 2017). Social justice leadership is context specific (Beyciogly & Ogden, 2017; Gairín & Rodriguez-Gómez, 2014; McNae, Morrison, & Notman, 2017; Potter, 2017a) and the head teachers need to develop a clear understanding of the meso and macro context within which they work. This is complex work, especially given the changing intersection of the macro, meso, and micro foci. These changes often depend on a specific issue and the complexity or simplicity of the system. Such activist work (Branson, Morrison, & McNae, 2015; Miller, Roofe, & Garcia-Carmona, 2019; Robinson, 2017) requires significant energy, commitment, and drive. As such, social justice leaders need to find ways to maintain their commitment and energy. At a more fundamental level, a conclusion drawn from the comparative analysis in this chapter, is that the head teachers have a secure set of core values which guide them in their social justice leadership philosophy and practices at the micro level (King & Travers, 2017).

The head teachers in this study have both a significant understanding of the specific factors that shape their social justice practice, and also the ability to recognize and create opportunities to develop the understandings and practices of others within the school community. This includes the communication of an aspiration of achievement for all pupils, as well as supporting the development of social justice attitudes, skills, and commitment of teachers. Important support factors identified by the head teachers at the micro level included engagement with professional networks, both within the school and with peers and colleagues within the wider system. Indeed, building networks and collaborative practice were identified as important strategies, not only in taking forward a social justice agenda but in sustaining social justice leaders themselves.

CONCLUSION

This chapter has synthesized the findings from eight education systems, voluntarily selected from over 20 countries contributing to the ISLDN, a collaborative network of researchers and practitioners collecting data from interviews with head teachers in varied contexts, utilizing a shared framework (Figure 4.1). This approach enables the analysis of comparative data for cross-cultural research, enhancing understandings of social justice leadership (Angelle et al. 2015; Dimmock & Walker, 2010) at macro, meso, and micro levels. In this chapter, the findings related to the third ISLDN research question provided the focus, analyzing factors that help and hinder the work of social justice leaders.

Theoharis (2010) likens the work of social justice school leaders to activist research. The head teachers in Theoharis' study were keenly aware of the barriers for learners in their schools and used a range of political strategies to leverage change. What the ISLDN analysis highlights is both the importance of head teachers addressing the factors in their school context but also the significance of meso and macro level factors, which hinder or facilitate such efforts. In the context of this book, published to mark the 10th anniversary of the ISLDN, this point of head teachers striving to be social justice leaders akin to activist research, resonates with the existence of the ISLDN. The process of our network of researchers, some of which are practicing school leaders, employing the methodology described in this chapter, has in itself contributed to social justice leadership. The opportunity for participant reflection enables school leaders to confront the realities of their daily working (Milner, 2015) and challenge inequalities. Indeed, a significant finding of the ISLDN research is that school leaders have been helped in making sense of the complexities in which they work (Potter, 2017b); the three levels of the ISLDN framework have enabled school leaders interviewed to be reflexive about their own contexts. Thus, in some small part, those head teachers have possibly enjoyed an element of empowerment, in their particular contexts, from our ISLDN process.

The context in which social justice leaders work is dynamic and subject to a range of influencing factors which can constrain or facilitate their work. These include characteristics of the school itself, and system structural aspects such as the connections and disconnections between the different system levels and the lines of communication and accountability across these levels. Social justice leadership requires an awareness of these contextual aspects, alongside a realization of the inherent political nature of this work, as policy rhetoric and practice realities coalesce, due to the messy nature of social justice policy implementation (Jones, Angelle, & Lohmann-Hancock, 2019). Social justice leaders have a readiness to engage in forms of leadership that seek to bring about change in attitudes and in practice in both the local and wider school community. Arguably, in working at the micro and meso levels, head teachers have the power and authority to empower others and to change practices, playing a significant role in shaping the conditions for learning (Forde & Torrance, 2017), exerting influence both across the school as an organization, and at the individual classroom and teacher level (Torrance & Forde, 2017). As such, they are held to account for socially just practices, positioned in relation to competition within the global marketplace which places education under increasing pressure to deliver improved services to meet the needs of society (Torrance & Angelle, 2019). In this endeavor, they need to be skilled at mediating within and between the meso and macro levels of the system, attuned to the contextualized needs and realities of the school. In doing so, head teachers will be able to negotiate the unjust local, national, and international contexts to better support the needs of marginalized children.

REFERENCES

Angelle, P. S. (2017). Constructions, enactments, articulations: The work of the IS-LDN social justice group. In P. S. Angelle (Ed.), *A global perspective of social justice leadership for school principals* (pp. xv–xx). Charlotte, NC: Information Age.

Angelle, P. S., Morrison, M., & Stevenson, H. (2015). 'Doing' social justice leadership: Connecting the macro and micro contexts of schooling. In J. Ryan & D. Armstrong (Eds.), *Working (with/out) the system: Educational leadership, micropolitics and social justice* (pp. 95–118). Charlotte, NC: Information Age.

Angelle, P. S., & Torrance, D. (2019). The significance of context in the enactment of social justice. In P. S. Angelle & D. Torrance (Eds.), *Cultures of social justice leadership: An intercultural context of schools* (pp. 195–207). Cham, Switzerland: Palgrave MacMillan.

Beyciogly, K., & Ogden, S. B. (2017). Social justice beliefs and behaviors: A cross-cultural look at Turkish and U.S. principals. In P. S. Angelle (Ed.), *A global perspective of social justice leadership for school principals* (pp. 111–126). Charlotte, NC: Information Age.

Bogotch, I., & Shields, C. M. (2014). Introduction: Do promises of social justice trump paradigms of educational leadership? In I. Bogotch & C. Shields (Eds.), *International handbook of educational leadership and social [in]justice* (pp. 1–12). London, England: Springer.

Branson, C. M., Morrison, M., & McNae, R. (2015). Tui tui tuituia–Weaving together: What can be generalised from these articles? [Special issue: Educational leadership for social justice]. *Journal of Educational Leadership, Policy & Practice, 30*(1), 119–128.

Cribb, A., & Gewirtz, S. (2005). Navigating justice in practice: An exercise in grounding ethical theory. *Theory and Research in Education, 3*(3), 327–342.

Dimmock, C., Stevenson, H., Bignold, B., Shah, S., & Middlewood, D. (2005). School community perspectives and their leadership implications. *Effective leadership in multi-ethnic schools*. Nottingham, England: National College for School Leadership.

Dimmock, C., & Walker, A. (2010). Developing comparative and international educational leadership and management: A cross-cultural model. *School Leadership and Management, 20*(2), 143–160.

Forde, C., & Torrance, D. (2017). Social justice leaders: Critical moments in headteachers'/principals' development. Special edition: 'Leadership Stories': Unlocking the Path to Social Justice Leadership. *Research in Educational Administration and Leadership, 2*(1), 29–52.

70 ▪ D. TORRANCE et al.

Gairín, J., & Rodriguez-Gómez, D. (2014). Leadership, educational development and social development. In I. Bogotch & C. Shields (Eds.), *International handbook of educational leadership and social [in]justice* (pp. 819–843). London, England: Springer.

Hajisoteriou, C., & Angelides, P. (2014). Education policy in Cyprus: From decision-making to implementation. In I. Bogotch & C. Shields (Eds.), *International handbook of educational leadership and social [in]justice* (pp. 895–909). London, England: Springer.

Jones, K., Angelle, P. S., & Lohmann-Hancock, C. (2019). Local implementation of national policy: Social justice perspectives from the USA, India, and Wales. In P. S. Angelle & D. Torrance (Eds.), *Cultures of social justice leadership: An intercultural context of schools* (pp. 169–194). Cham, Switzerland: Palgrave MacMillan.

King, F., Forde, C., Razzaq, J., & Torrance, D. (2019). Systems of education governance and cultures of justice in Ireland, Scotland and Pakistan. In P. S. Angelle & D. Torrance (Eds.), *Cultures of social justice leadership: An intercultural context of schools* (pp. 67–92). Cham, Switzerland: Palgrave MacMillan.

King, F., & Travers, J. (2017). Social justice leadership through the lens of ecological systems theory. In P. S. Angelle (Ed.), *A global perspective of social justice leadership for school principals* (pp. 147–165). Charlotte, NC: Information Age.

Lee, Y. L. B. (2010). *Managing complex change in a Hong Kong higher education institution: A micropolitical perspective.* Unpublished doctoral dissertation, University of Leicester, England.

McNae, R., Morrison, M., & Notman, R. (Eds.). (2017). *Educational leadership in Aotearoa New Zealand: Issues of context and social justice.* Wellington, New Zealand: NZCER Press.

Miller, P. (2016). *Exploring school leadership in England and the Caribbean: New insights from a comparative approach.* London, England: Bloomsbury.

Miller, P., Hill-Berry, N. P., Hylton-Fraser, K., & Powell, S. (2019). Social justice work as activism: The work of education professionals in England and Jamaica. *International Studies in Educational Administration, 47*(1), 3–19.

Miller, P., Roofe, C., & Garcia-Carmona, M. (2019). School leadership, curriculum diversity, social justice and critical perspectives in education. In P. S. Angelle & D. Torrance (Eds.), *Cultures of social justice leadership: An intercultural context of schools* (pp. 93–119). Cham, Switzerland: Palgrave MacMillan.

Milner, A. (2015). *Narrative as imagination: Storying an alternative discourse of teacher professionalism.* Paper presented at the annual meeting of the European Conference on Educational Research, Budapest, Hungary.

Morrison, M. (2017). Conceiving context: The origins and development of the conceptual framework. In P. S. Angelle (Ed.), *A global perspective of social justice leadership for school principals* (pp. 43–64). Charlotte, NC: Information Age.

Organisation for Economic Cooperation and Development. (2012). Equity and quality in education: Supporting disadvantaged students and schools. Paris, France: OECD.

Potter, I. (2017a). Change in context and identity: The case of an English school leader. In P. S. Angelle (Ed.), *A global perspective of social justice leadership for school principals* (pp. 231–249). Charlotte, NC: Information Age.

Potter, I. (2017b). Developing social justice leadership through reflexivity. In P. S. Angelle (Ed.), *A global perspective of social justice leadership for school principals* (pp. 293–302). Charlotte, NC: Information Age.

Robinson, K. (2017). Retracing the steps of the journey: A literature review of social justice leadership from a global context. In P. S. Angelle (Ed.), *A global perspective of social justice leadership for school principals* (pp. 21–41). Charlotte, NC: Information Age.

Ryan, J. (2010). Promoting social justice in schools: Principals' political strategies. *International Journal of Leadership in Education: Theory and Practice, 13*(4), 357–376.

Shields, C. M., & Mohan, E. J. (2008). High-quality education for all students: Putting social justice at its heart. *Teacher Development, 12*(4), 289–300.

Szeto, E., & Cheng, A. Y. N. (2018). How do principals practise leadership for social justice in diverse school settings? A Hong Kong case study. *Journal of Educational Administration, 56*(1), 50–68.

Theoharis, G. (2010). Disrupting injustice: Principals narrate the strategies they use to improve their schools and advance social justice. *Teachers College Record, 112*(1), 331–373.

Torrance, D., & Angelle, P. S. (2019). The influence of global contexts in the enactment of social justice. In P. S. Angelle & D. Torrance (Eds.), *Cultures of social justice leadership: An intercultural context of schools* (pp. 1–19). Cham, Switzerland: Palgrave MacMillan.

Torrance, D., & Forde, C. (2015). To what extent can headteachers be held to account in the practice of social justice leadership? [Special issue: Educational leadership for social justice]. *Journal of Educational Leadership, Policy and Practice, 30*(1), 79–91.

Torrance, D., & Forde, C. (2017). Policy and practice in social justice leadership in Scotland. In P. S. Angelle (Ed.), *A global perspective of social justice leadership for school principals* (pp. 187–208). Charlotte, NC: Information Age.

Young, M. (2017). In support of cross-national examinations of social justice leadership. In P. S. Angelle (Ed.), *A global perspective of social justice leadership for school principals* (pp. ix–xiv). Charlotte, NC: Information Age.

CHAPTER 5

THE INTERNATIONAL SCHOOL LEADERSHIP DEVELOPMENT NETWORK'S HIGH-NEEDS SCHOOLS STRAND

Ten Years of History

Jami Royal Berry
University of Georgia

Betty Alford
California Polytechnic State University

Mette L. Baran
Cardinal Stritch University

Karen Bryant
University of Georgia

Kristine Hipp
Cardinal Stritch University

Glady Van Harpen
University of Wisconsin Oshkosh

Educational Leadership for Social Justice and Improving High-Needs Schools, pages 73–92
Copyright © 2021 by Information Age Publishing
All rights of reproduction in any form reserved.

74 ■ J. R. BERRY et al.

As the International School Leadership Development Network (ISLDN) celebrates its 10-year anniversary, this chapter offers a reflection on the high-needs schools (HNS) strand of the project and highlights the studies and learnings that have grown from the research conducted over the life of the project. The chapter begins by offering the history of the HNS strand of the ISLDN. Next, it provides an overview of the HNS strand studies that have been conducted; the contexts in which they were situated; and an analysis of the common themes related to learning, leadership, and context. Then it moves into a discussion of the researchers' learning as a part of the overall project, inclusive of the voices of scholars who have been involved in the project since its inception, as well as those who have joined the work overtime. The chapter closes with recommendations for next steps for both the project and for those seeking to participate in an international professional learning community.

The ISLDN was developed as a joint initiative of the British Educational Leadership, Management, and Administration Society (BELMAS) and the University Council for Educational Administration (UCEA). Stimulated by the success of the International Successful School Principalship Project (IS-SPP), UCEA conference participants were invited to take part in a series of discussions as to what might be researched under the banner of the ISLDN. Those conversations produced a rich research initiative with two streams of interest, leadership in high-needs schools, and leadership for social justice, as the primary areas of focus. Over the first 10 years of the project, researchers have conducted work around the globe as members of the ISLDN, and this chapter focuses on the story of the HNS strand of the ISLDN work.

DEVELOPING THE RESEARCH PROTOCOL

The purpose of the ISLDN's work within the HNS strand was to determine various qualities of leadership critical to leading high-needs schools focusing on three areas: learning, leadership, and context. A secondary purpose of the work was to determine the qualities of leadership essential for leading high-needs schools coupled with contextual factors. Within the context of these parameters the project sought to identify school leaders working in a number of different cultural contexts to address the following research questions:

1. "What fosters student learning in high-needs schools?"
2. "How do principals and other school leaders enhance individual and organizational performance in high-needs schools?"
3. "How do internal and external school contexts impact individual and organizational performance in high-needs schools?"

School Leadership Development Network's High-Needs Schools Strand ■ 75

Several of the founding members of HNS strand developed a research protocol to provide network members with a comprehensive and universal tool to collect data in high-needs schools investigating learning, leadership, and context. The overall guide consists of interview protocols for principals, school staff members, school governing boards, parents, and students (Baran & Berry, 2015). It is recommended that the protocols be used in their entirety in order to gain a comprehensive detailed understanding of the factors at work in an individual school setting; however, researchers have used it in whole and in part.

Authors utilizing the research protocol were provided an operational definition of high-needs schools within the context of the school studied. While some researchers noted challenges in making contextual comparisons in that context can differ greatly from country to country, typically, high-needs schools identified shared one or more characteristics including a high percentage of families living in poverty, a high percentage of educators working outside their content areas, high turnover of staff and students, a high percentage of indigenous or marginalized populations, and/or a situational need based on an event. Additionally, researchers categorized the selected schools using one of the following two leader categories:

1. A new principal serving 0–3 years in the principal's position at the current school, or
2. A veteran principal having served more than 3 years in the current school.

Purposeful sampling was used in selecting various individuals from the school for their perspectives. The purpose of these interviews and/or focus groups was to validate the principal's work and learning outcomes for students. Data were collected in two phases:

- *Phase 1 (Pilot): Completed in 2014.* The draft research protocol was piloted in nine locations including Australia, China, Malaysia, Nepal, Sweden, and the United States, during the Spring and Summer of 2014. Revisions were subsequently made to the original protocol based on the feedback from participants including interviews with principals, teachers, staff, and parents.
- *Phase 2 (Research Using Updated Protocol): Commenced in 2015.* The main methods used to collect data for studies conducted in this phase included two individual interviews with the school leader; individual interviews with additional senior staff members such as assistant principals; individual interviews with teachers, and focus groups or interviews with parents and/or students.

76 ▪ J. R. BERRY et al.

The topics of leadership and learning are complex; hence, researchers were encouraged to explore a theoretical framework that supported the research questions coupled with the context of their individual school sites. The collective research, however, did not focus on one specific theoretical framework. Rather, a conceptual framework emerged that connected multiple contexts involving school leadership and high-needs schools. Therefore, addressing the topics through a multitude of lenses provided a more comprehensive picture of the complexities of high-needs school leadership in varying cultural contexts. This framework is reflected in the five themes in this work and seeks to understand researchers' roles in collaborative work.

OVERVIEW OF STUDIES CONDUCTED AND DISCUSSION OF COMMON THEMES

Since the establishment of the ISLDN, its members have contributed to the scholarship of leadership in high-need schools through global research utilizing the protocol highlighted above. A review of 13 studies conducted by 30 researchers in Australia, New Zealand, Belize, South Africa, and the United States revealed several key themes regarding successful school leadership in high-needs schools. As previously mentioned, the geographic scope of the high-needs research spanned four continents with one-quarter of the studies conducted within the United States. Six studies examined principal leadership in high-needs schools, four considered the educational context of high-needs schools, and three viewed leadership in high-needs schools through the lens of school performance. Qualitative methods were used in nine studies specifically employing interviews using the HNS protocol; three additional case studies and one review of historical literature pertaining to high-need schools constituted our review. These studies and reviews were conducted from 2014 to 2019.

Our review and analysis of these studies by different high-needs schools research teams identified five themes. These themes encompassed a range of concepts, including school culture and relationships, expectations for students, staff, and stakeholders, leadership styles, and data-driven decision-making, which are highlighted in the following sections.

Theme 1: Building a Caring Culture and Supportive Community Through Relationships

One strong and pervasive theme reflected across studies from around the world was the importance of leadership that fosters a caring culture and supportive community through relationships. Teachers perceived professional development opportunities and instructional feedback as effective leadership strategies for the development of a supportive learning community, especially when contrasted against traditional teacher evaluation methods (Kearney, Murakami, Bunch, Viamontes, & Campbell, 2018). Peer observations were found to reduce isolation and to promote collegiality. In a study of leadership in rural schools in the Southeastern United States (Klar, Huggins, Andreoli, & Buskey, 2019), the authors identified professional learning communities as a vehicle through which leaders supported teachers in instructional improvement efforts, stating, "Though not without their limitations, the collaborative, participant-centered, and job-embedded nature of professional communities has made them popular options for teacher and, more recently, leader professional development" (Klar et al., 2019, p. 4).

Two other American researchers in Georgia emphasized the importance of involving the entire community in the development and implementation of a supportive learning community. Aguedje (2017) asserted, "An empowered school leader, changes the occasional success of a few children of poverty to the consistent high performance of a culture focused on learning" (p. 8). Collaborative community building activities in this study included enlisting volunteers from the ranks of local civic, business, and governmental leaders and parents and using school buildings as community centers to bring stakeholders together. Savage (2017) posited that these activities addressed many of the barriers preventing parents in high-needs schools from active involvement in the school community. The employment of a parent liaison who facilitated a parent outreach center providing resources and programs for parents was highlighted as a strategy that increased parental engagement.

Theme 2: High Expectations for Student Learning

The importance of high expectations by the principal as instructional leader (Leithwood, Day, Sammons, Harris, & Hopkins, 2006; Waters, Marzano, & McNulty, 2003) was underscored by multiple studies reviewed. The researchers identified and clustered this as a second common theme of *high expectations for student learning and teacher performance.* Okilwa and Barnett (2019) studied leadership of a high-needs elementary school in South Texas that had sustained academic success over a 20-year period. One of the four principals who participated in semi-structured interviews described "the need for setting high expectations for everyone in the school, including teachers, students, parents, and support staff" (p. 155). In their study of an urban school in the upper Midwestern United States, Baran and Van Harpen (2019) noted, "A strong academic focus that demands high expectations for staff, students and families; consistency and rigor

78 ▪ J. R. BERRY et al.

regarding a highly structured standard curriculum, instructional strategies, and programs" (p. 119) were key in successfully turning around academic performance through a culture of learning. In a study of school leadership practices in New Zealand, Notman and Jacobson (2019) highlighted the central role of the head teacher in three quality early childhood centers. In a study of two successful principals of high-needs schools in California, Alford (2019) emphasized, "Willingness to *take a stand* in support of high expectations was illuminated by each principal's words and actions" (p. 93, emphasis in original).

Theme 3: The Importance of Understanding School and Community Context

A third theme present in the high-needs research was the importance principals placed on understanding their context, including demographics and the socioeconomic context of the school and the local community. The educational settings ranged from preschool to intermediate or middle level, with the schools being defined by their local educational governing bodies. The schools were located in rural, suburban, and urban settings. In most cases, the schools were serving a majority of students in a low socioeconomic range. In several of the schools, the majority or a high percentage of students were students of color (Alford, 2019; Baran & Van Harpen, 2019; Berry, Cowart Moss, & Gore, 2019; Chisholm, Waight, & Jacobson, 2019; Murakami & Kearney, 2019; Notman & Jacobson, 2019; Okilwa & Barnet, 2019. Given these factors, there was a richness in both the range of cultural diversity and in the need for leaders to understand the uniqueness of their communities in order to affect change and bring about school improvement.

The importance of school improvement, indeed school reform, as it relates to context was asserted by Elmore (2004), "Improvement is more a function of learning to do the right thing in the setting in which you work" (p. 73). Each of the 13 studies discussed a variety of contexts ranging from economic to political. In their research Berry et al. (2019) asserted, "In our model for High-needs School Leadership (HNSL), we argue that the effective principals in high-needs schools utilize contextualization, hypervigilance, and intentionality as they navigate their unique school climates and communities" (p. 144).

The engagement of stakeholders in decision-making through distributed leadership is a successful practice of leaders in high-needs, high-performing schools. Principals who demonstrate the skills to improve collaborative structures within their schools can more effectively implement and sustain

School Leadership Development Network's High-Needs Schools Strand ▪ **79**

change for school improvement. In a study situated in Georgia, Aguedje (2017) asserted, "It takes a highly-skilled leader to form, build the capacity of, and properly support a team of teachers, parents and, stakeholders that continuously desire to overcome social situations related to poverty" (p. 7). Additionally, Okilwa and Barnett (2019) found principals' own personal educational experiences played a role in understanding and modeling expectations for their school communities. It is this contextualization that differentiates leaders of high-need schools from those in more traditional school settings.

Theme 4: Adaptive Leadership

In viewing problems and questions facing high-needs schools across multiple contexts, it appears principals' actions reflect what Heifetz, Linsky, and Grashow (2009) termed "adaptive challenges" (p. 10). The work of remedying adaptive challenges, according to Heifetz (2010), "requires more than the application of current expertise, authoritative decision-making, standard operating procedures or culturally informed behaviors" (p. 73). In fact, the findings conducted by the high-needs group confirms that leaders of high-needs schools approach their challenges in adaptive ways.

In the United States, some school districts have embraced public charters in order to enable school leaders more innovative and creative approaches to teaching and learning. One such school district using public charters is the Milwaukee (Wisconsin, United States) Public Schools (MPS). The leader of one MPS school stated, "A school can't exist with the idea that we're going to tell kids that they are going to go to college and then treat them like they're going to prison" (Baran & Van Harpen, 2019, p. 111). In turn, the entire school was vision and mission-driven, with school leaders and teachers placing an equal, intentional, and consistent focus on character building with high standards for student behavior and academic excellence (Hipp & Baran, 2014). For example,

> Academically and behaviorally, students and staff at Lloyd chanted daily expressions that revealed a strong sense of unity, efficacy, and beliefs that mirrored the school's mission and vision both in and outside of the school's daily morning Assemblies and in classrooms. (Hipp & Baran, 2014, pp. 36–37)

Zip code would not define students' destinies; focus, effort, and consistency were key to creating and sustaining a culture of learning.

On the other side of the globe, the leaders of two Australian schools utilized the Department of Education Training's (DET) notion of having a

80 ▪ J. R. BERRY et al.

"high level of autonomy and flexibility . . . to undertake significant change" (Gurr, Drysdale, Longmuir, & McCrohan, 2019, p. 35). Examples included higher expectations for students and contractual agreements with faculty. Additionally, the researchers found capacity building and leadership development were important in the context of school improvement. Their finding supported how Heifetz et al. (2009) describe leadership "as a verb, and not a job" (p. 24).

Furthermore, a case study of a successful school leader in the Ganglands of Cape Town, South Africa, (Bryant, Berry, & Cevik, 2019) illustrated the importance of adaptive leadership as the school's leader opted to build a school on the gangs' battleground. She met with the leadership of each gang.

> Citing the need for a safe space for students to learn as well as the desire to honor the lives lost on all sides of the gang wars, she pleaded her case. Ultimately, every gang leader agreed to allow her to build The Leadership College on the former battlefield. (p. 120)

Finally, in a school located in Belize, Chisholm et al. (2019) found leaders went beyond traditional role responsibilities to serve the community through home visits and social welfare checks. One example of school leaders understanding the need for adaptation was the facilitation of an educational program called "Fish with Purpose" (p. 76), which capitalized on the country's tourism and unique aquatic ecology. This program not only integrated curricula, but also promoted entrepreneurship and sustainability for students and their community. These are a few examples of how school leaders, in this study, epitomized adaptive leadership in high-needs settings.

In all of the studies reviewed, the ability of school leaders to view problems as challenges, and to "get on the balcony" (Heifetz & Linsky, 2002, p. 51) to understand what was happening in their unique settings, promoted teaching and learning. The challenges facing high-needs schools are complex and require leaders who are able to adapt and conceptualize solutions which are different, in many cases, from those facing other public schools (Murakami, Notman, & Gurr, 2019).

Theme 5: Data-Based Decisions

A final theme that appeared in the studies was a reliance on data-based decisions. Data exists in many forms and influence decisions in schools worldwide. According to Kowalski, Lasley, and Mahoney (2008), "Data-based decision making is the process of compiling, reviewing, sharing, and using data to assist in improving schools and, particularly, enhancing student achievement" (p. 103). It is this focus on student achievement and accountability that is such a challenge to schools everywhere, but especially to those categorized as high-needs. Okilwa and Barnett (2019) reported how two principals in South Texas used summative and formative data in order to improve their schools. One of the principals in the study reported, "We had formative and summative data . . . so we studied the level of thinking required in the content areas [and] how they apply these concepts in problem-solving. So we did a lot of examining of the depth that knowledge had to be taught" (p. 160). It is important to note, however, it is difficult to compare student achievement school-to-school since assessments are unique to their geographic settings.

Several of the high-needs school studies reveal a commitment to academic excellence and increasing performance using governmental assessments; however, in some instances, there was a significant commitment to factors not easily measured by standardized assessments, such as parental and community engagement (Aguedje, 2017; Alford, 2019; Notman & Jacobson, 2019), collective responsibility (Okilwa & Barnett, 2019), core values (Berry et al., 2019; Bryant et al., 2019), high expectations (Baran & Van Harpen, 2019; Klar et al., 2019), building relationships (Baran & Van Harpen, 2019; Hipp & Baran, 2014), and overall school improvement (Gurr, Drysdale, Longmuir, & McCrohan. 2019). Although not statistically measurable, these data are captured in the qualitative methods and narratives of the high-needs school studies.

Summary of Themes

The five themes identified by high-needs schools researchers are a snapshot of the rich findings present in their collective work. The work qualitatively captures the narratives of schools that are different, based on geography and culture, and yet highlights the commonalities of high-needs leadership practice that exists among this unique set. In order to quantify narrative data and provide a broader sense of the many variables involved in these works, a word cloud (see Figure 5.1) is used. This analysis gathers textual findings from the research summaries offering a visual representation of anecdotal qualitative data from the 13 analyzed studies. The size of word in the graphic is an indicator of how often it appears in the text, thereby giving emphasis. The word cloud encapsulates key pieces of the high-needs schools' story including those related to pedagogy, community, and collaboration, which form the collective narrative from the studies.

Figure 5.1 Graphic conceptualization summary findings from 13 high-needs school studies. *Source:* Wordclouds.com, 2019.

VOICES OF RESEARCHERS

The following section shares the voices of HNS members regarding their experiences within the network that contributed to their participation and fostered their learning. How participants viewed the culture within the network including contributions of the network to their personal and professional growth as well as recommendations for next steps are discussed. These 15 researchers shared perspectives including reasons for network involvement, the development of a culture of learning, ways the network contributed to personal and professional growth, key learnings about leadership practice, and recommendations for next steps.

School Leadership Development Network's High-Needs Schools Strand ▪ **83**

Reasons for Network Involvement

When asked what prompted individuals to join ISLDN, they shared that their interest in international research on leadership in high-needs schools and the "space to connect with other scholars with similar interests" were predominant reasons. Some participants joined because another member invited them, while others responded to the open call for participation. Interviewees for this work emphasized the welcoming climate established by the network leaders as a key characteristic of the network. The keywords and phrases often expressed from participants were "welcoming" and a "shared interest in the topic being addressed by the network of school leadership in high-need schools through an international context." As an interviewee explained, "Just the notion that there is a community of people who are interested in learning how schooling processes are structured in different contexts was very appealing to me." Participants also expressed that they viewed "creating a community of international researchers as an important initiative." The network provided a "welcoming" environment in contrast to the university academic environment that practitioners who had recently transitioned to university teaching described as sometimes "hierarchical and not that welcoming." The open nature of membership in the network fostered a collegial rather than hierarchical culture for learning. One participant stated, "I saw the open call for participation and responded due to interest in the topic." However, the participant added that she continued to attend the network sessions because she found "a very welcoming environment of individuals who were also interested in successful principal leadership in high-need schools throughout international contexts." Another interviewee stressed:

> A big takeaway for me has been to reiterate the strength of the community of researchers working together. I think that to have a project where you have collaborators from throughout the world looking at common questions for common themes is really a way to build the capacity of the researchers as researchers, but also as educators who can extend their understanding immensely because they are able to look at situations through the eyes of many.

Some of the participants in the ISLDN had also been members of the International Successful School Principalship Project (ISSPP); however, that network was participation by invitation rather than open to new as well as experienced researchers. One participant who is a member of both groups expressed an interest to "confirm findings across both groups." New researchers recognized the value of their voices being heard and were encouraged to participate. An interviewee explained that encouragement from a senior faculty member resonated with her in her role as a clinical

84 ■ J. R. BERRY et al.

faculty member when he said, "Think about what you want your research agenda to be, and the stories you want to tell, and say 'yes' to the projects that help you get there." Some of the participants of the ISLDN network were graduate students who had been encouraged by their mentors or dissertation chairs to participate. One member noted that she joined because her advisor extended an invitation.

Preeminent scholars in the field and new scholars expressed that they "were accepted in the same way." The "shared interest in school leadership and how that plays out in other countries" was a strong joint research interest. As a former graduate student shared, "I was an international student, and I wanted to work with people from different countries. The network was a tremendous opportunity to participate with senior professors and researchers as a graduate student." Another scholar added:

> I was immersed among scholars who are interested in similar things. I felt very welcome, and I appreciated the network leader saying, "I'm glad you're here, and I think you have things to contribute." I appreciated the support that I received from the network leaders.

Leaders of the network were supportive, welcoming, and active in fostering research through ongoing email communication concerning upcoming opportunities as venues for sharing research.

The network maintained an ongoing structure with set meeting times and opportunities to present research through various venues from research symposiums at UCEA to international conferences at the British Educational Leadership, Management, and Administration Society (BELMAS), the New Zealand Educational Administration and Leadership Society (NZEALS), and the Congreso International de Organizacion de Instituciones Educativas (CIOIE), which were highly valued by participants. Participants appreciated that the network met consistently in a pre-conference session at UCEA each year that provided ongoing support for collaboration, giving a "space" for community building sessions.

Culture of Learning

Members developed the protocol for research, which was viewed as being beneficial in developing a culture of learning. On a weekend at Georgia State University in the United States, participants initially began the protocol development. The protocol was finalized in England and discussed at follow-up BELMAS and UCEA meetings. Members of the network highlighted the value of being part of this process. A member expressed the benefit of participating in developing the protocol by stressing, "The process expanded us, because it helped us to look at the issues we're working to address through the minds of many as opposed to just through our own lens."

The network provided opportunities for scholarship and presentation in multiple international settings as well as at annual UCEA conferences. The network leaders submitted symposium proposals at UCEA that combined paper submissions from network participants for a focus on shared themes. The network leaders also provided a symposium submission for an international educational leadership conference in Spain as well as in New Zealand and England. Additionally, individuals were encouraged to provide individual submissions. Network participants stressed that these opportunities were powerful benefits of the network. As one stressed, "The opportunities to present and learn together through conferences and shared presentations in symposiums promoted that culture of learning."

The network leaders went a step further in fostering collegiality and positive relationships by making reservations at restaurants near the UCEA sessions during one evening of the conferences and extending an invitation to all members of the network. The opportunity to meet informally and further network was extremely valuable and provided multiple opportunities for incidental learning to occur. Adult learning theorists (Marsick & Watkins, 2001) stated the importance of this learning to individual growth. Although these dinner sessions had no set agenda, they presented additional time for networking and sharing.

A culture of learning was developed in multiple ways. Through the structure of yearly face-to-face meetings, international conference participation, and informal gatherings at conferences, individuals who shared a goal of understanding school leadership in high-needs schools experienced growth in their knowledge and skills that then impacted their scholarship and university teaching. As one participant shared:

> This 10-year publication is a gift to one another and to the world. Our collaborative work, reflecting a broad professional learning community, is a model for other collaboratives. Amid our professional advancements, personal relationships have emerged that also sustain our work.

Personal and Professional Growth

Both new and experienced scholars spoke to their growth as researchers from participation in the network. The network experiences contributed to a sabbatical experience in Sweden for two interviewees, to the opportunity to observe successful high-needs schools in the United States, Spain, New Zealand, and the United Kingdom for others, and to the opportunity to research the important topic of school leadership in high-needs schools

86 ▪ J. R. BERRY et al.

through the use of a common protocol that was developed by the members. A researcher shared that his goal was "moving beyond aggregate information about what we know about effective school leadership to really look at what is unique about leading high-need schools. What does it take to get them off underperforming lists?"

Participants also spoke to the importance of how partaking in the network influenced their university teaching. For example, a researcher from the United States shared that she realized that prior to participating in the project, her lens was "Americanized." The opportunity to meet with researchers from other countries and visit schools where outstanding leaders in high-needs contexts throughout the world were facilitating success for students, was paramount to expanding her understanding. She explained, "This has been an eye-opening experience that has really expanded my understanding of what schooling is . . . and has reminded me that we are constantly learning." Another member noted, "The project helped to change my ethnocentric thinking and increased my understanding that leaders around the world share more commonalities than differences through their shared passion for education and for students." Perhaps the most heartening comment was from a member when she shared that the work had "been a pleasure and the highlight of my career."

Key Learnings About Leadership Practice

A deepened understanding of leadership in high-needs schools across multiple countries emerged for participants in the network. Important beliefs, practices, and processes of successful school leadership in high-needs schools were illuminated as were context-specific actions. An often-repeated theme emergent from the interviews was that school leadership must always be viewed as context-specific. As Hallinger (2016) offered, "Community contexts vary widely with respect to the needs, opportunities, resources, and constraints they present to school leaders" (p. 7). For example, two interviewees emphasized that natural disasters can influence a leader's next steps. An earthquake in Nepal or a hurricane in the United States influences leaders' actions and focus. External and internal constraints and/or supports influence a leader's actions, and as an interviewee explained, "Leaders often have no control over socio-economic issues of poverty that may be present." As another interviewee stressed, "We can change the trajectory of a student's life and change the trajectory of their communities." In doing this, she added, "It's important to involve the students and the students' voice and those of the family in a community to gain the perceptions of the key stakeholders." Specific needs are unique to particular contexts

School Leadership Development Network's High-Needs Schools Strand ▪ **87**

and engagement of all stakeholders in the improvement process is vitally important.

As many participants noted, leadership clearly needs to be understood from a contextual lens. One urged:

> Leaders are more effective in high need schools when they can connect with their communities, clearly understand the conditions affecting students and staff, set high expectations for student and teacher performance, and create a culture where teachers feel a collective responsibility to improve student performance.

As another ISLDN member explained, "What resonated as much as context was that there are also leadership practices that seem to trade across context, across cultures. One of those, for example, is how leaders invest in other people." School leaders in high-needs settings were responsive to specific needs present within their context, but multiple interviewees stated that there was a shared finding that these leaders' actions were driven by a personal passion and commitment to helping all students learn at high levels. They wanted their students to be able to succeed and have the same opportunities that those in schools not characterized as high-needs experience. A participant explained a key finding of the research on high-needs schools:

> We've found that the school leaders are really on the ground and in the classrooms and very involved in what's happening. They are not micromanaging things, but if they're asking people to take on leadership roles, they're supporting those people, they're in the classrooms, they're bringing instruction to the floor, and they are balancing the notion of high expectations with care for the individuals. As a principal said, "We can love the students, but they're going to learn, too."

Participants also reported that high-needs school leaders modeled authenticity and moral conviction in their actions with genuine respect and positive regard for all stakeholders. They listened to the needs that were expressed by stakeholders and analyzed data to assist in determining next steps. An interviewee stressed, "What I gleaned from what I heard people share from different places of work, passion matters." Interviewees stressed that successful school leaders in high-needs schools were modeling their commitment to ongoing learning by providing opportunities for professional development and collaboration. They actively engaged the community as partners, and there was a "feeling of family" within the school. They were concerned with the needs of the whole child, not just the students' academic success.

RECOMMENDATIONS FOR NEXT STEPS

As participants reflected on next steps for the network, they shared hopes that the collaborative would continue with established meeting times at BELMAS and UCEA and continued opportunities to investigate the issue of school leadership in high-needs contexts. In addition, hopes were expressed that attention would be given to providing greater outreach to involve additional scholars, including scholars of color, from non-English speaking contexts, and from countries that have not been well represented during the project's first 10 years. Additionally, participants shared that securing funding for wider visibility of the research findings and increasing the publication of the findings in practitioner venues to influence the ongoing improvement of practice were two ways to ensure the work not only continued, but also had a lasting impact in the field.

CONCLUSIONS

As the ISLDN celebrates its 10-year anniversary in 2020, this chapter offered a reflection on the HNS strand of the project and highlighted the studies and learnings that have grown from the research conducted over the life of the project. The chapter presented the history of the HNS strand of the ISLDN; provided an overview of the common themes related to learning, leadership, and context; and shared lessons learned by the researchers who have taken part in the international professional learning community that has grown out of the project.

Since the onset of the ISLDN work, the HNS research team clearly had input and ownership into developing the focus, understanding the concept, creating methods and assessments, and analyzing common findings across global school settings defined as HNS. The researchers, while not driven by a specific framework, sustained themselves by emerging into a unique professional learning community. Specifically, the culture established by the researchers reflects several Professional Learning Community (PLC) dimensions, including shared and supportive leadership, shared vision and values, collective learning and application involving shared personal practice, and supportive conditions—structures and relationships (Hord, 1997; Hipp & Huffman, 2010; Watson, 2014), which were similarly apparent in several of the successful high-need schools studied.

The researchers shared leadership by sharing responsibility within the team through an eagerness to learn from and support one another. The team's productivity and effectiveness reflect what Hord and Hirsh (1998) observed, "Learning is restricted to what the PLC members know and the

School Leadership Development Network's High-Needs Schools Strand ■ 89

skills that members can share ... as long as the expertise to address a need or goal resides in the group" (p. 34).

Shared vision and values were apparent through an unalterable focus on building lateral capacity around a common goal reflective of the purpose of the project and the integrity of the work at hand and commitment to excellence. Learning collectively and applying new knowledge was continuous in the personal and professional growth expressed by the researchers as they shared knowledge, experience, and practices while co-writing, co-presenting, analyzing data, creating manuscripts for publication, field testing the interview protocol, and continually refining their work.

The supportive conditions that exist add depth to the concept of "the broader community" (Kelley & Shaw, 2009) by revealing how such a community can be built and sustained within an international context over the course of time. Regularly scheduled meetings, conferences, work groups, networking dinners, collaborative writing and, co-presenting have been apparent in several contexts across countries and continents. Moreover, each member has contributed to the sustainability of self and project by respecting and trusting one another.

The HNS team has not wavered from the focus of the work and understanding of the challenges that hinder growth in affecting student achievement across a variety of cultural contexts. What has emerged over the last 10 years is evidence of professional researchers/practitioners advancing "the concept of a PLC from a 'brick and mortar,' building-based community to one that has no tangible physical boundaries" (Hipp & Weber, 2008, p. 1).

The story of this work is truly a testament to the scholars who originally envisioned it as an inclusive international collaboration aimed at disseminating knowledge about leadership in high-needs schools and to those who have participated in the telling of the stories of courageous leaders from varied contexts throughout the world. The research these scholars have conducted has broadened the collective understanding of leadership in high-needs schools, context, and community to advance student achievement. Perhaps equally important, the structures created through the support of BELMAS and UCEA have provided a collaborative model for scholars across other contexts to work with one another in telling the important stories within their fields, while simultaneously building relationships with one another.

REFERENCES

Aguedje, T. L. (2017). *How principals manage time, mindsets, and communities to benefit children of poverty* (Doctoral dissertation). Retrieved from Scholarworks@ Georgia State University, Atlanta.

Alford, B. (2019). Leadership practices for equity and excellence: An exploratory narrative of two principals of high-need elementary schools in California. In E. Murakami, D. Gurr, & R. Notman (Eds.), *Educational leadership, culture, and school success in high-need schools* (pp. 85–101). Charlotte, NC: Information Age.

Baran, M. L., & Berry, J., (2015). *The International School Leadership Development Network (ISLDN) high needs schools group research protocol and members' guide.* Unpublished manuscript.

Baran, M. L., & Van Harpen, G. (2019). Creating a culture of leadership in a high-need inner-city USA school: The unique leadership challenges. In E. Murakami, D. Gurr, & R. Notman (Eds.), *Educational leadership, culture, and school success in high-need schools* (pp. 103–128). Charlotte, NC: Information Age.

Berry, J. R., Cowart Moss, S., & Gore, P. (2019). Leadership in high-needs/high performing schools: Success stories from an urban school district. In E. Murakami, D. Gurr, & R. Notman (Eds.), *Educational leadership, culture, and school success in high-need schools* (pp. 131–148). Charlotte, NC: Information Age.

Bryant, K. C., Berry, J. R., & Cevik, S. (2019). A South African high-needs school: A case of context driven by history. *International Journal of Educational Leadership Preparation, 14*(1), 113–127.

Chisholm, L., Waight, N., & Jacobson, S. (2019). School leadership for social justice and STEM: Findings from a high-need secondary school in Belize. In E. Murakami, D. Gurr, & R. Notman (Eds.), *Educational leadership, culture, and school success in high-need schools* (pp. 65–83). Charlotte, NC: Information Age.

Elmore, R. (2004). *School reform from the inside out.* Cambridge, MA: Harvard University Press.

Gurr, D., Drysdale, L., Longmuir, F., & McCrohan, K. (2019). Successful school leadership that is culturally sensitive but not culturally constrained. In E. Murakami, D. Gurr, & R. Notman (Eds.), *Education leadership, culture, and school success in high-need schools* (pp. 25–43). Charlotte, NC: Information Age.

Hallinger, P. (2016). Bringing context out of the shadows of leadership. *Educational Management, Administration and Leadership, 46*(1), 5–24. https://doi.org/10.1177/1741143216670652

Heifetz, R. A. (2010, Spring). Adaptive work. *The Journal Kansas Leadership Center,* 72–77.

Heifetz, R. A., & Linsky, M. (2002). *Leadership on the line: Staying alive through the dangers of leading.* Boston, MA: Harvard Business Press.

Heifetz, R. A., Linsky, M., & Grashow, A. (2009). *The practice of adaptive leadership: Tools and tactics for changing your organization and the world.* Boston, MA: Harvard Business Press.

Hipp, K. K., & Baran, M. L. (2014, November). A preliminary study of one urban school's turnaround effort involving learning, leadership, and internal and external contexts. Paper presented at the annual UCEA Convention, Washington, D.C.

Hipp, K. K., & Huffman, J. B. (2010). *Demystifying professional learning communities: School leadership at its best.* Lanham, MD: Rowman & Littlefield Education.

Hipp, K. K., & Weber, P. (2008). Developing a professional learning community among urban school principals. *Journal of Urban Learning, Teaching and Research, 4,* 46–56.

Hord, S. L. (1997). *Professional learning communities: Communities of continuous inquiry and improvement.* Austin, TX: Southwest Educational Development Laboratory.

Hord, S. M., & Hirsh, S. A. (1998). Making a promise a reality. In A. M. Blankstein, P. D. Houston, & R. W. Cole (Eds.), *Sustaining professional learning communities* (pp. 23–40). Thousand Oaks, CA: SAGE.

Kearney, W., Murakami, E., Bunch, K., Viamontes, C., & Campbell, A. (2018). Leadership advocacy towards teacher and student success: Addressing inequities and opportunities in a rural district. *Rural Society, 27*(2), 143–156. https://doi.org/10.1080/10371656.2018.1477512

Kelley, C. J., & Shaw, J. J. (2009). *Learning first: A school leader's guide to closing achievement gaps.* Thousand Oaks, CA: Corwin Press.

Klar, H. W., Huggins, K. S., Andreoli, P. M., & Buskey, F. C. (2019). Developing rural school leaders through leadership coaching: A transformative approach. *Leadership and Policy in Schools,* 1–21. https://doi.org/10.1080/15700763.2019.1585553

Kowalski, T. J., Lasley, T. J., & Mahoney, J. W. (2008). *Data driven decisions and school leadership: Best practices for school improvement.* Boston, MA: Pearson.

Leithwood, K., Day, C., Sammons, P., Harris A., & Hopkins, D. (2006). *Seven strong claims about successful school leadership.* Nottingham, England: National College of School Leadership.

Marsick, V. J., & Watkins, K. E. (2001). Informal and incidental learning. In S. B. Merriam (Ed.), *The new update on adult learning theory* (pp. 25–34). San Francisco, CA: Jossey-Bass.

Murakami, E., Kearney, W. K. (2019). Principals in high-performing, high-poverty, minority-serving schools in Texas. In E. Murakami, D. Gurr, & R. Notman (Eds.), *Educational leadership, culture, and success in high-need schools* (pp. 3–24). Charlotte, NC: Information Age.

Murakami, E., Notman, R., & Gurr, D. (2019). Sustaining a culture of academic success in a high needs elementary school. In E. Murakami, D. Gurr, & R. Notman (Eds.), *Educational leadership, culture, and school success in high-need schools* (pp. xi–xix). Charlotte, NC: Information Age.

Notman, R., & Jacobson, S. (2019). School leadership practices in early childhood education: Three case studies from New Zealand. In E. Murakami, D. Gurr, & R. Notman (Eds.), *Educational leadership, culture and success in high need schools* (pp. 169–184). Charlotte, NC: Information Age.

Okilwa, N. S., & Barnett, B. (2019). Sustaining a culture of academic success in a high-needs elementary school. In E. Murakami, D. Gurr, & R. Notman (Eds.), *Educational leadership, culture, and school success in high-need schools* (pp. 149–167). Charlotte, NC: Information Age.

Savage, B. C. (2017). *Leadership practices that support parental involvement in one high needs elementary school* (Doctoral dissertation). Retrieved from Scholarworks@ Georgia State University, Atlanta.

Waters, T. J., Marzano, R. J., & McNulty, B. A. (2003). *Balanced leadership: What 30 years of research tells us about the effect of leadership on student achievement.* Aurora, CO: Mid-continent Research for Education and Learning.

Watson, C. (2014). Effective professional learning communities? The possibilities for teachers as agents of change in schools. *British Educational Research Journal, 40*(1), 18–29.

Worldclouds.com (2019). *Graphic conceptualization of a summary of finding from 13 high needs studies.* Retrieved from https://www.wordclouds.com

CHAPTER 6

REVIEW OF METHODOLOGICAL APPROACHES IN STUDIES OF HIGH-NEEDS SCHOOLS ACROSS MULTINATIONAL CONTEXTS

Nathern S. A. Okilwa
University of Texas at San Antonio

As the International School Leadership and Development Network (IS-LDN) celebrates its 10th anniversary of collaborative work, it is worth exploring the nature and state of the scholarly work produced by the network. Before delving into reviewing the scope of the ISLDN scholarship, a brief description of what constitutes the ISLDN work is important—a more detailed evolution of the network is discussed in Chapters 2–5. The ISLDN comprises two scholarship strands: high-needs schools (HNS) and social justice leadership (SJL). The HNS strand focuses on the leadership required to improve outcomes in schools that are defined as exhibiting

Educational Leadership for Social Justice and Improving High-Needs Schools, pages 93–112
Copyright © 2021 by Information Age Publishing
All rights of reproduction in any form reserved.

one or more of these characteristics: (a) high percentage of individuals from families with incomes below the poverty line; (b) high percentage of school teachers not teaching in the content area in which they were trained to teach; (c) high teacher/leader turnover rate; (d) high percentage of non-native language speakers; (e) high percentage of historically/socially excluded groups; (f) high percentage of indigenous groups; (g) high percentage of students with learning differences; (h) lack of access to basic physical infrastructure; and/or (i) situational needs based on unforeseen events (e.g., natural or manmade disasters; Baran & Berry 2015; Gurr & Drysdale, 2018). Scholars in the HNS strand are generally guided by questions about (a) leadership, such as "In what ways do school leaders enhance individual and organizational performance?"; (b) learning, such as "In what ways can student learning be fostered?"; and (c) context, such as "How do the internal and external contexts impact individual and organizational performance?" In an effort to investigate these questions, the HNS protocols describe the three main data collection methods as interviews, observations, and school-related documents.

The second strand, SJL, is concerned with exploring social justice leaders in different countries and settings to determine how the school leaders form their views, understand social justice within their own context, and initiate and implement a social justice agenda (Angelle, 2017). Guiding questions for this strand include: (a) "How do social justice leaders make sense of 'social justice'?"; (b) "What do social justice leaders do?"; (c) "What factors help and hinder the work of social justice leaders?"; and (d) "How did social justice leaders learn to become social justice leaders?"

For the purpose of this review, the focus is on HNS strand. The goal of this chapter is to review studies conducted by scholars of the HNS strand to better understand the methodological approaches utilized in these studies. In order to conduct a meaningful review of the work, Hallinger (2013) provides a useful conceptual framework for systematic reviews of educational leadership and management research. I, therefore, start with a brief discussion of Hallinger's conceptual framework, which provides a structure for the rest of this chapter.

HALLINGER'S CONCEPTUAL FRAMEWORK FOR SYSTEMATIC REVIEWS

Hallinger (2013) chronicles the evolution of research reviews in the field of educational leadership and the importance of conducting systematic research reviews. He argues that his framework is an effort to acknowledge how "research reviews serve both to describe and demarcate the advancement of knowledge over time" (p. 132). Additionally, research reviews "play a critical role in the advancement of knowledge by highlighting milestones of progress along particular lines of inquiry" (p. 127). Indeed, the two IS-LDN strands have achieved significant milestones over the past decade—numerous presentations of research at conferences and published articles, book chapters, and books. This volume is further evidence of that milestone as well. Hallinger points out that past reviews were often prompted by a perception of a problem with a focus on substantive, methodological, and/or conceptual issues. This current review of the methodological approaches of HNS studies comes not from a problem orientation but rather as a survey of methodological landscape. Instead of an arbitrary approach to conducting research reviews, Hallinger proposes a conceptual framework for systematic reviews of leadership and management scholarship that responds to five major questions: (a) "What are the central topics of interest, guiding questions, and goals?"; (b) "What conceptual perspective guides the review's selection, evaluation, and interpretation of the studies?"; (c) "What are the sources and types of data employed for the review?"; (d) "How are data evaluated, analyzed, and synthesized in the review?"; and (e) "What are the major results, limitations, and implications of the review?" Consequently, the rest of this chapter is organized based on Hallinger's (2013) five-question conceptual perspectives.

Question 1: What Are the Central Topics of Interest, Guiding Questions, and Goals?

In response to this question, Hallinger (2013) suggests that reviewers need to explicitly articulate their thematic focus and purpose in the form of specific questions/goals. This chapter focuses on a review of methodological approaches and procedures pertinent to HNS scholarship. A focus on methodological review is consistent with past studies (e.g., Bridges, 1982; Hallinger, 2011; Hallinger & Heck, 1996; Murphy, 1988) that have considered this research component critically important. Therefore, the chapter centers on the different components of methodology to include the research approach (qualitative, quantitative, or mixed methods), research questions, participants, site/locale, data collection, and data analysis.

Question 2: What Conceptual Perspective Guides the Review's Selection, Evaluation, and Interpretation of the Studies?

Hallinger (2013) argues it would be a "fallacy to suggest that systematic reviews are value neutral" (p. 132). Therefore, my choice of methodological

96 ▪ N. S. A. OKILWA

approaches as a focus of this review is consistent with my belief that the scope of the research methods is a depiction of the quality of the study and believability of the findings or relevance of the evidence (Gough, 2007). Research methods articulate the plan or strategy the researcher undertakes in an effort to pursue answers to the research question(s) or hypothesis (Gough, 2007). Researchers suggest the methods section should be thorough, explicit, and transparent enough to allow for any of these three types of replication:

> (a) *exact replication*—a previous study is replicated using the same population and the same procedures; (b) *empirical replication*—a previous study is replicated using the same procedures but a different population; and (c) *conceptual replication*—a previous study is replicated using the same population but different procedures. (Aguinis & Solarino, 2019, p. 1292)

With regard to HNS scholarship, researchers have replicated studies in their various geographic and cultural contexts utilizing a common protocol and the three core guiding questions (about leadership, learning, and context) outlined above. While acknowledging the contextual uniqueness, one of the goals is to learn potential similarities and differences of schooling in these contexts.

Question 3: What Are the Sources and Types of Data Employed for the Review?

Hallinger (2013) suggests delimiting scholarship for inclusion in a review using justifiable criteria (e.g., sources such as journal articles, dissertations, books, conference papers; time period; search-type—selective, bounded, or exhaustive) that produces substantial and high quality literature. I, therefore, delimited this review to studies conducted by researchers within the HNS strand; searches for published articles were purposively confined to outlets known to the author and in consultation with members within the network. The main sources of articles and book chapters appeared in Murakami, Gurr, and Notman's (2019) edited book, *Educational leadership, culture, and success in high-need schools*; the special issue of *International Studies in Educational Administration* (Volume 46, No. 1, 2018); ISLDN website homepage (https://isldn.weebly.com/); and the special issue of *Management in Education* (Volume 28, No. 3, 2014). However, articles in *Management in Education* were not included because they were written as a summary and did not follow the traditional format of an empirical study report, thus, the methods section (the focus of this current review) is missing from those articles. I also checked references listed in these articles and book chapters for additional studies for inclusion. Additionally, I checked conference paper presentations (mainly at UCEA), not for inclusion, but as a source of information to track published studies.

The main criterion for making the final selection of studies for inclusion in this current review was published original empirical studies conducted within HNS settings in a variety of national contexts. Hallinger (2013) also reinforces the need to explicate the process of reading, extracting information, and generating codes and themes from the data. For this review, Table 6.1 represents the main methodological information extracted from HNS scholarship to include authorship, study approach, participants, site/locale, and data collection/analysis.

Question 4: How Are Data Evaluated, Analyzed, and Synthesized in the Review?

Hallinger (2013) suggests "the nature of the data gleaned from the 'review database' will determine the types of data analysis and synthesis" to be employed (p. 135). A thorough evaluation, analysis, and synthesis provide another level of screening for relevance and quality of the studies under review. However, for the purpose of my review of HNS studies, I was not particularly concerned about exclusion on the basis of quality. Studies were included so long as they met the basic inclusion criteria mentioned above because my goal was to provide a general survey of the methodological landscape of HNS studies. I analyzed the articles and book chapters that I identified for this review by focusing on the type of research approach (qualitative, quantitative, or mixed methods) employed, conceptual framework/perspectives, research questions or purpose statement, participants, site/locale, data collection methods, and data analysis.

Question 5: What Are the Major Results, Limitations, and Implications of the Review?

Hallinger (2013) points out the importance of clearly articulating what was learned from the review of studies (i.e., the findings or results). In addition, he provides some guidelines to augment the response to the question posed here, which include (a) a clear statement of results, actionable conclusions, and the conditions under which the findings apply; (b) the design of the research review; and (c) the implications of the findings. In this section, I present Table 6.1, which lists studies included in this current review (N = 18) and highlights critical information extracted from the studies in response to methodological components: Study approach, conceptual framework/perspectives, research questions or purpose statement,

TABLE 6.1 Empirical Studies Conducted by ISLDN Scholars

Authorship	Study Approach/RQ	Participants	Site/Locale	Data Collection/Analysis
1. Alford (2019)	• Qualitative: exploratory narrative • Purpose: To identify the leadership practices that foster learning in two successful high-need elementary schools.	2 female elementary school (ES) principals	2 high-need ES: >85% ethnic minority (i.e., majority Hispanic); >85% low SES; 36% ELs Locale: Southern California, United States	• In-depth interviews, field notes of on-site observations, document reviews • Conducted open & axial coding for themes using iterative, recursive process
2. Alford & Gautam (2014)	• Qualitative: exploratory narrative study • RQ: In what ways was each head teacher's (principal's) development fostered for successful school leadership? What were the challenges of the local context of Nepal?	2 male secondary school head teachers; members of Nepalese Ministry of Education	Low income secondary schools (urban & rural) w/ high achievement Locale: Nepal, South Asia	• Interviews w/ head teachers, school documents, and field notes • Conducted open & axial coding for themes
3. Baran & Harpen (2019)	• Qualitative case study • RQ: What fosters student learning in high-needs schools?	1 male principal, dean of students, academic dean, & chief operation office	K–8 charter school with 97% free/reduced lunch Locale: Milwaukee, Wisconsin	• Interviews (Phase 1 & 2) • Utilized descriptive & pattern codes
4. Berry, Moss, & Gore (2019)	• Qualitative case study • Utilized the high-needs schools leadership model • RQ: What fosters student learning in high-needs schools? How do school leaders enhance individual and organizational performance in high-needs schools? How do internal and external school contexts impact individual and organizational performance in high-needs schools?	>15 educators (including 2 female principals)	High-need: 1 elementary school (ES) and 1 middle school (MS) Locale: Southeastern United States	• Interviews with >15 educators; document analysis • Thematic analysis consistent with high-needs schools leadership model

(continued)

TABLE 6.1 Empirical Studies Conducted by ISLDN Scholars (Continued)

Authorship	Study Approach/RQ	Participants	Site/Locale	Data Collection/Analysis
5. Gurr, Drysdale, Clarke, Wildly (2014)	• Qualitative case study • RQ: (not clearly reported)	Principals, leadership team, middle-level leaders (not fully clarified)	Secondary college school Locale: Australia	• Multiple perspective interviews • Analysis procedures—not stated
6. Gurr, Drysdale, Longmuir & McCrohan (2018)	• Qualitative: multiple perspective observational case studies • Employed Hallinger's (2016) multi-context instructional leadership • RQs: What are the characteristics and practices of principals leading under-performing schools and what influences these? Who else contributes to the leader-ship of these schools and what are their contributions? How does the context in-fluence the performance of these schools?	3 principals (1 female, 2 male), senior & middle level leaders, teachers, parents, students, and school council members	3 secondary schools: 2 educationally advantaged & 1 educationally disadvantaged Locale: Victoria, Australia	• Interviews, relevant school-related documents • The process of data analysis not articulated
7. Gurr, Drysdale, Longmuir, & McCrohan (2019; duplicate of Gurr et al., 2018)	• Qualitative: multiple perspective observational case studies • Utilized Hallinger's (2018) context and culture framework • RQs: What are the characteristics and practices of principals leading under-performing schools and what influences these? Who else contributes to the leader-ship of these schools and what are their contributions? How does the context in-fluence the performance of these schools?	3 principals (1 female, 2 male), senior & middle level leaders, teachers, parents, students, & school council members	3 underperforming secondary schools: 2 educationally advantaged & 1 disadvantaged contexts Locale: Victoria, Australia	• individual or group interviews, observations, relevant school-related documents *Note:* No dedicated section on methods—lacks thorough description of methods

(continued)

TABLE 6.1 Empirical Studies Conducted by ISLDN Scholars (Continued)

Authorship	Study Approach/RQ	Participants	Site/Locale	Data Collection/Analysis
8. Jacobson & Notman (2018)	• Qualitative case study • Conceptual framework of core practices of successful school leadership • Purpose: To examine the practices of three ECE leaders engaged in increasing parental involvement at centers serving diverse, high-needs communities in New Zealand (NZ)	3 head teachers (all female), teachers, and parents	3 early childhood centers across the SES spectrum (low to high) Locale: New Zealand	• Interviews, government, and school documents • Process of data analysis not clearly articulated
9. Medina, Martinez, Murakami, Rodriguez, & Hernandez (2014)	• Qualitative approach • Purpose: Exploration of leadership in high-need schools	2 principals (2 female)	2 elementary schools Locale: Texas	• Interviews • Dialogic narrative *Note:* No methods section
10. Murakami & Kearney (2019)	• Qualitative: criterion sample & phenomenological design • Employed advocacy leadership framework • RQ: How do principals in high-performing high-poverty minority serving schools in Texas enhance performance at the individual and organizational levels?	4 principals (2 female & 2 male)	High-need (85/85/85): 3 ES & 1 charter MS in South Central Texas	• Focus group, interviews, classroom observations, and school public documents • A priori coding for themes consistent with advocacy leadership framework *Note:* provided details about site, participants, data collection, & analysis.

(continued)

TABLE 6.1   Empirical Studies Conducted by ISLDN Scholars (Continued)

Authorship	Study Approach/RQ	Participants	Site/Locale	Data Collection/Analysis
11. Murakami, Kearney, Scott, & Alfaro (2018)	• Single case study • Utilized ISLDN framework for the study of high needs schools • RQ: In what ways does the leadership team plan strategies that can be effective in turning around a high-needs school?	1 principal (female), 1 school counselor, 1 social worker, 1 parent liaison, 2 parents, & 14 teachers.	High-need ES Locale: Texas	• Interviews, on-site observations, school-related documents • Hierarchical analysis of interventions consistent with each of the strategic areas of improvement
12. Notman & Jacobson (2019)	• Case study methodology • Conceptual framework of core practices of successful school leadership • Objective: To determine whether key participants—teachers, parents, and leaders themselves—believe the leader played a key role in the center's success.	3 head teachers (all female), teachers, & parents (not fully clarified)	3 early childhood centers across the SES spectrum (low to high) Locale: New Zealand	• Interviews, government, & school documents, and ethnographic notes
13. Okilwa & Barnett (2017)	• Qualitative approach • Change management and sustainability framework • RQ: How does a high-need school sustain academic improvement over time?	principal (female), 2 teachers, 2 parent representatives	1 elementary school Locale: Texas	• Quantitative archival school data • Interviews • Descriptive statistics and comparative endemic data analysis

(continued)

TABLE 6.1   Empirical Studies Conducted by ISLDN Scholars (Continued)

Authorship	Study Approach/RQ	Participants	Site/Locale	Data Collection/Analysis
14. Okilwa & Barnett (2018)	• Qualitative approaches • Multidimensional conceptual framework of context • RQ: How did four successive principals read and respond to a high-needs elementary school context that enabled them to turn around and/or sustain academic performance?	4 principals (all female), 3 veteran teachers, 2 parent leaders	1 high-need elementary school Locale: Texas	• Semi-structured interviews • Comparative data analysis consistent with the multidimensional conceptual framework of context
15. Okilwa & Barnett (2019)	• Qualitative case study • Theoretical constructs of leadership succession and change management • RQ: How did principals enhance individual and organizational performance in the school? What fostered student learning in the school?	4 principals (all female), 3 veteran teachers	1 elementary school Locale: Texas	• Interviews (individual and group) • Data analysis using comparative coding for emerging themes
16. Oliveira & Carvalho (2019)	• Quantitative & qualitative designs • Employs school management framework • RQ: How do principals manage their jobs considering their high-need situations, focusing on student learning (or not)?	2 principals (1 female, 1 male); management teams, 5–6 teachers	2 schools (grade levels not defined): high SES & mixed middle class & working class Locale: Rio de Janeiro, Brazil, South America	• Survey GESQ2014 for quantitative analysis • Interviews, principal shadowing, observation—management team/teacher meeting • Analytical procedures not clearly explicated

(continued)

TABLE 6.1 Empirical Studies Conducted by ISLDN Scholars (Continued)

Authorship	Study Approach/RQ	Participants	Site/Locale	Data Collection/Analysis
17. Torres-Arcadia, Rodríguez-Uribe, & Mora (2018).	• Qualitative case study • Utilized ISLDN framework for the study of high-needs schools • RQs: How do principals and other school leaders enhance individual and organizational performance in high-needs schools? How do internal and external school contexts impact individual and organizational performance in high-needs schools?	3 principals (2 female, 1 male); at least 3 teachers & support staff; parents; students	3 inner city schools (2 elementary schools & 1 secondary school) Locale: Sonora, Jalisco, & Yucatan in Mexico	• Semi-structured interviews; focus groups • Multiple case study analysis was used, conducted open coding system; used triangulation—member checking
18. Waight, Chisolm, & Jacobson (2018)	• Naturalistic case study • RQs: What are the roles of school leaders in a high-needs secondary school in Belize? How were these roles aligned with the goals of STEM? How is the STEM curriculum enacted in a high-needs secondary school in Belize? What were students' experiences with STEM related courses?	2 administrators (female); 2 teachers; 15 students (6 male & 9 females)	1 rural secondary school Locale: Belize, Central America	• In-depth individual interviews with school leaders, STEM teachers & students; classroom observations; field notes • Used interpretive data analysis and triangulation

Note: RQ = Research Question; SES = Social Economic Status; EL = English Learners; STEM = Science, Technology, Engineering, & Mathematics.

104 ▪ N. S. A. OKILWA

participants, site/locale, and data collection and analysis. The following sections are organized around these components.

STUDY APPROACH

Study designs should be consistent with the types of questions that are asked, which is apparent in the HNS research questions examining (a) the ways school leaders enhance individual and organizational performance, (b) how student learning is fostered, and (c) how the internal and external contexts impact individual and organizational performance. In examining these questions, all the studies I reviewed for this chapter follow the qualitative tradition, which is consistent with the design of the HNS protocol. The protocol heavily relies on qualitative interviews (individual or group) for data collection, coupled with observations and school related documents.

According to Brooks and Normore (2015), "In order to choose an appropriate design, scholars must have a clear understanding of: what they are studying and which design is most appropriate for that topic, phenomenon, dynamic, person, or place" (p. 799). The HNS strand is clearly concerned about student learning, the role of school leadership, and the influences of internal and external contexts (Gurr & Drysdale, 2018). Questions that emerge from these areas of the schooling process as framed by the HNS strand predominantly lend themselves to qualitative approaches. The Oliveira and Carvalho (2019) study (#16—see Table 6.1) is the only study that introduced an element of quantitative analysis; however, only as part of the identification process for the final sites for their study. Otherwise, data collection from their focus study participants was qualitative—interviews, shadowing, and observations.

PARTICIPANTS

Given that ISLDN's work is concerned about the contribution of school leadership on student learning, every study included at least one principal (or head teacher). It is worth noting that a significant majority of the principals in the studies reported here were women. In addition to the principals, other leadership team members, teachers, parents, and/or students were interviewed. Collecting perceptions of various stakeholders, besides principals and head teachers, triangulates the data collection process. Most of the studies I reviewed articulated the use of triangulation as a means to assure increased validity of the findings (Creswell & Creswell, 2018). Mertler (2020) suggests that "Triangulation is a process of relating multiple sources of data in order to establish their trustworthiness or verification of the consistency of the facts while trying to account for their inherent biases" (p. 13). Mertler introduces the term "polyangulation" as a true representation of the multiplicity of sources used in the process of achieving the purposes of triangulation (p. 13). Triangulation or polyangulation can also be achieved by employing multiple research designs such as mixed method approaches—quantitative and qualitative. Three studies (Alford, 2019; Medina, Martinez, Murakami, Rodriguez, & Hernandez, 2014; Murakami & Kearney, 2019) only conducted interviews with principals; however, observations and school documents or records also were collected.

SITE/LOCALE

In examining the sites and national location of the ISLDN studies considered for this review, two main observations stand out. First, many HNS studies were conducted in elementary school settings—6 out of the 18 studies in this current review were exclusively conducted at the elementary school. One study was conducted in a K–12 setting. Furthermore, three studies were secondary schools; however, the grade levels were not clearly stipulated. Additionally, two studies did not address the type of school setting. Finally, the study conducted in an Early Childhood Center stands out because it is the only study at that educational level. As a second observation, half of the studies were conducted in the United State—9 out of 18 in this review. The other half are distributed between Nepal, Australia, New Zealand, Brazil, Mexico, and Belize.

DATA COLLECTION AND ANALYSIS

HNS studies included in this review reflect similar methods of data collection and analysis across grade levels and national contexts. This is consistent with the purpose of the protocol, which advances the use of interviews (individual or group), observations, and school-related documents. In their discussion of these methods common to qualitative educational leadership studies, Brooks and Normore (2015) note that these methods allow researchers flexibility in the sequence of questioning. However, researchers need to be cognizant of the potential peril of elite interviews—interviews conducted with/by those at the top of the organization or social structure (Harvey, 2010; Marshall, 1984). For instance, HNS studies seem to involve less student, parent, and community voices—7 out of 18 studies interviewed parents, and of those seven only three engaged with the students. The underrepresentation of student and parent perspectives needs to be addressed. Additionally, with regard to focus groups as a method of

106 ▪ N. S. A. OKILWA

data collection, researchers should give thoughtful consideration to group dynamics: "How are these dynamics likely to influence the data collection process?" For instance, 6 out of 18 studies reported utilizing group interviews. In addition, observations are another common data collection method—7 out of 18 studies I reviewed conducted observations. Given considerations for potential influence on data collection due to group dynamics and power interplay, it is imperative for researchers to be explicit, thorough, and transparent in their description of the research methods in general (Aguinis & Solarino, 2019).

LIMITATIONS

One main limitation of this review is the exclusive focus on the methodological approaches of the ISLDN studies. However, this review is not alone on this focus (see Berkovich & Eyal, 2017; Hallinger, 2011). While fundamentally important, examining the methodological approaches used is only one slice of otherwise major research projects, which have to be interpreted in the context of a holistic study design. In addition, this review is in no way comprehensive. The search sources were delimited and I may have missed other studies for inclusion.

REFLECTIONS AND CONCLUSION

As ISLDN's HNS scholars celebrate this 10-year milestone of collaborative research and scholarship, surveying the work thus far, such as what I have done by focusing on methodological approaches, is appropriate. The methods section could be considered a roadmap needed to arrive at the right destination or a recipe to produce a delicious meal. Therefore, in pursuit of answers to research questions of interest, the methodological design needs to be thorough, explicit, and transparent (Aguinis & Solarino, 2019). As earlier noted, methodological evaluation is consistent with past, similarly positioned reviews (e.g., Berkovich & Eyal, 2017; Bridges, 1982; Hallinger, 2011; Hallinger & Heck, 1996; Murphy, 1988). This exercise gives us an opportunity to highlight predominant research practices and trends, as well as potential gaps that can collectively inform HNS scholarship, especially as we chart the course for the future.

First, gaps emerge in areas such as school levels—most of the research projects are disproportionately concentrated on elementary or primary grades with limited representation of secondary grades. For the review articles that identified their study sites by level, 60% of the sites are elementary or primary schools while 40% are considered secondary. Besides the well

Review of Methodological Approaches Across Multinational Contexts ▪ **107**

acknowledged organizational and structural differences akin to elementary and secondary schools, some scholars have pointed to other important considerations. For example, due to the organizational differences, prescriptions for effective elementary schools do not quite fit secondary schools (Firestone & Herriott, 1982). If this is the case, more studies are needed to unveil effective practices specific to secondary school settings.

Second, there is an underrepresentation of male principals or head teachers in the schools researched—based on studies included in the review that reported the gender of the principal or head teacher, 81% were female while 19% were male. Existing studies that examine male and female school leadership cite myriad issues (e.g., representation in leadership position, differences in leadership styles, interplay of culture and gender, stereotypes, perceptions, and treatment) moderated by gender (Coleman, 2005, 2007; Gray, 1987; Krüger, 2008; Law, 2013; Sanchez & Thornton, 2010; Shaked, Glanz, & Gross, 2018). Given HNS scholars operate in a variety of international contexts with varied cultural perceptions and interpretations of gender, there is reason to pay attention to this variable in the study of school leadership and management.

Third, student, parent, and community voices tend to be overlooked—as noted earlier, seven studies interviewed parents and only three obtained students' perspectives. If the work we do is about students, then whenever possible, involving students and their parents in understanding their schooling experiences is important. Mitra (2008) correctly notes, "To improve student achievement, it makes sense to go straight to the source—students. Students can not only share opinions about their classroom experiences, but also play a significant role in school improvement efforts" (p. 20). The exclusion of students and their families in the decision-making processes in schools (Lac & Mansfield, 2018) should not be perpetuated by ignoring their views in the knowledge production that seeks to improve schools. The benefits of including these voices are well documented (Cook-Sather, 2007; Lac & Mansfield, 2018; Lumby, 2007; McKenna & Millen, 2013; Mitra, 2006, 2008).

Finally, most of the studies in this review emanate from the United States or Western societies (82%). Multiple national contexts of HNS scholarship provides an opportunity to explore "emerging approaches to conceptualizing the study of school leadership internationally and to explore leadership practices and effects in a wide range of national contexts" (Hallinger & Huber, 2012, p. 361). There is a need to expand HNS international representation. Furthermore, these studies lack demonstrable utility for practitioners and policy makers. Research should bridge theory and practice and HNS scholarship has the potential to impact policy and practice contextual nature of the work (Levačic & Glatter, 2001).

108 ▪ N. S. A. OKILWA

I agree with other scholars (e.g., Aguinis & Solarino, 2019; Hallinger, 2013; Trainor & Graue, 2014) that rigorous methodological approaches are the backbone of high quality (or lack thereof) empirical educational research. Therefore, to maintain research quality across the broad and diverse international educational landscape that the HNS consortium represents, scholars in our field of educational leadership and management point to a number of quality control elements worthy of our attention. For instance, attending to norms of rigor such as validity, reliability, trustworthiness, triangulation, and transferability are important (Brooks & Normore, 2015). Moving forward, questions worth asking ourselves to ensure rigor does not elude us include: What is the role of theory in the design and implementation of research studies? Are there enough data to support significant claims? Did we spend enough time to gather interesting and significant data? Is the context or sample appropriate given the goals of the study? Did we use appropriate procedures in terms of field note style, interviewing practices, and analysis procedures (Gough, 2007; Trainor & Graue, 2014; Tracy, 2010)?

Another important consideration for the HNS research team is whether there are alternative methodologies that should be included in their corpus of work? (see Todd, 2018). As we continue to interrogate this phenomenon of HNS, there is high interest globally to find solutions to the "wicked problems" (Grint, 2005, p. 1473) that continue to challenge the educational process of underserved children and youth across nations. The current work of HNS scholars sheds some light on the convergence and divergence of education issues while cognizant of context. To increase their voice in the policy discourse surrounding the high-needs schooling process within the various contexts in which HNS work is being conducted, these scholars may consider exploring other methodologies, such as quantitative approaches, which are often privileged at the policy discourse table. To that end, to situate future HNS work for potential policy discourse, I find Berkovich and Eyal's (2017, p. 485) methodological recommendations useful:

- Developing more mixed method and quantitative studies.
- Choosing "cleaner" participant profiles and instructional units, abandoning a sampling design based on multiple/mixed school affiliation.
- Adopting more diverse conceptual models in quantitative research . . . as well as longitudinal designs and non-individual levels of analysis that better differentiate between effects related to leaders and those related to the perceptions of individuals followers.

In summary, this exploratory methodological review of HNS studies was intended to reveal the trends, predominant practices, and potential gaps in this research to date. The HNS project framework lends itself to qualitative

Review of Methodological Approaches Across Multinational Contexts ▪ **109**

research traditions, which have produced significant knowledge. There is, however, a need to strengthen current methods as well as explore alternative methodological approaches that will collectively position HNS scholars to have greater influence across contexts in which the work is conducted. Furthermore, there is a need for further collaboration to increase the representation of knowledge production from non-U.S. or, for that matter, non-Western contexts. For instance, ISLDN scholars should consider collaborating with other research consortia such as the Commonwealth Council for Educational Administration and Management (CCEAM). Their membership reflects many developing nations in the world, which could provide opportunities to recruit scholars in underrepresented global regions. In addition, our colleagues can jointly seek research-funding opportunities with scholars from regions with limited resources required to engage in major research projects. In general, for the ISLDN to live up to its nomenclature, international representation and reach needs to be expanded.

REFERENCES

Aguinis, H., & Solarino, A. M. (2019). Transparency and replicability in qualitative research: The case of interviews with elite informants. *Strategic Management Journal, 40*(8), 1291–1315.

*Alford, B. (2019). Leadership practices for equity and excellence: An exploratory narrative of two principals of high-need elementary schools in California. In E. Murakami, D. Gurr, & R. Notman (Eds.), *Educational leadership, culture, and success in high-need schools* (pp. 85–101). Charlotte, NC: Information Age.

*Alford, B., & Gautam, C. (2014). Beliefs and actions influencing student achievement in successful high-need secondary schools: Voices of head teachers in Nepal. In S. Harris & J. Mixon (Eds.), *Building cultural community through global educational leadership* (pp. 130–145). Ypsilanti, MI: National Council of Professors of Educational Administration.

Angelle, P. S. (Ed.). (2017). *A global perspective of social justice leadership for school principals.* Charlotte, NC: Information Age.

Baran, M. L., & Berry, J. R. (2015). *The International School Leadership Development Network's (ISLDN) high needs schools group research protocol and members' guide.* [Unpublished document]. British Educational Leadership, Management, and Administration and the University Council for Educational Administration.

*Baran, M. L., & Harpen, G. V. (2019). Creating a culture for learning in a high-need inner-city USA school: The unique leadership challenges. In E. Murakami, D. Gurr, & R. Notman (Eds.), *Educational leadership, culture, and success in high-need schools* (pp.103–128). Charlotte, NC: Information Age.

Berkovich, I., & Eyal, O. (2017). Methodological review of studies on educational leaders and emotions (1992–2012): Insights into the meaning of an emerging research field in educational administration. *Journal of Educational Administration, 55*(5), 469–491.

110 ▪ N. S. A. OKILWA

*Berry, J. R., Moss, S. C., & Gore, P. (2019). Leadership in high-need/high performing schools: Success stories from an urban school district. In E. Murakami, D. Gurr, & R. Notman (Eds.), *Educational leadership, culture, and success in high-need schools* (pp. 131–148). Charlotte, NC: Information Age.

Bridges, E. (1982). Research on the school administrator: The state-of-the-art, 1967–1980. *Educational Administration Quarterly, 18*(3), 12–33.

Brooks, J. S., & Normore, A. H. (2015). Qualitative research and educational leadership: Essential dynamics to consider when designing and conducting studies. *International Journal of Educational Management, 29*(7), 798–806.

Creswell, J. W., & Creswell, J. D. (2018). *Research design: Qualitative, quantitative, and mixed methods approaches* (5th ed.). Los Angeles, CA: SAGE.

Coleman, M. (2005). Gender and secondary school leadership. *International Studies in Educational Administration, 33*(2), 3–20.

Coleman, M. (2007). Gender and educational leadership in England: A comparison of secondary headteachers' views over time. *School Leadership and Management, 27*(4), 383–399.

Cook-Sather, A. (2007). What would happen if we treated students as those with opinions that matter? The benefits to principals and teachers of supporting youth engagement in school. *NASSP Bulletin, 91*(4), 343–362.

Firestone, W. A., & Herriott, R. E. (1982). Prescriptions for effective elementary schools don't fit secondary schools. *Educational Leadership, 40*(3), 51–53.

Gough, D. (2007). Weight of evidence: A framework for the appraisal of the quality and relevance of evidence. *Research Papers in Education, 22*(2), 213–228.

Gray, H. L. (1987). Gender considerations in school management: Masculine and feminine leadership styles. *School Organization, 7*(3), 297–302.

Grint, K. (2005). Problems, problems, problems: The social construction of "leadership." *Human Relations, 58*(11), 1467–1494.

Gurr, D., & Drysdale, L. (2018). Leading high needs schools: Findings from the International School Leadership Development Network. *International Studies in Educational Administration, 46*(1), 147–156.

*Gurr, D., Drysdale, L., Clarke, S., & Wildy, H. (2014). High need schools in Australia: The leadership of two principals. *Management in Education, 28*(3), 86–90.

*Gurr, D., Drysdale, D., Longmuir, F., & McCrohan, K. (2018). The leadership, culture and context nexus: Lessons from the leadership of improving schools. *International Studies in Educational Administration, 46*(1), 22–44.

*Gurr, D., Drysdale, D., Longmuir, F., & McCrohan, K. (2019). Successful school leadership that is culturally sensitive but not context constrained. In E. Murakami, D. Gurr, & R. Notman (Eds.), *Leadership, culture, and school success in high-need schools* (pp. 25–43). Charlotte, NC: Information Age.

Hallinger, P. (2011). A review of three decades of doctoral studies using the principal instructional management rating scale: A lens on methodological progress in educational leadership. *Educational Administration Quarterly, 47*(2), 271–306.

Hallinger, P. (2013). A conceptual framework for systematic reviews of research in educational leadership and management. *Journal of Educational Administration, 51*(2), 126–149.

Hallinger, P., & Heck, R. H. (1996). Reassessing the principal's role in school effectiveness: A review of empirical research, 1980–1995. *Educational Administration Quarterly, 32*(1), 5–44.

Hallinger, P., & Huber, S. (2012). School leadership that makes a difference: International perspectives. *School Effectiveness and School Improvement, 23*(4), 359–367.

Harvey, W. S. (2010). Methodological approaches for interviewing elites. *Geography Compass, 4*(3), 193–205.

*Jacobson, S., & Notman, R. (2018). Leadership in early childhood education: Implications for parental involvement and student success from New Zealand. *International Studies in Educational Administration, 46*(1), 86–101.

Krüger, M. L. (2008). School leadership, sex and gender: Welcome to difference. *International Journal of Leadership in education, 11*(2), 155–168.

Lac, V. T., & Mansfield, K. (2018). What do students have to do with educational leadership? Making a case for centering student voice. *Journal of Research on Leadership Education, 13*(1), 38–58.

Law, W. W. (2013). Culture, gender and school leadership: school leaders' self-perceptions in China. *Compare: A Journal of Comparative and International Education, 43*(3), 295–322.

Levačic, R., & Glatter, R. (2001). 'Really good ideas'? Developing evidence-informed policy and practice in educational leadership and management. *Educational Management & Administration, 29*(1), 5–25.

Lumby, J. (2007). Parent voice: Knowledge, values and viewpoint. *Improving Schools, 10*(3), 220–232.

Marshall, C. (1984). Elites, bureaucrats, ostriches, and pussycats: Managing research in policy settings. *Anthropology and Education Quarterly, 15*(3), 235–251.

McKenna, M. K., & Millen, J. (2013). Look! Listen! Learn! Parent narratives and grounded theory models of parent voice, presence, and engagement in K–12 education. *School Community Journal, 23*(1), 9–48.

*Medina, V., Martinez, G., Murakami, E., Rodriguez, M., & Hernandez, F. (2014). Principals' perceptions from within: Leadership in high-need schools in the United States. *Management in Education, 28*(3), 91–96.

Mertler, C. A. (2017). *Action research: Improving schools and empowering educators* (5th ed.). Thousand Oaks, CA: SAGE.

Mitra, D. L. (2006). Student voice from the inside and outside: The positioning of challengers. *International Journal of Leadership in Education, 9*(4), 315–328.

Mitra, D. L. (2008). Amplifying student voice. *Educational Leadership, 66*(3), 20–25.

Murakami, E., Gurr, D., & Notman, R. (Eds.). (2019). *Educational leadership, culture, and success in high-need schools* (pp. 3–23). Charlotte, NC: Information Age.

*Murakami, E., & Kearney, W. S. (2019). Principals in high-performing, high-poverty, minority-serving schools in Texas. In E. Murakami, D. Gurr, & R. Notman (Eds.), *Educational leadership, culture, and success in high-need schools* (pp. 3–23). Charlotte, NC: Information Age.

*Murakami, E. T., Kearney, W. S., Scott, L., & Alfaro, P. (2018). Leadership for the improvement of a high poverty/high minority School. *International Studies in Educational Administration, 46*(1), 2–21.

112 ▪ N. S. A. OKILWA

Murphy, J. (1988). Methodological, measurement, and conceptual problems in the study of instructional leadership. *Educational Evaluation and Policy Analysis, 10*(2), 117–139.

*Notman, R., & Jacobson, S. (2019). School leadership practices in early childhood education: Three case studies from New Zealand. In E. Murakami, D. Gurr, & R. Notman (Eds.), *Educational leadership, culture, and success in high-need schools* (pp. 168–184). Charlotte, NC: Information Age.

*Okilwa, N. S., & Barnett, B. G. (2017). Sustaining school improvement in a high-need school: Longitudinal analysis of Robbins Elementary School (USA) from 1993 to 2015. *Journal of Educational Administration, 55*(3), 297–315.

*Okilwa, N. S., & Barnett, B. G. (2018). Four successive school leaders' response to a high-needs urban elementary school context. *International Studies in Educational Administration, 46*(1), 45–85.

*Okilwa, N. S., & Barnett, B. G. (2019). Sustaining a culture of academic success at a high-needs elementary school. In E. Murakami, D. Gurr, & R. Notman (Eds.), *Leadership, culture, and school success in high-need schools* (pp. 149–167). Charlotte, NC: Information Age.

*Oliveira, A. C. P., & Carvalho, C. P. (2019). Principals' work in high-need schools: Findings from Rio de Janeiro. In E. Murakami, D. Gurr, & R. Notman (Eds.), *Educational leadership, culture, and success in high-need schools* (pp. 45–61). Charlotte, NC: Information Age.

Sanchez, J. E., & Thornton, B. (2010). Gender issues in K–12 educational leadership. *Advancing Women in Leadership, 30*(13), 1–15.

Shaked, H., Glanz, J., & Gross, Z. (2018). Gender differences in instructional leadership: How male and female principals perform their instructional leadership role. *School Leadership & Management, 38*(4), 417–434.

Todd, L. (2018). Imagining methodology: Doing educational leadership research differently. *Management in Education, 32*(1), 50–52.

*Torres-Arcadia, C., Rodríguez-Uribe, C., & Mora, G. (2018). How principals lead high needs schools in Mexico. *International Studies in Educational Administration, 46*(1), 123–146.

Tracy, S. J. (2010). Qualitative quality: Eight "big-tent" criteria for excellent qualitative research. *Qualitative Inquiry, 16*(10), 837–851.

Trainor, A. A., & Graue, E. (2014). Evaluating rigor in qualitative methodology and research dissemination. *Remedial and Special Education, 35*(5), 267–274.

*Waight, N., Chisolm, L., & Jacobson, S. (2018). School leadership and STEM enactment in a high needs secondary school in Belize. *International Studies in Educational Administration, 46*(1), 102–122.

* Indicates studies that are part of the methodological review.

PART II

CROSS-STRAND AND CROSS-COUNTRY COMPARISON

CHAPTER 7

FROM THE MOUTHS OF BABES

Policy Recommendations From P–12 Students

Keneisha Harrington
Clemson University

Britt-Inger Keisu
Umeå University, Sweden

Björn Ahlström
Umeå University, Sweden

Parker M. Andreoli
Clemson University

Hans W. Klar
Clemson University

Educational Leadership for Social Justice and Improving High-Needs Schools, pages 115–133
Copyright © 2021 by Information Age Publishing
All rights of reproduction in any form reserved.

115

116 ▪ K. HARRINGTON et al.

Children and youth are the cornerstones of any education system. However, educational leaders often construct schools and educational environments without student input. In recent years, scholars have begun to note the importance of centering student voice in policy development (Lac & Mansfield, 2018), and have encouraged practitioners to empower their students as leaders and agents of change (Mitra & Gross, 2009; Mansfield, Welton, & Halx, 2012). The extant literature on student voice highlights the need for youth representation in educational policy development (Smyth, 2006). In addition, the oppressive nature of the power dynamics involved in policy creation and implementation call for a critical approach to policy analysis (Young & Diem, 2017). As Lac and Mansfield (2018) noted, "Schools and districts cannot establish equitable learning outcomes for all students when leaders continually ignore, belittle, or deny the voices of historically marginalized students, parents, and families" (p. 51). Therefore, it is imperative that we not only listen to the voices of students, but that we respond to their voices by implementing policies and practices that *they feel* are beneficial to themselves as learners and will help improve *their* schools. At the macro level, school reform is a response to the current policy environment. At the micro level, schools and districts implement policies to improve schools. It is with this view that we conceptualized our study.

The purpose of this chapter is to critically examine students' perspectives of school-level policies intended to improve the learning environments of a high needs elementary school in the United States and an upper secondary school in Sweden focused on gender equity and diversity, using a lens that centers student voice. We used critical policy analysis (Young & Diem, 2017) as a framework to analyze existing data gathered from students about their schools and the function of school leadership amidst reform efforts. In doing so, we sought to answer the research question: "What can school leaders learn from students' voices during times of school improvement and social justice-oriented reforms in their schools?" The issues and ideas vocalized by students showcase the value they bring to educational decision-making.

LITERATURE REVIEW

The International School Leadership Development Network (ISLDN) began 10 years ago as a joint effort of the British Educational Leadership, Management, and Administration Society (BELMAS) and the University Council for Educational Administration (UCEA) to facilitate international research on school leadership development (Baran & Berry, 2015). The ISLDN is comprised of two strands, leadership for high-needs schools and leadership for social justice. We begin this section of the chapter with a brief discussion of leadership for high-needs schools and leadership for social justice.

LEADERSHIP FOR HIGH-NEED SCHOOLS

In the ISLDN, high-needs schools are those with characteristics that could precipitate significantly negative effects on student learning outcomes. According to the ISLDN Members' Guide (Baran & Berry, 2015), these influences could include a high percentage of students living in poverty, high teacher or leader turnover, a substantial lack of resources, and a natural or man-made disaster. Effective school teachers and leaders are critical to the success of all schools. In high-needs schools, effective school leadership is essential in meeting the environmental challenges that can negatively impact teaching and learning in them. Recognition of the importance of effective school leaders is evident in both Sweden and the United States. Much of this recognition is grounded in research dating back to the effective schools movement (Edmonds, 1979; Levine & Lezotte, 1990). The research associated with this movement suggested that effective schools require leaders with a strong instructional focus (Edmonds, 1979; Hallinger & Murphy, 1986). More recently, scholars have identified the benefits of school leaders positively influencing student learning by enacting core sets of instructional and transformational school leadership practices (Day, Gu, & Sammons, 2016). These core practices include setting direction, developing people, redesigning the organization, and managing the instructional program (Louis, Leithwood, Wahlstrom, & Anderson, 2010).

Leaders in high-needs schools must work to enact this combination of instructional and transformational leadership practices whilst simultaneously balancing concerns for school and community members and the accountability demands placed upon them (Peck & Reitzug, 2014). In reviewing ISLDN case studies, Gurr & Drysdale (2018) noted that researchers commonly reported that effective leaders in high-needs schools can achieve this balance by adapting core leadership practices to suit their unique contexts. According to Bredeson, Klar, and Johansson (2011) this adaptation can be best achieved when school leaders have a high level of contextual literacy. Given that students and their views are an enormous, but frequently overlooked aspect of the school context, through this research we illustrate the importance of students' views of leadership practices in a high-needs school that is undergoing instructional reforms.

LEADERSHIP FOR SOCIAL JUSTICE

Social justice has its roots in the notion of power and unequal power relations. By attending to inequalities in schools, it is possible to reveal those who are marginalized (Angelle, Ärlestig, & Norberg, 2015; Larson & Murtadha, 2002). Furthermore, when focusing on inequalities, one can

118 ▪ K. HARRINGTON et al.

identify structures of power that promote some groups of students and act as barriers for others. This knowledge is a prerequisite for leaders endeavoring to provide an equitable education for all students. Leadership for social justice is, thus, the practice of principals who prioritize and are "committed to reducing inequalities" (Angelle, 2017, p. 308).

As social justice and socially responsive leadership can be understood in different ways in different contexts, it is important to understand this concept in relation to the Swedish educational system. As a welfare state, one of Sweden's fundamental tasks is to provide equal education for all citizens in order to achieve both social and academic objectives within a safe and secure environment. The Swedish curriculum states that schools should rest on a foundation based on democratic values, and activities within schools and should be designed according to these values (Lgy 11, 2011). The goals of this policy can be divided into two categories: social objectives and civic objectives. Social objectives refer to topics like bullying and how to treat other people. Schools should actively work against bullying, racism, and inequality between sexes and all other forms of insulting behaviors or attitudes (SFS, 2010). Civic objectives focus on topics related to democracy and how society functions.

When relating social justice to the Swedish educational system we can see that, as in all Nordic countries, Australia, the United States, and the United Kingdom, these policies are increasingly formulated within a broader equality and anti-discrimination framework that covers sex, ethnicity, religious or other beliefs, disability, sexuality, gender identity, and age (SFS, 2008; Skjeie & Langvasbråten, 2009). Principals in Sweden have the responsibility of designing and implementing policies of gender equality and diversity that align with the Swedish discrimination and education acts (SFS, 2008, 2010). Therefore, our point of departure in the Swedish case study is in how students perceive gender equality and diversity work in their school.

THEORETICAL FRAMEWORK

Student Voice

There are multiple interpretations of the term "student voice" and its related terms, and we recognize the limitless possibilities for the integration of student voice into the educational leadership field (Lac & Mansfield, 2018). However, for the purpose of this study we make an important distinction between student voice and student agency. We view student voice as the expression of thoughts, feelings, and desires of students that can help develop student leaders and aid in educational decision-making. We consider student agency to be the ability of students to bring about change through expressing their voices, and we see it as a prerequisite for personalized learning defined by students' choices and voices. Therefore, in this study we focus on student voice as a critical component of educational policy making and school reform.

The term student voice is often used to describe students having an impact on matters that affect their lives and work environments (Lansdown, 2006). The concept of student voice emerged in the 1960s and 1970s as part of the student power movement and then transformed to student participation and voice initiatives in schools (Mager & Nowak, 2012). The core assumption among scholars that focus on student voice is that students have a perspective that teachers and other adults in schools do not have (Cook-Sather, 2006). Hence, students are perceived as experts because they have firsthand knowledge and experiences of the reforms and their influences on the teaching and learning environments in their schools.

In Sweden, students are supposed to be active participants in their learning (SFS, 2010). The Swedish curriculum states that it is not enough to give students knowledge about societal and democratic values. Education is meant to be provided in a democratic manner where students can develop traits and characteristics which are important when they, as adults, become active participants in a democratic society (Lgy 11, 2011). According to Serriere and Mitra (2011), the United States has been rather sluggish in prioritizing student voice, taking the view that children are citizens in training and have not yet fully stepped into their democratic rights. The ever-growing accountability movement in the United States has stifled student voices as the social and civic outcomes of schools are often forgotten when placed beside the need to meet academic standards (Serriere & Mitra, 2011). However, in recent years, student voice has become increasingly important to educators and educational stakeholders around the country.

There are many positive effects when students' voices are included in educational decision-making, such as promoting their civic habits (Fielding, 2001), social and emotional well-being (Coombes, Appleton, Allen, & Yerrell, 2013), social negotiation and judgement skills (Rayner, 2003), academic achievement (Lenoir, 2011), and motivation (Cumings Mansfield, Welton, & Halx, 2018). Furthermore, seeking students' input can increase their sense of belonging and reduce exclusion from school (Finn, 1993). This approach challenges dominant assumptions, policies, and practices in education that tend to marginalize students' voices (Anderson & Graham, 2016). In this study, student voice served as a guiding framework for the development of our research questions and our methods in conjunction with critical policy analysis (CPA).

120 ■ K. HARRINGTON et al.

Critical Policy Analysis

Scholars have spent years analyzing policy creation and implementation with traditional policy analysis techniques (Levinson, Sutton, & Winstead, 2009). In recent decades, CPA has developed as a response to the accountability movement (Young & Diem, 2017), and as a framework to address concerns that traditional policy analysis typically ignores, such as inequity and issues of power (Diem, Young, & Sampson, 2018). Critical policy analysis can be used to illuminate and investigate the inherent positions of power and ideologies held by educational leaders and policymakers. Scholars of CPA generally focus their studies on the distinctions between policy rhetoric and policy in practice, the origins and development of policy, the unequal power distribution policies create, and participation in policy decisions by marginalized groups (Young & Diem, 2017). As we sought to examine policies from the lens of students who are marginalized stakeholders in the context of education policy, CPA served as a critical part of the framework for the analysis of our findings.

METHODS

In this chapter, we report the findings of a multi-site case study (Merriam, 2009) of students' experiences and understandings of policy changes in two schools undergoing school-level improvement efforts, one focused on instructional improvements, and one focused on gender equity and diversity. To answer our research question, we purposefully selected Peach Tree Elementary School (PTES) in the United States and West Side Upper Secondary School (WSUSS) in Sweden to examine student voice in two differing contexts. In 2018, we conducted semi-structured interviews and focus groups (Patton, 2015) with students in both schools using protocols adapted from the ISLDN. In addition to the questions from the ISLDN protocols, we specifically asked questions intended to illustrate students' experiences and understandings of the policies as well as their recommendations for improving them. For example, we asked students to describe their dream school and to tell us how they felt their schools could be improved. The questions in the protocols used in both countries were similar, though tailored specifically for their respective aims.

At PTES, we conducted semi-structured interviews with six students who had been recommended by the principal. The students were in the fourth or fifth grade at the time of the study and most of them had been at the school since Kindergarten. The students were selected on the basis that they were familiar with the changes that had occurred at PTES in recent years and were willing to participate in an interview with a single member of the research team. At West Side, four focus groups were held with 16 students, all 18 years of age and in their final year of school. The focus groups consisted of between two and five students. Two of the focus groups were single gender, and two were mixed gender. In total, seven students were female, and nine were male. To form the focus groups, four students who were selected by the principal on the basis that they were familiar with the reforms, were communicative, and would be confident in expressing their views. Each of these students was then invited to select between one and four friends to join the focus group. The purpose of this recruitment strategy was to create a relaxed atmosphere in which students would feel comfortable sharing their views about the reforms as they were already familiar with the other members of their group. All interviews and focus groups were audio recorded and transcribed in their entirety.

We analyzed transcripts of the interviews using multiple rounds of coding (Saldaña, 2013). We first used inductive coding to independently develop preliminary sets of codes. Research team members then conferred with their compatriots to discuss the developing findings and conducted an additional round of coding as a group. Next, our entire research team conferred to discuss the themes from each case and the similarities and differences between the cases. We then conducted a final round of coding using the following concerns of CPA as a part of the analytical framework:

> Regarding the policy, its roots, and its development...the distribution of power, resources, and knowledge as well as the creation of policy "winners" and "losers"...regarding social stratification and the broader effect a given policy has on relationships of inequality and privilege. (Young & Diem, 2017, p. 4)

Peach Tree Elementary School

Peach Tree Elementary School is in a small, rural town in the southeastern United States, where nearly 1 in 5 families live in poverty. Peach Tree serves approximately 350 students. Sixty-three percent of students are African American, 26% are White, 5% are Hispanic, 5% are of two or more races, and 1% is Asian. In recent years, the school underwent many changes with a new principal, leadership team, and school improvement efforts that ultimately resulted in the school being removed from the state's list of Priority Schools, the lowest performing, high-needs schools, as measured by students' performance on state-mandated exams. Our study examined how the school-level policies that were put in place to improve learning outcomes were viewed and understood by the students themselves. These policies primarily related to the school-wide implementation of a program designed to improve teaching practices. As a result of this initiative, significant changes were seen at the

122 ▪ K. HARRINGTON et al.

school that led to a refocusing on teaching and curricular reforms, intensive teacher professional development, and increased expectations for students, teachers, and family members (Klar et al., 2019).

West Side Upper Secondary School

West Side Upper Secondary School is one of the largest upper secondary schools in Sweden. It is in a mid-sized municipality in Sweden and has approximately 2000 students. As an upper secondary school, WSUSS offers several programs of study to students in Grades 10 to 12. West Side was one of four secondary and upper secondary schools involved in a larger, social justice-oriented project which connected gender equality and diversity with systematic quality work in Swedish schools. Systematic quality work, the Swedish term describing continuous school improvement efforts, is an aspect of Sweden's increasing accountability context. West Side was selected for this study because it was criticized severely by the Swedish School Inspectorate in relation to matters concerning gender equity and diversity. As a result of this criticism, the school was in the process of initiating efforts intended to improve gender inequality and views of diversity at the school. Therefore, WSUSS provided a timely and relevant look into the perspectives of students experiencing the effects of policies implemented in response to macro-political influences on their daily school experiences.

FINDINGS

In this section, we present the findings of our data analysis to illustrate how students in these schools experienced and understood policy changes at the school level. In doing so, we also attempt to highlight what school leaders can learn from students' voices during times of school improvement and social justice-oriented reforms in their schools. We begin by examining the case of PTES, then WSUSS.

Peach Tree Elementary School

At PTES, we discovered that even elementary school students are aware of the environmental changes caused by policy reform. While the students were likely not aware of the changes in policy and practice taking place due to the school being placed on the state's list of priority schools, interviews with them revealed that they experienced and understood policy at the school level based on changes in their environment. We categorized these changes in four ways: physical, social-emotional, instructional, and relational. Examining the context in which students understood policy through these lenses allowed us to identify direct and indirect recommendations for school leaders.

Physical Changes

The reform at PTES led to changes in the physical environment of the school. Students viewed changes in the physical space as positive. The students recognized changes such as the paint color on the walls, new technology in classrooms, and even the cleanliness of the building. Students discussed the posters on the wall, the anchor charts and artwork in their classrooms, and the way the physical space made them feel. One student talked about their classroom environment saying: "It's better to learn in, because if it was just a boring room with just white walls and a whiteboard, then it would just not be fun."

In addition, students recognized the importance of safety in their physical space. Participants highlighted the importance of attending a school where they felt physically safe and they knew bullying was not tolerated. This indirect recommendation for anti-bullying policies at school offers critical insight into the value students place on safety and what school safety means in an increasingly technological, and in some cases violent, society.

Social-Emotional Changes

The students at PTES also experienced social-emotional environmental changes during this time of school reform. One of the recurring themes across the data was the feeling of security while students were in school and in their classrooms. Students discussed how safe they felt at PTES and how comfortable they were. One participant said: "This is a really nice school. You'll really feel comfortable here. Nobody's going to make me feel bad here." Another student echoed this sentiment saying the following about the classroom environment: "It feels real safe, [because] we're around people that we know and we can trust." In the context of this study, we recognized security as meaning something different from safety in that the students felt emotionally secure enough to share their thoughts and ideas in class and with their peers at school.

The elementary school students not only articulated how they felt in their school, but they explained how their classrooms were "safe spaces" for disagreements and arguments between students. One student said, "Some people in my class, they don't like each other. But, my teacher, she's like 'Get in a group and tell [each other] how you feeling.' And then at the end we give each other a big hug." In recent years, instructional practice and policy discourse in the United States has begun to shift towards social-emotional learning. Students who participate in classroom circles and engage in conversations about their feelings with other students have shown improvement academically, socially, and in terms of classroom conduct.

In addition, students noted that receiving praise motivated them to set goals for academic success. Students shared the belief that the motivation and confidence that their teachers had in them to succeed was one of the things that helped them to not only enjoy but to do well in school. Several students recounted stories of how younger students wrote motivational cards and made posters to encourage them during state-mandated testing. The positive feelings associated with receiving encouragement from the school community influenced student's learning, effort in the classroom, and achievement. Student recognition of the importance of these issues points to the necessity of more social-emotional learning practices in schools.

Instructional Changes

Some of the changes that students seemed most impacted by were the changes in the instructional environment. Students noticed changes in teaching staff and paid close attention when teachers changed teaching grade levels or subjects. They were also aware of a difference in instructional activities used by teachers. They discussed teachers' use of new technology in the classroom, and how teachers used more engaging learning activities than they did before. One student expressed disdain for the teaching and learning strategies used prior to the school reform saying, "As long as we don't go back to worksheets. Before we had all the fun technology and stuff, we just did worksheets." Students discussed field trips, collaborative learning and engaging in class activities and games as fun and important parts of their learning. They also shared how being engaged in the classroom helped them retain more information. It was clear that students appreciated a variety of learning activities in the classroom. This finding suggests educational leaders should encourage professional development for teachers focused on student engagement.

Relational Changes

Relational changes were reflected in students' responses to changes in their relationships with students, staff, and other people as a result of the policy changes at their school. A majority of the students described how "friendly" the principal and teachers at their school were. One student said, "The people that work here are very friendly. The principals are friendly, the teachers are friendly, and some of the students here, they're friendly, too." The feeling that the people they were surrounded by in their school were friendly led to students believing that people cared about them. The students interviewed at PTES felt cared for and they felt their needs were met.

The students also had a clear understanding of kindness and were genuinely concerned about the treatment of other students. They advocated for anti-bullying practices and talked about how important they felt it was to help others. The relationships students cultivated with each other seemed to mirror the relationships they had with adults in the school building—relationships that were built through trust and kindness.

Lastly, students associated effort with success, but they also recognized the contributions of others in their success. The importance of teachers, principals, their peers, and their families in their academic success was evident throughout the interviews. The students viewed their school community as a family, and they took responsibility for the success of the entire school. This family mentality was illustrated by a student when they said, "It takes everything. Parents and teachers, and principals, and even the teachers that aren't my teachers, it takes all of them for everybody to be successful." The students recognized that learning does not happen in a vacuum, and that their learning and success took place within a community.

West Side Upper Secondary School

At WSUSS, the students provided descriptions of how their school organized for social justice through gender equality and diversity work. Based on their experiences, we highlight three ways the students were engaged in and impacted by this work: theme days, an annual student survey, and the integration of social justice in teaching practices. Further, we conclude this section with an analysis illustrating how the school's policies and practices related to social justice can be described as "flash mob activities."

Theme Days
During the interviews at WSUSS, we asked students how their school organized diversity and gender equality work. One typical activity students described was holding theme days. As one student noted,

> I can say that the work we can see and notice are special theme days, arranged once a year . . . one thing that is evident at these theme days is that not everyone is engaged in this activity and the students are not super interested [in] or even attend these days.

A typical activity on a theme day was watching a movie or listening to a lecture that addressed topics related to social justice. The students expressed that they were neither engaged, nor involved in the planning of these days. Further, they noted that there was no follow up or discussion of theme days. The students also described a feeling of detachment to these days and noted that they were designed from an adult perspective rather than from a student perspective. This detachment led to declining engagement and participation during these days.

Annual Student Survey

Another activity organized by the school was an annual student survey related to ethics, and factors in the psychosocial work environment, such as sexual harassment and bullying. The students discussed getting little or no feedback on the results of the survey and they did not feel that the results led to any major changes or that they were used for organizational development. One student said, "The survey is done because it has to be done." Another student replied,

> It's not because they want to gather information. It is because it will look good somewhere else, like in a report. Then, it is like this, "If you students fill out this form and we got a hundred percent return rate, you will have a break." Then, many of the students just quickly and sloppily answer the survey because it doesn't feel relevant.

Students also noted that the surveys were too extensive, and that they were handed out at the end of classes and the follow up was scarce to nonexistent. Similar to theme days, this detachment led to disengagement for students. If youth perspectives are truly valued in developmental efforts, creating new ways of gathering student experiences is critical. A survey, even if taken seriously, can only provide limited data about a subject; a school leader needs additional information to understand how to translate student voices to actual measures.

Integrating Social Justice in Teaching

As described in prior sections, the students perceived that the school's work with social justice issues was an activity "on the side." However, the students expressed that these topics should be treated more seriously, and they expressed the need for integrating social justice into teaching as illustrated in the following quote:

> Don't bother with the theme days...don't use the money on some fancy lecturer. Use the resources to integrate these issues into teaching and what happens in the classroom, all the time. It should be an ongoing topic and it should be included in every course, in every subject in order to reach every student.

Notwithstanding the students' critiques of these practices, we found that students were very interested in social justice issues, but they had never been given the opportunity to talk about them freely. They seemed to want to discuss these issues and they expressed the need to have a say in matters that concerned them daily. Students did not want the conversations with us to end, as indicated by them saying things like, "We have never talked like this before," emphasizing their desire to be heard in relation to these issues. Their visions for an ideal school included social justice at the forefront and as an integrated part of everyday practices. Furthermore, they felt these practices should be enacted regardless of sex, ethnicity, religious or other beliefs, disability, sexuality, gender identity, and age.

Social Justice Work: A Flash Mob Activity

An analogy fitting the description of policy and practice at WSUSS is the cultural phenomenon of flash mobs. Flash mobs consist of large groups of people suddenly gathering in public spaces to perform pre-arranged acts only to dissipate as quickly as they had gathered once the performance has ended. Just like the short-term effect of a flash mob, a theme day or a survey did not challenge the complex power relations the gender equality and diversity work intended to address. Moreover, the work did not become an integrated part of daily practices at the school. The students perceived these activities as an alibi for doing the actual work. Therefore, flash mobs are an appropriate analogy for gender equality and diversity at WSUSS. Organizing gender equality and diversity work without considering and engaging the student voices led to a feeling of "What's in it for us?" among students.

DISCUSSION

The data from this study were derived from two different contexts. In the case of WSUSS, students were able to articulate their feelings, needs, and wants at an advanced level. They understood the actions driven by policy changes taking place at their school, and they developed opinions about the practices as a result of those changes. In the case of PTES, although the elementary students did not understand the specific policy changes taking place, they were aware of and affected by the changes in their environment. While the cases were different, our findings revealed several similar themes. First, the students in both cases had opinions about how their instructional environment should be facilitated. Students at PTES recognized the importance of being engaged in their learning, and of having supportive, collaborative learning environments. Students at WSUSS advocated for more integrated and consistent social justice learning experiences. Students at both WSUSS and PTES also prioritized issues of safety. Students at WSUSS noted the importance of safety, freedom, and harassment, while PTES students supported anti-bullying movements. Lastly, students in both cases wanted their voices to be heard and valued. These similar themes underwrite the importance of including student voices in educational decision-making. In

128 ▪ K. HARRINGTON et al.

this section we further discuss our findings in the context of CPA and offer recommendations for practicing school leaders.

Critical Policy Analysis

To understand and analyze policies and practices at PTES and WSUSS, we used the lens of CPA. In doing so, we focused on three areas of concern identified by Young and Diem (2017), policy, power, and social stratification. The first area of concern relates to the policy, its roots, and its development. Neo-liberal logics had an impact in relation to our findings. Neoliberalism can be described as the marketization and financialization of politics, an ideology or a policy, and with it the introduction of new kinds of governance and technology for control (Larner, 2000). One central logic of neoliberalism often identified is the logic of detail (Dahl, 2009). It emphasizes rationalization, governed by the control of time; codification; standardization and division, and governance of details. In the case of WSUSS, this logic is revealed when organizing for social justice through theme days and surveys. These important issues are boiled down to a checklist, completed once a year. This logic reduces the professionalism teachers achieved through their education and contradicts the ethos of their profession. In the U.S. case, the accountability movement, a manifestation of neoliberalism (Ambrosio, 2013), impacted what was taught and how it was taught in classrooms, detracting from a focus on social-emotional learning.

In relation to the second concern, the distribution of power, and the third concern, social stratification, it is evident that policy and practice are derived from the perspective of the privileged adults. When the experiences and knowledge of students are silent or not considered, there might be several losers (Cook-Sather, 2006). The school risks not taking all valuable aspects of knowledge into consideration when developing goals and strategies for organizational development efforts. In such a scenario everyone loses, and the organization might not get the prerequisite information needed to reach its full potential. The impact of not considering student perspectives could be seen in the Swedish case when students reported that the theme days were designed without their input, which led to their feelings of disengagement from the activities. In the U.S. case this finding was echoed when students discussed their negative feelings about the former instructional practices which were derived from what were once considered "best practices."

Students, who are less privileged and more vulnerable than adults in the decision-making process, find their time in school can be challenging. In relation to learning or social justice, they need their voice to be heard and taken into consideration. If these voices are heard, they might provide

From the Mouths of Babes ▪ **129**

principals and teachers with the necessary tools to promote student learning and social justice for all students in schools.

Recommendations for School Leaders

In our conceptualization of this research study we sought to identify specific recommendations for school leaders based on the voices of students. Through an understanding of how the students at PTES understood policy changes around them and problematized school issues we gleaned three recommendations from students:

- Cultivate physically safe and emotionally secure learning environments.
- Consider that student engagement is critical to student learning.
- Create a school climate that values teamwork and kindness.

In the United States, policies related to school safety and resource allocation have historically been determined by micro and macro levels of school leadership, including the federal government and the U.S. Department of Education. However, our analysis leads us to believe that not only can students articulate school-level policy concerns, but that they also have the capacity to offer solutions and recommendations as well. While these suggestions may be considered best practices, having students' perspectives helps school leaders gain a contextual understanding of their environment and allows them to be more effective in their school improvement efforts.

The critical nature of student voice also applies to the case in Sweden. When students at WSUSS discussed specific practices that took place at their school, they were able to problematize certain aspects and make recommendations to improve them. Although unintentional, students' recommendations have connections to policy that should be taken into consideration by school leaders. These recommendations include:

- Systematize policy and practice through integrating social justice in teaching.
- Treat challenges and problems professionally, rather than hiding or trivializing students' experiences.
- Build trustworthy relationships between students and adults and consider students to be valuable knowledge producers.

By listening to student's voices and addressing their concerns, the privilege and power that comes with being an adult decreases and shifts to students. In order to facilitate these organizational changes, courage on behalf of

130 ■ K. HARRINGTON et al.

teachers and leaders is required. These recommendations from the "mouths of babes" in both the United States and Sweden can develop and strengthen leadership practice while addressing issues of unequal power in schools.

CONCLUSION

Our work as educational leaders should begin and end with students in mind. As the primary recipients of our services and participants in a democratic society, students should be valued as stakeholders throughout the educational process. This process includes policy creation and implementation. Despite their age differences, students in our study were not only able to recognize issues and problematize them within the context of their schools, but they also offered solutions and recommendations that could help social justice and school improvement efforts more broadly. Ultimately, the students were concerned about their learning environments, they wanted to feel safe in school, and they wanted their voices to be heard and valued. Their valuable insights highlight the critical nature of including student voices in all aspects of educational decision-making, including policy development.

The collaboration of researchers, students, and school leaders around policy development could potentially lead to more equitable and socially just school policies and practices when they take account of students' voices. As school leaders around the world seek to make impactful changes in their environments, they would be well advised to consider student voice in school improvement and social justice-oriented reforms in their schools.

REFERENCES

Ambrosio, J. (2013). Changing the subject: Neoliberalism and accountability in public education. *Educational Studies, 49*(4), 316–333. https://doi.org/10.1080/00131946.2013.783835

Anderson, D. L., & Graham, A. P. (2016). Improving student wellbeing: Having a say at school. *School Effectiveness and School Improvement, 27*(3), 348–366.

Angelle, P. S. (2017). Moving forward. In P. Angelle (Ed.), *A global perspective of social justice leadership for school principals* (pp. 303–319). Charlotte, NC: Information Age.

Angelle, P., Ärlestig, H., & Norberg, K. (2015). The practice of socially just leadership: Contextual differences between US and Swedish principals. *International Studies in Educational Administration, 44*(2), 21–37.

Baran, M. L., & Berry, J. R. (2015). The International School Leadership Development Network (ISLDN) high needs schools group research protocol and members' guide. (Unpublished Manuscript).

Bredeson, P. V., Klar, H. W., & Johansson, O. (2011). Context-responsive leadership: Examining superintendent leadership in context. *Educational Policy Analysis Archives, 19*(18), 1–28. Retrieved from https://epaa.asu.edu/ojs/article/view/739

Cook-Sather, A. (2006) Sound, presence and power: "Student voice" in educational research and reform. *Curriculum Inquiry, 36*(4), 359–390.

Coombes, L., Appleton, J. V., Allen, D., & Yerrell, P. (2013). Emotional health and well-being in schools: Involving young people. *Children & Society, 27*(3), 220–232.

Cumings Mansfield, V., Welton, A., & Halx, M. (2018). Listening to student voice: Toward a more holistic approach to school leadership. *Journal of Ethical Educational Leadership, Special Issue 1,* 10–27.

Dahl, H. M. (2009). New public management, care and struggles about recognition. *Critical Social Policy, 29*(4), 634–654.

Day, C., Gu, Q., & Sammons, P. (2016). The impact of leadership on student outcomes: How successful school leaders use transformational and instructional strategies to make a difference. *Educational Administration Quarterly, 52*(2), 221–258. https://doi.org/10.1177/0013161X15616863

Diem, S., Young, M. D., & Sampson, C. (2018). Where critical policy. Meets the politics of education: An introduction. *Educational Policy, 33*(1), 3–15. https://doi.org/10.1177/0895904818807317

Edmonds, R. (1979). Effective schools for the urban poor. *Educational Leadership, 37,* 15–24.

Fielding, M. (2001). Students as radical agents of change. *Journal of Educational Change, 2,* 123–141.

Finn, J. D. (1993). *School engagement and students at risk.* Washington, DC: Department of Education, National Center for Educational Statistics.

Gurr, D., & Drysdale, L. (2018). Leading high needs schools: Findings from the international school development network. *International Studies in Educational Administration, 46*(1), 147–156.

Hallinger, P., & Murphy, J. F. (1986). The social context of effective schools. *American Journal of Education, 94*(3), 328–355. https://doi.org/10.1086/443853

Klar, H. W., Moyi, P., Ylimaki, R. M., Hardie, S., Andreoli, P. M., Dou, J., . . . Buskey, F. C. (2019). Getting off the list: Leadership, learning, and context in two rural, high-needs schools. *Journal of School Leadership, 30*(1), 1–22. https://doi.org/10.1177/1052684619867474

Lac, V. T., & Mansfield, K. C. (2018). What do students have to do with educational leadership? Making a case for centering student voice. *Journal of Research on Leadership Education, 13*(1), 38–58. https://doi.org/10.1177/1942775117743748

Lansdown, G. (2006). International developments in children's participation. In K. Tisdall, J. Davis, & A. Prout (Eds.), *Children, young people and inclusion.* Bristol, England: Policy Press.

Larner, W. (2000). Neo-liberalism, policy, ideology, and governmentality. *Studies in Political Economy, 63*(1), 5–25.

Larson, C. L., & Murtadha, K. (2002). Leadership for social justice. In J. Murphy (Ed.), *The educational leadership challenge: Redefining leadership for the 21st century* (pp. 134–161). Chicago, IL: University of Chicago Press.

132 ▪ K. HARRINGTON et al.

Lenoir, G. C. (2011). *Study and analysis of academic skills of newcomer high school students who are foreign born in central Texas* (Doctoral Dissertation). Austin: The University of Texas.

Levine, D. U., & Lezotte, L. W. (1990). *Unusually effective schools: A review and analysis of research and practice*. Madison, WI: National Center for Effective Schools Research and Development.

Levinson, B. A. U., Sutton, M., & Winstead, T. (2009). Education policy as a practice of power: Theoretical tools, ethnographic methods, democratic options. *Educational Policy, 23*(6), 767–795.

Lgy 11. (2011). *Läroplan för gymnasieskolan* [Curriculum for upper secondary school]. Stockholm, Sweden: Utbildningsdepartementet.

Louis, K. S., Leithwood, K., Wahlstrom, K. L., & Anderson, S. E. (2010). *Learning from leadership: Investigating the links to improved student learning*. Minneapolis: University of Minnesota, Center for Applied Research and Educational Improvement. Retrieved from http://www.wallacefoundation.org/knowledge -center/school-leadership/key-research/Documents/Investigating-the -Links-to-Improved-Student-Learning.pdf

Mager, U., & Nowak, P. (2012). Effects of student participation in decision making in school: A systematic review and synthesis of empirical research. *Educational Research Review, 7*(1), 38–61.

Mansfield, K. C., Welton, A., & Halx, M. (2012). Listening to student voice: Toward a more inclusive theory for research and practice. In C. Boske & S. Diem (Eds.), *Global leadership for social justice: Taking it from field to practice* (pp. 21–41). Bingley, England: Emerald.

Merriam, S. B. (2009). *Qualitative research: A guide to design and implementation*. San Francisco, CA: Jossey-Bass.

Mitra, D. L., & Gross, S. J. (2009). Increasing student voice in high school reform: Building partnerships, improving outcomes. *Educational Management Administration & Leadership, 37*(4), 522–543. https://doi.org/10.1177/1741143209334577

Patton, M. Q. (2015). *Qualitative research and evaluation methods* (4th ed.). Thousand Oaks, CA: SAGE.

Peck, C., & Reitzug, U. (2014). School turnaround fever: The paradoxes of a historical practice promoted as a new form. *Urban Education, 49*(1), 8–38. https:// doi.org/10.1177/0042085912472511

Rayner, S. (2003). Democracy in the age of assessment: Reflections on the roles of expertise and democracy in public-sector decision-making. *Science and Public Policy, 30*(3), 163–170.

Saldaña, J. (2013). *The coding manual for qualitative researchers* (2nd ed.). London, England: SAGE.

Serriere, S., & Mitra, D. (2011). Critical issues and contexts of student voice in the United States. In C. Day (Ed.), *The Routledge international handbook of teacher and school development* (pp. 223–229). New York, NY: Routledge.

SFS. (2008). *Svensk författningssamling* [Swedish Codes of Statutes], Diskrimineringslag [The Discrimination Act], 2008, 567.

SFS. (2010). *Svensk författningssamling* [Swedish Codes of Statutes], Skollagen [The school law], 2010, 800.

Skjeie, H., & Langvasbråten, T. (2009). Intersectionality in practice? Anti-discrimination reforms in Norway. *International Feminist Journal of Politics, 11*(4), 513–529.

Smyth, J. (2006). Educational leadership that fosters "student voice." *International Journal of Leadership in Education, 9*(4), 279–284. https://doi.org/10.1080/13603120600894216

Young, M. D., & Diem, S. (Eds.). (2017). *Critical approaches to education policy analysis: Moving beyond tradition.* Cham, Switzerland: Springer.

CHAPTER 8

LEADING SUCCESSFULLY IN HIGH-NEEDS CONTEXTS

Australian and New Zealand Cases

David Gurr
University of Melbourne, Australia

Lawrie Drysdale
University of Melbourne, Australia

Fiona Longmuir
Monash University, Australia

Kieran McCrohan
University of Melbourne and Wesley College, Australia

Rachel McNae
University of Waikato, New Zealand

Michele Morrison
University of Waikato, New Zealand

Sylvia Robertson
University of Otago, New Zealand

Educational Leadership for Social Justice and Improving High-Needs Schools, pages 135–152
Copyright © 2021 by Information Age Publishing
All rights of reproduction in any form reserved.

136 ▪ D. GURR et al.

This chapter explores Australian and New Zealand research from the International School Leadership Development Network (ISLDN). From Australia, a group of four scholars focused on the high-needs strand. In a paper published in a special issue of *Management in Education*, Gurr, Drysdale, Clarke, and Wildy (2014) presented the cases of two principals, one from a metropolitan school in Melbourne, Victoria and the other from a remote school in Western Australia. These cases were based on research and familiarity of the researchers with the principals, rather than full ISLDN case studies. Subsequently, the Victorian group expanded to include doctoral students Longmuir and McCrohan, and conducted four multiple perspective case studies using the ISLDN high-needs research protocol and that of the International Successful School Principalship Project (ISSPP; Gurr, Drysdale, Longmuir, & McCrohan, 2018, 2019; Longmuir, 2017, 2019); it is findings from these cases that are reported in this chapter.

From New Zealand, a number of scholars have contributed 23 qualitative case studies to both the social justice and high-need schools research strands over a period of 7 years from 2010 to 2017. In the North Island, University of Waikato colleagues conducted studies of primary, intermediate and secondary principals whose work advances the cause of social justice (Branson, 2017; Branson, Morrison, & McNae, 2016; McNae, 2017; McNae, Morrison, & Notman, 2017; Morrison, 2017; Morrison, Branson, & McNae, 2015) while, in the South Island, University of Otago colleagues researched early childhood centers, primary schools, and secondary schools in high-needs contexts (Notman, 2010, 2011, 2012, 2017; Notman & Henry, 2011; Robertson, 2017, 2018).

Many of the New Zealand social justice cases have strong indigenous and regional perspectives and some of the high-needs cases extend to early childhood settings. The Australian high-needs cases represent metropolitan schools in various states of educational challenge, but which are all on improvement journeys. This chapter considers these findings and perspectives to arrive at a view of commonalities and differences intended to guide leadership for social justice and high needs.

The conceptual framework that guides this discussion uses the four element leadership framework developed by Leithwood and colleagues (Leithwood, 2012; Leithwood, Harris & Strauss, 2010). This includes setting directions, developing people, redesigning the organization, and improving the instructional programs. This is essentially a combined transformational and instructional leadership view with the *setting direction* and *developing people* elements similar to the transformational component of Bass' (1990) view of transformational leadership, and *redesigning the organization* and *improving the instructional programs*, having many similarities to instructional leadership.

Leading Successfully in High-Needs Contexts ■ **137**

CONTEXT CONSIDERATIONS

Australia and Victoria

Australia, like many countries, has a history of colonization and extensive, controlled and humanitarian immigration, with country prosperity partly tied to continued population growth. The last 70 years has seen migration move from an Anglo-Celtic emphasis to include, in succession, an emphasis on migrants from Europe, Asia, and Africa. Of the more than 9,000 schools in Australia, in 2016, 65.4% of students attended a free and secular government school, 20.2% a Catholic school, and 14.4% attended a range of independent schools (Australian Bureau of Statistics, 2017).

Government schools in the state of Victoria have a long history of relatively high levels of self-management beginning with the establishment of school councils in 1975 (Anderson, 2006; Gurr, Drysdale, & Walkley, 2012). In recent years, however, there has been considerable system influence through the construction of compulsory curriculum and improvement frameworks. The Framework for Improved Student Outcomes (FISO: www.education.vic.gov.au/fiso) influences school work through the articulation of four major areas (excellence in teaching and learning, positive climate for learning, professional leadership, community engagement in learning) and 16 strategies that influence student achievement, engagement and well-being. Schools use this framework to plan for improvement and report on progress annually to the government and school community.

In terms of the preparation and development of school leaders, we (Gurr & Drysdale, 2015) and others (e.g., Jensen, Hunter, Lambert, & Clark, 2015; Watterston, 2015a, 2015b) have noted the lack of a clear national framework and the reliance of support for school leaders through systems, universities, service organizations, other providers and the support of colleagues and senior leaders in schools. A school leader in Australia needs to rely mostly on self-identification and self-management in which individuals decide that they want to pursue leadership opportunities, and then seek out the support and experiences to help them.

New Zealand

Signed in 1840, between Māori chiefs and representatives of the British Crown, Te Tiriti o Waitangi (Treaty of Waitangi) is considered New Zealand's founding document. This compelled colonizers to officially recognize the mana (status) and rights of indigenous inhabitants and, more recently, to uphold the principles of partnership, protection, and participation in

138 ▪ D. GURR et al.

all spheres of government, including the education system. From its indigenous and bicultural origins, New Zealand has become an increasingly diverse multicultural nation, comprising approximately 4.9 million people, of whom 14.9% identify as Māori; 74% as being of European descent; 11.8% as Asian; 7.4% as Pacific peoples; and 1.2% as Middle Eastern, Latin American, and African (Statistics New Zealand, 2013).

Public provision of compulsory schooling is free and secular, with the majority of students attending state primary, intermediate, and secondary schools. Enrolment rates in early childhood education (ECE) are relatively high. In 2015, 94% of 4-years-olds, 89% of 3-year-olds, and 65% of 2-year-olds were enrolled in kindergartens and ECE centers, the majority of which are privately owned and government subsidized (Norgrove & Scott, 2017). Since 1985, students have had the option of attending mainstream English/bilingual or Kura Kaupapa (Māori language immersion) schools. Approximately 10% of students pay attendance dues to attend state integrated special character (typically religious faith) schools, while just under 5% of students pay full tuition fees to attend private schools.

Educational disparity is evident in low outcomes for Māori and Pacific students, and young people from low socioeconomic backgrounds. Educational leaders thus play a pivotal role in challenging discriminatory discourses, advocating for those least well served by the education system, and reducing disparities in access, opportunity, and outcome. However, formal leadership preparation is limited. During the last 5 years, programs to develop aspiring and first time principals were disbanded and an experienced principals' program was trialed but not implemented. In 2018, a new leadership strategy was published (Education Council, 2018), but it is not yet clear what influence this will have on educational disparity.

In state schools, educational governance is highly devolved and enacted since 1989 by over 2,500 Boards of Trustees. These are groups of locally elected parent representatives who together with the principal: establish strategic direction; monitor and evaluate student achievement; oversee the employment and management of staff, property, finances, curriculum, and administration; and, ensure compliance with legal and policy requirements. The New Zealand education system is undergoing major change with the biggest revamp of education policy since 1993 (Ministry of Education, 2019). The new initiatives are designed to better support minority and marginalized groups, focus school boards and principals on core education roles, provide better support and guidance for teachers and parents, and allow schools to be more responsive to community needs (Ministry of Education, 2019).

Leading Successfully in High-Needs Contexts ▪ **139**

THE NEW ZEALAND CASES

The four New Zealand case studies reported in this chapter comprise an early childhood setting and primary school from the high-needs research strand, and an intermediate and secondary school from the social justice strand. Common to all four cases is a concern for vulnerable children, a commitment to building vibrant culturally responsive pedagogies of relations, and a determination to challenge discriminatory discourse and practice within and beyond school gates. The four leaders, Sonya (ECE leader), Whetu (Year 1–8 primary school principal), Emma (Year 7–8 intermediate school principal), and James (Year 9–13 secondary school principal) bring diverse life and teaching experience to their formal leadership roles. Sonya and Whetu are experienced leaders, while Emma and James (pseudonyms) are first time principals. For additional information about the cases, please see Branson (2017), Morrison et al. (2015), Notman (2017), and Robertson (2017).

Setting Directions

It was evident that clear educational vision and a strong service ethic underpinned strategic leadership enactment in all four contexts. Emma, for example, believed she had the moral responsibility to love, value, and grow all young people, stating that "doing the right thing and keeping everyone's dignity intact in the process" was an important aspect of her leadership approach. Whetu similarly believed that students must remain at the center of learning, declaring "children's ideas and strengths need to be tapped into... the school is about the kids; not the teachers." This shaped his leadership in ways that centered attention on the actions of social justice leadership to meet these needs. Being a "big picture" thinker and strategic planner, he was also able to provide clear direction.

Similarly, Sonya's actions at her early childhood center sought to draw the teachers' attention back to the needs of the child. She used reflective questions with her staff to grow leadership of learning, for example, "Tell me what learning is happening for the children here." James firmly believed his leadership actions shaped the school direction and were critical to reversing "low corporate self-esteem" amongst students and staff in a "highly competitive school environment." He also encouraged students to bring their full selves to the schools context, believing that students should not have to "leave their Māoriness at the gate." Overall, each of the four leaders sought to bring people together through focusing on the needs of learners in their care. These leaders recognized a personal and professional responsibility to grow the capabilities and strengths of others.

140 ▪ D. GURR et al.

Developing People

Sonya saw herself and her early childhood center as advocates for the families in attendance. She not only encouraged her staff to forge partnerships with parents to meet the children's learning needs, but also provided for the social and emotional needs of the parents. This holistic approach highlighted the importance of trust and positive relationships. Collaboration between staff and parents was of importance, but Sonya also took a more direct leadership approach when needed. She questioned the teaching practice of her staff, but supported this approach by investing in the resources needed for staff professional learning (Notman, 2017).

Whetu faced the challenge of merging two schools in a high-needs setting. Key to this process was the establishment of positive relationships with staff and the local community. Also important was the initial collaboration that took place in order to identify a set of values that would be enacted by everyone. Modelling high expectations based on these values was imperative to Whetu and he consistently "walked the talk." Whetu sought positive outcomes and came to see any disagreements as opportunities "to reflect on our policies and our practices at school and how we react to situations in the future" (Robertson, 2017, p. 154). He viewed all experience whether positive or negative as an opportunity for critical reflection and learning.

Emma identified the importance of building trust when leading for social justice. She used dialogue and open to learning conversations as foundational strategies for building race consciousness and exposing deep-set beliefs. Also important was critical reflection on the routines, rituals, and practices that marginalize students within the school setting. She noted, "We challenge social issues collectively." Emma championed professional learning such as field trips to local landmarks and *marae* (communal meeting places) to strengthen teacher awareness of local history and geography. She sought to make deliberate appointments of teachers steeped in *te reo* (language) and *tikanga* (customs), particularly those with local *iwi* (tribal) affiliation. In this way, she enabled the infusion of indigenous ways of knowing into every aspect of school life.

James prioritized challenging fixed mindsets saying: "That's the journey that we as a staff, who are predominantly White, middle-class, have to make if social justice is going to be our bottom line here." He encouraged risk taking and experimentation, even when unsuccessful. Also important was the distribution of leadership opportunities to staff, and he noted, "I come under the leadership of our kaitiaki [assistant principal leading Māori strategy]. He takes the lead and I am the learner under his chieftainship." These strategies led to the creation of professional capital and collective wisdom. As with the other New Zealand leaders, when challenged with developing

Leading Successfully in High-Needs Contexts ▪ **141**

self and others, James saw collaboration based on shared values and moral purpose, as key to leadership for social justice in high-needs settings.

Redesigning the Organization

Securing greater equity in education involves disrupting the status quo, shifting cultural and professional norms, and aligning new and existing systems in the pursuit of socially just practice and outcomes. Engaging disenfranchised members of the school community was a high priority for the case study leaders. Emma sought guidance from local *iwi* elders. Perceiving parents as cultural experts and partners in the education process was fundamental to opening communication and establishing *manaakitanga* (hospitable and respectful relationships). James sought *whānau* views, engaging a Māori researcher to make personal contact with families. The four action points arising from a *whānau hui* (meeting) formed the agenda for the newly constituted Māori strategic team, led by an assistant principal from, and with the blessing of, local *iwi*.

Initiatives to improve student relationships included PB4L (Positive Behavior for Learning) and restorative justice processes. An ethic of care underpinned James' decision to mix rather than stream Year 9 classes, as a precursor to vertical classes, and a *tuakana-teina* model saw senior students mentoring juniors. Recognizing the importance of *whanāungatanga* (belonging) and the need to address "issues that students have without being deficit about it," he prioritized student mentoring and voice. A respected *kaumatua* (elder) initiated an ongoing conversation with Year 10 students with the intention that every student had a "significant other" with whom they can discuss their goals, dreams, and aspirations.

At the staff and system level, James commented that redesigning the organization involved the creation of a physical environment that encouraged collaborative planning, cross-curricular professional learning groups that disrupted historical and staid group-think, data analysis that enabled measurement of effect size and optimal resource allocation, and the broadening of self-review processes to include relational trust surveys. Whetu also prioritized relationships. During the merger, and in the months following it, he collaborated with the school staff, students, and community in the redesign of the school. Maintaining high visibility and transparent change processes were key factors in Whetu's leadership approach.

While actions that tighten vision and system alignment are straightforward in theory, multiple and ongoing tensions made these fraught in practice. Case study leaders had to pursue equity in a competitive education environment, and academic acceleration in a relationally precarious one. This required them to manage their emotions and still their impatience.

142 ▪ D. GURR et al.

Charged with leading an unpopular school merger and uniting two disparate groups of primary and intermediate school staff, Whetu realized that establishing a common set of values would be a necessary prerequisite to collaboration and the determination of change priorities. Sonya saw the need to support her staff with ongoing opportunities for professional development. James discerned systemic tensions in the drive to maintain school roll and reputation:

> We lose privileged parents at our peril...there is a certain sense of inequity in that we look to court those parents in order...keep the performance of this school above the national average. So it's systemic in its very nature and that is difficult.

He saw a critical part of his leadership as mediating personal urgency for change, the expectations of policy makers, and staff morale.

Improving Instructional Programs

New Zealand case study principals exercised direct and indirect instructional leadership to varying degrees, depending on contextual factors including size and circumstance. Differences in enactment are best illustrated by the intermediate and secondary case studies. Recent experience as a regional curriculum adviser and assessment for learning facilitator positioned Emma well to "lead from the front" in modelling the professionalism and pedagogy expected of teachers. This included co-constructing a "dialogue covenant" to guide professional conversations, upskilling teachers on the philosophy and key competencies underpinning the revised national curriculum, introducing and integrating collaborative planning processes, evaluating a range of assessment tools, and honing teachers' data interpretation skills. Emma's direct involvement in instructional matters reinforced for staff the presence of a principal "who knew and understood curriculum and what instruction actually looks like, rather than a leader completely removed from the chalk face." As one teacher commented, "Everything that we do in our classrooms is modelled from above...they're walking the talk."

In terms of curriculum delivery, New Zealand schools have considerable latitude in designing learning experiences that reflect the interests of their constituents. Given a school demographic in which 27% of students identify as Māori, and official language status, Emma perceived the introduction of a school wide second language program focusing on *te reo* (Māori language) as a "no-brainer." Having developed internal capacity through instructional leadership and strategic staff placement within teaching teams, she saw her next task as the "celebration of culture" through authentic learning contexts.

In secondary schools, direct instructional leadership is less common with principals typically distributing curriculum responsibility to heads of subject disciplines, hence James' comment that "hiring the right staff is one of the most important things I can do." As a precursor to extending pedagogical practice school wide, he supported faculty heads to develop curriculum sub-levels within Year 9 subjects. Cross-curricular professional learning groups meet with a view to accelerating the learning of students within particular classes, and departments meet to accelerate student learning within subject disciplines. As a consequence, an assisted general learning program has been disbanded and students reintegrated in mainstream classes, with attendant improvements in their academic and social well-being. Learning progression data also enabled more accurate measures of teaching performance. The senior leadership team and heads of department (HODs) collectively engaged in rigorous self-review processes that exposed variance within and across departments, and spurred "laggards" into action.

In conclusion, the New Zealand case studies reveal commonality and difference in leaders' lived experience. The complexity of change leadership for social justice is such that considerable overlap between each of the four themes exists. Furthermore, constructs such as Leithwood's (2012) do not fully encapsulate the embodied nature of leading change in high-needs contexts and the manner in which leaders make sense of this complex endeavor; this is explored in the discussion.

THE AUSTRALIAN CASES

Case studies were undertaken in four schools in Melbourne, Australia. These schools were secondary schools with students from ages 12 to 18 and were within the Victorian state government school system. The four schools were selected based on a history of low performance, as determined by declining enrolments and lower than expected average attainment on national testing measures. At the time of data collection, each of the four schools had demonstrated improvement on these measures. Two of the four cases, Fairview High School with Robyn and Tilverton College with Michael (all school and principal names are pseudonyms) were schools that served communities of relatively high economic advantage and the other two cases, Northern College with Peter and East Meadows College with Kate, were schools that served communities of relatively low economic advantage. All four schools could be described as having had challenges to their viability and had either experienced or considered closure. Michael, Peter, and Kate were externally appointed principals who led the improvement after

144 ▪ D. GURR et al.

the periods of decline. Robyn, at Fairview, was an internal appointment to the principal position after being in leadership roles since the school was reopened 5 years earlier. For additional information about research on these schools please refer to Gurr and Drysdale (2018), Gurr et al. (2018, 2019), and Huerta Villalobos (2013).

Setting Directions

In each school, there was a clarity of purpose evident that was important to initiating an improvement agenda that responded to past critical circumstances of decline. Each principal led from a standpoint of strong vision and purpose based on new ideas that were translated into new directions for each school. These were (a) the student-first focus at Tilverton; (b) student-centered learning and staff development focus at Fairview; (c) two-for-one focus to catch-up learning and leadership development at Northern; and (d) rebranding the school to make it a school of choice and connecting with community at East Meadows.

It was evident across the four schools that the directions selected were well supported by staff and the community. This quote from a teacher at Tilverton demonstrates how the clarity of vision shaped their work:

> We have a very clear vision and that's important. I think that that is driving us because we know where we want our kids to be . . . For me it's a focus point. It's like, ok well we're supporting learners, is it individualized . . . So, I can actually sit there and say, am I doing this? So that's a really good driving factor and it is really good to focus you and to guide you in what you are doing . . . The end point is quite clear. The vision is very, very clear.

This clarity in the direction of each school supported the leaders to manage the complexity of the work that was required for school improvement, particularly in these contexts of decline and crisis. Northern College exemplified complexity as a large three-campus school that was a merger of three smaller, failing schools. Peter used his appointment and the opening of the new, merged school to develop structures and operational processes that resonated with the vision of the school of developing high expectations of students and improved teacher capacity. He understood the history of "failure" that haunted the local community and that school expectations were low. In consultation with the leadership team, the principal used the mantra—"Two years of learning in one for all students"—to exemplify the vision and raise expectations. This catchphrase heightened the need to secure a guaranteed and viable curriculum, a shared instructional model and demanded a commitment from all staff to the school's improvement journey.

Developing People

Each school had a focus on developing the capability of everyone to contribute to improvement. One of the key strategies was getting the right people into the right seats on the bus, to use an analogy of Collins (2001). Initially, this involved strong recruitment and selection processes. Opportunities to employ new staff as enrolments increased were welcomed and the principals used the clear vision and directions to facilitate discussions about how staff aligned with the proposed improvement programs. At Fairview, Robyn explained, "When you recruit staff, what is the 'fit'? It's not that the person is not capable or would be unable to contribute but it is the cultural fit of 'is this person right for our organization?'" While at Northern College, Peter viewed staff recruitment as a way to bring educational equity to his students by actively recruiting the staff best suited to the positions available.

These leaders developed the capacity of the people that they had "on the bus" through a focus on both teacher and leadership development. In each of the cases, it was evident that a team of leaders supported the principals and assisted with the distribution of the improvement momentum throughout the schools. Although different in each setting, all four schools had a formal leadership structure that was important to the success of initiatives and the sustainability of change. At Northern College, Peter ensured that support and clear direction was provided for the leadership group for organizational structures and provision of in house and external professional learning so that these middle leaders could operate with agency within their own areas of responsibility.

At Northern College, East Meadows, and Tilverton, where the externally appointed principals were faced with the need for urgent change, the initial approach was authoritative and direct. They each had the support of a close circle from their respective leadership teams. The small number of other leaders relied upon by each new leader increased as relationships developed and there were some key new appointments to positions such as assistant principals. Over time, the focus on developing people spread more broadly across the staff.

In terms of their own development, all four principals had a pathway that prepared them for their principalships. Peter and Michael had been principals, whilst Kate and Robyn had extensive time through assistant principalships to develop their pedagogical, curriculum, and leadership skills. None relied on external programs for professional development, but all were life-long learners. Due to Tilverton's innovative approaches to teaching and learning, Michael became popular as a speaker and the school was regularly visited by local, national, and international educators, and the school provided dedicated professional learning programs.

146 ▪ D. GURR et al.

Redesigning the Organization

The theme of redesigning the organization is particularly relevant and interesting in these four cases, due to the fact that all of the schools were recovering from a period of crisis that had threatened their existence, albeit to varying degrees. The critical circumstances that each school had faced provided a springboard for urgent redesign to occur. Fairview High School and Northern College had a specific mandate to reinvent as a new entity and Robyn and Peter were well supported by the Victorian government education system. This included provision of funding for new buildings and for access to external consultants. Using these resources, they restructured many arrangements from changing timetabling, introducing sub-school structures, and developing consistent instructional models.

At the other two schools, East Meadows and Tilverton, Gail and Michael were appointed as a last resort to combat decline and avoid closure. This provided validation for radical redesign of the organizations, based on the ideas that each leader brought to the school. Using imminent demise to offset associated risks, fast-paced, disruptive changes were successfully implemented and these two principals rapidly altered the organization of each school.

All four principals were recognized for their capacity to access and mobilize resources from their networks to support the redesign of their schools. They reached out to the local school communities (which in some cases were depleted due to declining enrolments) and used their connections from within the Victorian Education Department to improve resources, facilities, and introduce new learning programs for their schools. For example, Peter had a close relationship with the regional director that ensured the needed physical resources were provided in a timely manner, and also allowed him to get approval for controversial programs such as student yearly progression based on results. Further, Kate's work exemplified the use of connections and networks to support the redesign of the organization. She built strong relationships with businesses and community organizations. As well as these relationships leading to new learning opportunities for students, they were also important to rebuilding the reputation of the school. She was adamant that schools needed to connect with their communities for the benefits of the students and the school stressing that "Schools can't be silos anymore... you need links with the outside world to challenge you more. Business and industry links are the only way to do this. You cannot become insular."

Improving Instructional Programs

In the early phase of the improvement at each school, the principals all identified that inconsistent practice and varied expectations were apparent.

To address these inconsistencies, they focused on the implementation of new instructional approaches and there were a number of common features in how this was achieved. Firstly, the development and communication of explicit expectations was prioritized. At Northern College and East Meadows, there was a focus on the implementation of a consistent, guaranteed, and viable curriculum that ensured variation was minimized and that all students had access to strong curriculum experiences. At Tilverton, Fairview, and East Meadows, the instructional approach included a focus on student voice and agency with options for students to develop their own learning journeys through greater subject choice and control over classroom experiences.

As already described, recruitment and selection contributed to the way that the leaders were able to improve the instructional programs. By employing teachers who were well informed of the expectations and committed to the approach of each school, consistency and quality of the instructional programs were enhanced. The selected instructional approaches were supported by adjustments to organizational arrangements. For example, at Fairview, timetabling was adjusted to provide longer periods of learning, and at Northern, targeted professional development was implemented with a focus on mentoring and coaching. East Meadows College employed team teaching structures in core subject areas, creating opportunities for students to choose what level of support and/or direct instruction they required.

As the new instructional programs were consolidated, teachers, and students at Tilverton and East Meadows, were given agency to make decisions that would continually develop and improve the selected programs. The combination of agency and clear expectations supported collective efficacy and often innovative responses to problems of practice across the schools.

CONCLUSIONS

These eight cases provide different perspectives on leading successfully in challenging contexts. From New Zealand there was a stronger focus on exploring the social justice dimension of principal leadership, and partly this was because members from New Zealand research group were involved in the social justice strand of the ISLDN. The Australian cases were all from Melbourne and all were part of the high-needs strand of the ISLDN, and so there was not the focus on exploring social justice, albeit it was evident in their narratives. The Leithwood (2012) four element leadership framework provided common lenses to view the cases. Drawing on this analysis, and despite the diversity in contexts, four leadership themes emerged.

148 ▪ D. GURR et al.

Clarity of Purpose

These principals brought a clarity of purpose to their schools, through establishing shared and agreed visions/directions and providing strong principal leadership to achieve these. Principal leadership was central to all the improvement efforts, and this leadership typically had a social justice orientation with clear moral purpose, high expectations for all, and a strong sense of organizational efficacy and agency—these school communities believed that they could succeed beyond the expectations of the surrounding context.

Leadership practices that enabled strong direction for each school centered on a capacity to relate to others and strengthen the avenues of influence through which the espoused directions could be translated to action. These leaders' abilities to balance a commitment to their own values and ideas with reflexive and relational practices that responded to nuances of context, and the values and ideas of others, were key to ensuring that the selected directions were elevated to the shared visions that underpinned the culture of each school.

Relationships

Relationships were central to the work of the principals, and indeed to all in the schools. Staff were viewed as being central to improvement efforts, and staff selection and development, aligned with and guided by school direction, was crucial to success. Building trust amongst all members of the school community and gaining genuine collaboration were important, especially through connecting explicitly and meaningfully with families and community. Connection with indigenous culture was especially important in the New Zealand context. Teacher and leadership development centered not only on developing skills and capacities, but also on fostering agency that led to impactful work. In terms of leadership preparation, many of the principals seemed to have had a professional path that led them inextricably to the principalships described in the cases—they had established a leadership reputation in other principal or assistant principal roles, and so had a clear sense of the responsibility and possibilities of their roles. Professional support during their principalship came from various sources, including education departments, critical friends, communities and families, universities and from the ongoing feedback gained from school success, informal feedback, and the day-to-day school interactions. The principals sought support and feedback, and, through this, knew that their schools were improving and that their work was impactful.

Taking Action

In many of the cases, crises led to an urgency for improvement. Principals were often selected for their capacity to access and mobilize resources from the networks they had developed in their careers. Relationships were again important in how the schools improved—harnessing extra resources from an education department, connecting with local families and communities to enlist their support, and fostering positive relationships with students. In many cases, there was a deliberate cultivation of disruptive strategies to improve the school, and perhaps the most extreme case was that of Tilverton, which thrived on continuous change driven by an unrelenting focus on student learning needs. Whilst there were strong change orientations, there was also a sense of patience about change, with most principals acknowledging that major change takes time (especially culture change). Again, the exception was Tilverton, which needed to transform quickly to survive.

Leading Learning

In most of the schools, there was a transformation in teaching and learning. In some cases the principals had clarity about the type of teaching and learning they envisaged was needed for success; in other cases, this was developed as school improvement progressed. Inconsistent teaching practices and varied expectations of students were common in the schools prior to an improvement orientation. To improve the schools there was development and communication of explicit and agreed expectations, targeted staff recruitment where possible, both direct and indirect leadership of the teaching and learning program, development of teacher agency, and, in many cases, student agency for program decisions. Many initiatives were inextricably linked to context, such as the development of Māori language programs in New Zealand schools to reflect the strong indigenous culture.

FUTURE DIRECTIONS

The ISLDN title suggests a research focus on leadership development, yet the cases presented here are relatively silent on this. In both Australia and New Zealand, given the lack of consistent approaches and resourcing, together with an emphasis on self-identification and self-management, it is perhaps unsurprising that our cases have little to offer in terms of advice about formal leadership preparation and development. Delving more deeply into leaders' roles in developing people, themselves included, would however surface important insights into leadership development. In posing

150 ▪ D. GURR et al.

the question, "How did social justice leaders *learn* to become social justice leaders?" researchers in the social justice leadership strand have probed aspects of being and becoming as leaders. Given that personal and professional formation are integral to leadership enactment (the doing), we suggest that greater emphasis on this avenue of inquiry across the ISLDN network, and leadership research more generally, would enhance empirical and theoretical understanding.

Life history and narrative approaches lend themselves well to this form of research (Shamir, Dayan-Horesh, & Adler, 2005; Slater, 2011). Dimmock and O'Donoghue (1997), for example, explored leadership using life history portraits of six successful secondary school principals in Western Australia, who were regarded as being innovative, based on peer and community recommendations. They showed how the personal and professional life histories of the principals helped to explain the elements of their leadership that were important to school success, such as personal vision, seizing opportunities, goal-setting, using research literature, understanding their own values and having a clear sense of moral purpose, understanding and using symbolism, questioning the status quo, balancing vision and processes, maintaining pressure for change and including all the stakeholders. While these elements are evident in the cases described in this chapter, understanding more deeply how life and career experiences translate into successful leadership practice would be valuable for leadership preparation.

REFERENCES

Anderson, M. (2006). *Being a school councillor in a government secondary college in Victoria: Constructions of role and* meaning (Doctoral dissertation). The University of Melbourne, Melbourne, Australia.

Australian Bureau of Statistics. (2017). *4221.0—Schools, Australia, 2016.* Canberra, Australia: Australian Bureau of Statistics. Retrieved from http://www.abs.gov .au/ausstats/abs@.nsf/mf/4221.0

Bass, B. M. (1990). From transactional to transformational leadership: Learning to share the vision. *Organizational Dynamics, 18*(3), 19–31.

Branson, C. M. (2017). Affective leadership: An illustration of the emotional side of social justice leadership. In R. McNae, M. Morrison, & R. Notman (Eds.), *Educational leadership in Aotearoa New Zealand: Issues of context and social justice* (pp. 46–60). Wellington: New Zealand Council for Educational Research Press.

Branson, C. M., Morrison, M., & McNae, R. (2016). In search of seamless education. In S. Gross & J. Shapiro (Eds.), *Democratic ethical educational leadership: Reclaiming school reform* (pp. 138–143). New York, NY: Routledge.

Collins, J.C. (2001). *Good to great: Why some companies make the leap . . . and others don't.* New York, NY: HarperCollins

Dimmock, C., & O'Donoghue, T. (1997). *Innovative school principals and restructuring. Life history portraits of successful managers of change.* London, England: Routledge.

Education Council. (2018). *The leadership strategy for the teaching profession of Aotearoa New Zealand: Enabling every teacher to develop their leadership capability.* Wellington, New Zealand: Education Council.

Gurr, D., & Drysdale, L. (2015). An Australian perspective on school leadership preparation and development: Credentials or self-management? *Asia Pacific Journal of Education, 35*(3), 377–391.

Gurr, D., & Drysdale, L. (2018). Leading high need schools: Findings from the International School Leadership Development Network. *International Studies in Educational Administration, 46*(1), 147–156.

Gurr, D., Drysdale, L., Clarke, S., & Wildy, H. (2014). High needs schools in Australia. *Management in Education, 28*(3), 86–90.

Gurr, D., Drysdale, L., Longmuir, F., & McCrohan, K. (2018). Leading the improvement of schools in challenging circumstances. *International Studies in Educational Administration, 46*(1), 22–44.

Gurr, D., Drysdale, L., Longmuir, F., & McCrohan, K. (2019). Successful school leadership that is culturally sensitive but not context constrained. In E. Murakami, D. Gurr, & R. Notman (Eds.), *Educational leadership, culture, and success in high-need schools* (pp. 25–44). Charlotte, NC: Information Age.

Gurr, D., Drysdale, L., & Walkley, D. (2012). School-parent relations in Victorian schools. *Journal of School Public Relations, 33*(3), 172–198.

Huerta Villalobos, M. (2013). *The role of the critical friend in leadership and school improvement* (Master of Education Thesis). The University of Melbourne, Melbourne, Australia.

Jensen, B., Hunter, A., Lambert, T., & Clark, A. (2015). *Aspiring principal preparation, prepared for the Australian Institute for Teaching and School Leadership.* Melbourne, Victoria: Australian Institute for Teaching and School Leadership.

Leithwood, K. (2012). The four essential components of the leader's repertoire. In K. Leithwood & K. S. Louis (Eds.), *Linking leadership to learning* (pp. 57–67). San Francisco, CA: Jossey Bass.

Leithwood, K., Harris, A., & Strauss, T. (2010). *Leading school turnaround. How successful leaders transform low-performing schools.* San Francisco, CA: Jossey-Bass.

Longmuir, F. (2017). *Principal leadership in high-advantage, improving Victorian secondary schools* (Doctor of Philosophy Thesis). The University of Melbourne, Melbourne, Australia.

Longmuir, F. (2019). Resistant leadership: Countering dominant paradigms in school improvement. *Journal of Educational Administration and History, 51*(3), 256–272. https://doi.org/10.1080/00220620.2019.1583172

McNae, R. (2017). Leading turnaround schools: Surfacing hope in times of crisis. In R. McNae, M. Morrison, & R. Notman (Eds.), *Educational leadership in Aotearora New Zealand: Issues of context and social justice* (pp. 29–45). Wellington: New Zealand Council for Educational Research Press.

McNae R., Morrison, M., & Notman, R. (Eds.). (2017). *Educational leadership in Aotearoa New Zealand: Issues of context and social justice.* Wellington: New Zealand Council for Educational Research Press.

152 ▪ D. GURR et al.

Ministry of Education. (2019). *Supporting all school to succeed. Reform of the tomorrow's schools system.* Wellington: New Zealand Ministry of Education.

Morrison, M. (2017). 'I wasn't really a decile 1- person': Deliberate enactment of social justice leadership in a high-needs context. In R. McNae, M. Morrison, & R. Notman (Eds.), *Educational leadership in Aotearoa New Zealand: Issues of context and social justice* (pp. 73–87). Wellington: New Zealand Council for Educational Research Press.

Morrison, M., Branson, C., & McNae, R. (2015). Multiple hues: New Zealand school leaders' perceptions of social justice. *Journal of Educational Leadership Policy and Practice, 30*(1), 4–16.

Norgrove, A., & Scott, D. (2017) *How does New Zealand's education system compare?* Wellington, NZ: Ministry of Education.

Notman, R. (2010). Who lies within? The personal development of educational leaders. *Journal of Educational Leadership, Policy & Practice, 25*(2), 17–29.

Notman, R. (Ed.). (2011). *Successful educational leadership in New Zealand: Case studies of schools and an early childhood centre.* Wellington: New Zealand Council for Educational Research Press.

Notman, R. (2012). Intrapersonal factors in New Zealand school leadership success. *International Journal of Educational Management, 26*(5), 470–479.

Notman, R. (2017). Holistic leadership in a high-needs early childhood centre. In R. McNae, M. Morrison, & R. Notman (Eds.), *Educational leadership in Aotearoa New Zealand: Issues of context and social justice* (pp. 130–142). Wellington: New Zealand Council for Educational Research Press.

Notman, R., & Henry, D. A. (2011). Building and sustaining successful school leadership in New Zealand. *Leadership & Policy in Schools, 10*(4), 375–394. https://doi.org/10.1080/15700763.2011.610555

Robertson, S. (2017). Leading a school merger in a high needs setting. In R. McNae, M. Morrison, & R. Notman (Eds.), *Educational leadership in Aotearoa New Zealand: Issues of context and social justice* (pp. 143–158). Wellington: New Zealand Council for Educational Research Press.

Robertson, S. (2018). A New Zealand principal's perceptions of identity and change. *Leading & Managing: Journal of the Australian Council of Educational Leaders, 24*(1), 33–46.

Shamir, B., Dayan-Horesh, H., & Adler, D. (2005). Leading by biography: Towards a life-story approach to the study of leadership. *Leadership, 1*(1), 13–29. https://doi.org/10.1177/1742715005049348

Slater, C. L. (2011). Understanding principal leadership: An international perspective and a narrative approach. *Educational Management Administration & Leadership, 39*(2), 219–227. https://doi.org/10.1177/1741143210390061

Statistics New Zealand. (2013). *Major ethnic groups in New Zealand.* Retrieved from https://www.stats.govt.nz/infographics/major-ethnic-groups-in-new-zealand

Watterston, B. (2015a). *Environmental scan: Principal preparation programs, prepared for the Australian Institute for Teaching and School Leadership.* Melbourne: Australian Institute for Teaching and School Leadership.

Watterston, B. (2015b). *Preparing future leaders: Effective preparation for aspiring school principals.* Melbourne: Australian Institute for Teaching and School Leadership.

CHAPTER 9

A COMPARISON OF SOCIAL JUSTICE LEADERSHIP MEANING AND PRAXIS

The Interplay of Unique Social Cultural Contexts in Turkish, Palestinian, and Lebanese High-Needs Schools

Khalid Arar
Texas State University

Deniz Örücü
Baskent University, Turkey

Julia Mahfouz
University of Colorado-Denver

Educational Leadership for Social Justice and Improving High-Needs Schools, pages 153–172
Copyright © 2021 by Information Age Publishing
All rights of reproduction in any form reserved.

153

154 ▪ K. ARAR, D. ÖRÜCÜ, and J. MAHFOUZ

The Middle East (ME) is a region characterized by diverse languages, dialects, cultures, religions, and political upheaval; where the context is turbulent with the influx of refugees and economic problems and the region's delicate balance in terms of wars and conflicts (Arar, Brooks, & Bogotch, 2019). Given such features of traditional societies (Oplatka & Arar, 2016; Sun & Leithwood, 2017) in the ME, this chapter attempts to address calls for reconceptualizing social justice (SJ) leadership, reflecting the significance of the local contexts grounded substantially in the culture and structure of these societies.

Therefore, to contribute to the research of ISLDN in comparing SJ practices of leaders in high-needs schools from different nations (Angelle, Morrison, & Stevenson, 2015; Arar, Beycioglu, & Oplatka, 2017; Barnett & Stevenson, 2015; Bryant, Cheng, & Notman, 2014; Gurr, Drysdale, Clarke, & Wildy, 2014; Morrison, McNae, & Branson, 2015), we seek to examine and compare the meanings and praxis of SJ leadership of school principals in three high-needs schools in the ME, based on three case studies in Turkey, in the divided city of Jerusalem, and in Lebanon. Taking a comparative stance, we believe, will contribute to how SJ is understood and implemented by school principals in diverse situations characterized as high-needs schools in the ME. Specifically we aim to answer the following questions: (a) "How are the principals' perceptions of SJ enacted and applied in their schools and communities?" and (b) "How do the cultural, social, and national contexts of high-needs schools influence perceptions and the implementation of SJ leadership?"

We relied on Angelle et al.'s (2015) conceptual framework for macro-micro examination of school contexts; which suggests that the school is "nested within a set of micro factors which were, in turn, nested within a set of macro factors" (Morrison, 2017, p. 46) and influenced by characteristics of SJ leadership (Bogotch, 2002; Theoharis, 2007). Investigating the practices and strategies by school leaders in these ME contexts assumes great importance when considering how SJ leadership (Arar et al., 2017; DeMatthews, 2018; Fraser, 2008) can adopt new ways to cater for the diversity and complexity. In this chapter we briefly provide our conceptual framework, followed by discussions of the contexts, methodology, findings, and conclusions.

CONCEPTUAL FRAMEWORK: MACRO/MICRO EXAMINATION OF HIGH-NEEDS SCHOOLS AND SOCIAL JUSTICE LEADERSHIP

The meaning of high-needs school is about the challenge and risk factors embedded within the school as a result of various serious phenomena occurring in the wider socio-political environment (Weldon, 2012). ISLDN

A Comparison of Social Justice Leadership Meaning and Praxis ■ **155**

studies have identified high-needs schools as possessing (Baran & Berry, 2015; Murakami, Kearney, Scott, & Alfaro, 2018):

1. a high percentage of individuals from families with incomes below the poverty line;
2. a high percentage of school teachers not teaching in the content area in which they were trained to teach;
3. a high teacher/leader turnover rate;
4. a high percentage of non-native language speakers;
5. a high percentage of historically/socially excluded groups;
6. a high percentage of indigenous groups;
7. a high percentage of students with learning differences;
8. a lack of access to basic physical infrastructures; and/or
9. a situational high-need based on an event such as a natural or man-made disaster. (p. 3)

Such challenging situations lead to inequities (Barnett & Stevenson, 2015). Hence, an understanding of the contextual factors by school leaders is critical in meeting the realities of such schools (Klar & Brewer, 2013).

Angelle et al.'s (2015) framework in understanding the high-needs schools and the related leadership praxis involves the general context about the society and the school's communities as well as its more specific education-focused context. The sociocultural dimensions and discourses help describe the national contexts and characteristics that interplay on macro and micro levels. Angelle and Torrance (2019) suggest that constructions of SJ are highly dependent on the context in which it takes place, while perspectives are "inextricably linked to social contexts within which models of justice make sense to the people involved" (Harris, 2014, p. 98).

SJ is a complex culturally loaded construct subject to various interpretations (Jean-Marie, Normore, & Brooks, 2009) especially in high-needs schools with religious, political, and ethnic differences, which are detailed through the cases in this chapter. SJ is a means of fixing inequities (Marshall & Ward, 2004), whereby SJ leadership is associated with the leaders' ability to change a school's culture at micro level, reflecting the wider societal inequities and injustices. However, the micro, meso, and macro contexts reinforce one another when in resonance and work against one another when out of phase, resulting in either amplifying or limiting the efforts of those aiming to affect change (Ogden, 2017).

School leaders in high-needs schools are pivotal in addressing injustice. SJ leaders seeking to disrupt long-standing systems of privilege in their school communities, promote change and encourage compassion and reflection (Berkovich, 2014). Leadership in high-needs schools necessitates certain values and principles for SJ, such as "concern for the

156 ▪ K. ARAR, D. ÖRÜCÜ, and J. MAHFOUZ

common good, participation, justice, equity, respect for the value and dignity of individuals, and their cultural traditions" (Murillo, Krichesky, Castro, & Hernández, 2010, p. 177). Gurr and Drysdale (2018), elaborating on the complex relationship between the leader and context, provide two perspectives on this complexity: (a) you cannot remove a leader from their context and expect to measure their effectiveness, or (b) the context defines the leader's approach and the required leadership style to match the situation. In the next section, we will portray the characteristics of the contexts we investigate.

COUNTRY CONTEXTS: TURKEY, PALESTINE, AND LEBANON

Turkey

Turkey, with a population of over 80 million, has a centralized and bureaucratic education system. The Ministry of National Education (MoNE) is the central authority overseeing all procedures through its provincial directorates. Compulsory education totals 12 years, with 4 years elementary, 4 years middle school, and 4 years high school levels, initiated in 2012. School principals are selected through an exam, and legally not required to study educational administration. Their authority and autonomy at school level are limited because of the centralized structure.

The compulsory school levels accommodate 53,870 public and 11,694 private schools and 4 distance education schools serving 17,885,248 students through more than 1 million teachers (MONE National Education Statistics, 2018). This massive system has diverse challenges such as financial and infrastructural problems, school access, teacher and principal preparation, curriculum content, regional differences, and school absence (Education Reform Initiative Report, 2018). The recent challenge added is the sudden arrival of the massive number of Syrian students (Arar, Örücü, & Küçükçayır, 2019). What began as Syrians as guests who were provided with emergency help in 2011, has transformed into over 3.5 million Syrians under "temporary protection" today, putting the education system under considerable strain. The number of registered Syrian children at school age was, by September 2018, about 1,234,439 while 736,628 are enrolled in schools (MONE, 2018). The system operates in two school types for the Syrian students. The first is temporary education centers (TECs) within the camps or attached to the public schools, and the second is direct placement inclusively in the public schools (Arar & Örücü&Ak-Küçükçayır, 2020).

Palestine/Jerusalem

Israel has a population of 9.29 million, 74.2% of whom are Jewish and 21.0% are Arab (Central Bureau of Statistics, 2019). Israeli society is divided into social, national, and political enclaves. The Arab population continually contends with an identity conflict as citizens of the officially defined Jewish state (Arar, 2012). Education in Israel is segregated with four distinct sub-educational systems: the state education system, the Jewish religious state education system, the Arab education system, and the ultra-orthodox Jewish education system (Gibton, 2011).

The Arab educational system serves 26% of the children, separate and distinct from the Jewish educational system. Classes are taught in Arabic and the state schools implement 80% government-dictated curriculum content, ignoring the narratives of the Arab population (Arar, 2012). Since Israel's occupation of the West Bank in 1967, Jerusalem has functioned as a divided city with clear distinctions between the western part of the city, which is designated as occupied territory by the UN. The number of Palestinian students studying in Jerusalem is 109,481 (The Association for Civil Rights in Israel, 2017). The education provision for Palestinian children in East Jerusalem is a daily struggle in a state of conflicting policies concerning the precarious status. The divided city is continually troubled by violent clashes between Jewish Israelis and Palestinian Arabs (Koren, 2017). This is the reality in which Palestinian schools function, with some of them being encompassed by walls, while their teachers and students are forced to pass through checkpoints commuting to schools.

Lebanon

Schools in Lebanon are mainly of three types: public institutions, subsidized private institutions, and tuition-based private institutions. General education is comprised of several successive components: kindergarten (optional); cycles I and II (Grades 1–6); cycle III (Grades 7–9), which concludes with the Brevet exam as a prerequisite before progressing to the next cycle; and cycle IV (Grades 10–12; Banque Bemo, 2014). Various education services are divided among several ministries, but the Ministry of Education and Higher Education (MEHE) is the major national body that oversees all levels of public and private education (MEHE, 2011).

As a pluralistic, diverse society, Lebanon struggles with social injustice across all communities, mirrored in the educational system (Bahous & Nabhani, 2008) such as the discrepancy in the quality of education between public and private schools. Despite the high tuition fees, more than 50% of

158 ▪ K. ARAR, D. ÖRÜCÜ, and J. MAHFOUZ

the student population attend private schools to receive quality education (Mahfouz, El Mehtar, Osman, & Kotok, 2019). Therefore, public schools are the only option for communities of high needs and students of low socioeconomic status (SES). This results in multilayered social injustice reflected through several factors. Lebanon is proud of teaching three languages, Arabic, English, and French; yet, public schools, especially in rural areas without enough language teachers, struggle with it. Another socioeconomic inequity stems from the geographical positions of these schools, with huge inconsistency in resource allocation between rural and urban schools. Rural schools struggle with poor resources (Greenfield & Akkary, 1998) and neglect from the government. Social injustice is also reflected in the centralized decision-making within the MEHE, while schools face political and religious pressures from the communities they live in, which obstructs their operations. For example, principals do not have the authority to assess teacher performance, are not part of the hiring and firing process, and have to conform to the MEHE's decisions neglecting the pressures of the political and religious systems.

METHODOLOGY

This cross-cultural comparative case study (Marshall & Rossman, 2012) utilized narrative analysis for a more robust conceptual, methodological, and analytical approach (Dimmock & Walker, 2010). Three case schools were identified in Turkey, Palestine and Lebanon (one school from each) following the criteria of high-needs schools provided by ISLDN (Baran & Berry, 2015). The Lebanese and Turkish schools have a high percentage of students with incomes below the poverty line while the Palestinian school has a high percentage of students of historically and socially excluded communities within a contested political environment. During 2018 we conducted semi-structured interviews with the school principals of the selected schools and shadowed them for a year. The interview questions addressed the participants' professional background, the ways principals make sense of SJ within their high-needs schools, the factors that facilitate or hinder the work of a SJ leader, and the various ways of implementing SJ leadership in specific high-needs schools.

Data was transcribed in Arabic in Lebanon and Palestine, and in Turkish in Turkey, and then translated to English. The analysis process entailed developing emergent codes, searching for recurrent experiences, feelings, and behaviors, highlighting distinct narratives, finding relationships among various categories and sub-categories in the data, and finally identifying the central themes. Principles of comparative analysis (Strauss & Corbin, 1998) guided the coding process, including comparison of any coded element

A Comparison of Social Justice Leadership Meaning and Praxis ▪ **159**

in the emergent categories and sub-categories. Structured analysis and peer review enhanced trustworthiness and reliability (Marshall & Rossman, 2012). The use of systematic data collection procedure contributed to the credibility and authenticity of the data. Pseudonyms were used to ensure anonymity. We provide detailed information on the case school contexts and principals under the findings section for an easier track of each case with their related findings.

FINDINGS

Three themes emerged: reflecting the ways principals make sense of SJ, the factors that hinder their SJ implementations, and ways of implementing SJ leadership. Following the contextual descriptions, the findings of each case is presented. All the principals' names are fictitious.

Turkish School and the School Principal, Alp

Turkish school (TS) is a public primary school in the outskirts of a big town and has a mixed student population of nearly 1,000 Turkish, Syrian, and a small group of Russian and Ukranian students. The main challenges are cultural differences, integration, poverty, stark contrasts in the SES of the students, school absence, and the limited teacher capacity for inclusive education. Turkish parents resist the presence of foreign students in the same classroom with their children and pressure the principal into separating classrooms into homogenous units. The principal, Alp, is a male who also suffered from educational inequalities during his childhood. As he himself articulated, he has a "greater understanding of SJ" through his "personal experience as a school principal" and previously his "disadvantaged childhood." He tries to balance the diverse needs in his school community to cope with poverty, prejudice, and other barriers, especially confronting refugee students.

The Story of Alp

Coming from a very poor family, Alp had to leave home early to go to a boarding school to study, as well as be a child worker. He recalled the impact of his teacher, who created opportunities for him, and he narrated his drive of SJ in this respect:

> I was working in the fields trying to attend the school. My teacher introduced me to some influential friends of hers. I'm grateful for their help. One of

160 ▪ K. ARAR, D. ÖRÜCÜ, and J. MAHFOUZ

them provided funding for me, the other placed me in a boarding school. Some classmates were well-off. I never forget my struggle, which urges me to work for equality.

SJ leadership, for Alp, meant saving futures through sharing resources, reducing inequalities, and recognizing and respecting each student, building compassion, dialogue and affection. He made sense of SJ through addressing the inequalities stemming from social class, poverty, ethnicity, and marginalization. He focuses on building a school culture that would facilitate inclusive educational practice for better integration of Syrian students:

> I rely on humanism rather than on sole bureacratic tasks. I believe all students deserve the same rights regardless of their nationality or financial status. I am doing my best for my kids. Here, we have traumatic war-torn students from Syria and impoverished Turkish children. Too many challenges!When the Syrians first arrived, I thought this should be my mission to provide the opportunity for a brighter future for these children.

As he had to deal with this harsh reality, he also had to fight with the societal prejudice in the community emphasizing his SJ commitment and values:

> Turkish parents refused to have their children placed together with the Syrians in the same class. They didn't mind other nationalities, but they did for the Syrians. I held several meetings; tried some simulation games to have them emphasize. We used to get money from the parents to support school. We cannot legally get it from the Syrians because they are under temporary protection. I also banned getting money from the Turkish parents to be fair. I tried to instill the idea that we are all equal in God's eye.

Alp's social interaction skills through which he builds a community of supporters facilitated his SJ pursuit. He articulated his main strategy as "playing the modern Robin Hood without weapons":

> Living here for many years, I have a lot of wealthy friends and acquaintances. We have limited resources. We don't receive extra funding for the Syrians as TECs do from the Ministry...I created my own resources through raising charity.

When he was first assigned to this school, it was nearly shattered. Then, he found different resources and built it up while prioritizing the needs of teachers and students. Before providing and renovating all classrooms and spaces for everyone, he did not allocate an office for himself for nearly 2 years.

Poverty and deprivation are SJ issues for him. For example, a student was often absent to accompany her parents collecting garbage. There were also

A Comparison of Social Justice Leadership Meaning and Praxis ▪ **161**

some girls whose families resisted their schooling. To address these issues, he mobilized his network for funds and paid home visits to persuade parents. He also persuaded the local mosque's Imam (leader of the Muslim community) to emphasize the importance of schooling, especially for the education of girls during Friday prayers. He was content with his achievement:

> I have students both Turkish and Syrians, who have to help their families collect garbage. When they don't turn up in the school, I go and find them on the streets collecting garbage. To stop all this, I arranged a system of charity among my social circles to provide them financial help. Since then, these children attend school regularly and they are happy.

However, he is worried about their future:

> Here, I do my best to empower them while trying to reduce inequalities. I don't know how they will survive in the secondary school and further. I am worried if they leave school after the primary grades. This requires system-wide measures and personal dedication of educators. I will follow the students at-risk as much as I can through my personal network with secondary schools here but I, alone, cannot handle all who move away, I can't track them. Every educator has to be sensitive about this issue all around Turkey. Education is the only way for them to survive.

Alp's SJ endeavor is also related with his policy mediation skills. Despite his limited formal autonomy, he negotiated with the Ministry officials to reconcile the formal expectations with the realities of his school. For example, foreign students had language barriers, hindering their achievement. Moreover, some suffered from post-war trauma, having difficulties in adaptation. Alp prioritized the psychological and language needs of these students and provided extra language courses and psychological support negotiating with the Ministry.

His SJ practices range from mobilizing resources to engaging the internal and external school community to eliminate inequalities. This was shaped and developed through his personal experience and the culture he was brought in.

Palestinian School and the School Principal, Khalil

Palestinian school (PS) is in East Jerusalem, in a residential area of a multi-religion neighborhood. Students are from low socioeconomic strata, mostly from Muslim families while few are Christian. The school competes with two financially advantaged neighboring schools. There are 680 students in six grades from Grade 7 to Grade 12. The school is divided

162 ■ K. ARAR, D. ÖRÜCÜ, and J. MAHFOUZ

into junior and senior high school. Some students and teachers live across the separation fence between East and West Jerusalem, and have to cross through security checkpoints supervised by soldiers to reach the school. The school suffers from chronic understaffing; for example, there are no psychologists and only one counselor for the school.

The principal, Khalil, is a male living in the same neighborhood. He holds an MA in education administration from a Palestinian university. He conservatively preserves his Palestinian identity while reconciling the demands of the Israeli Ministry and different restrictions of the Jerusalem municipality. Under political and religious conflict, with a fragmented education system, the reality in Jerusalem acts to the detriment of the school's educational climate and functioning. Khalil has to defend his staff and students from verbal abuse in encounters with Israeli soldiers at the checkpoints on their way to school. The soldiers sometimes even enter the school. Moreover, a shooting incident left the staff and students with post-traumatic symptoms and serious tension, and incidents of physical violence in the school's immediate environment occur.

The Story of Khalil

Khalil's vision of SJ is mainly constructed through his life in Jerusalem:

> I grew up in Jerusalem, embracing different religions, cultures, and peoples. Jews and Arabs; secular, religious, and ultraorthodox Jews; Christians, and Muslims living together, with many possibilities and equally many risks. It is a multi-faceted city and its different demographic, political, and economic dimensions are interwoven causing a dynamic that often erupts into legal and even physical conflicts. Here I grew to understand multiculturalism, to find ways for equal representation of different beliefs, while trying to find a path for dialogue and acceptance.

Similar to Alp, Khalil voiced the impact of his underprivileged childhood on his SJ formation:

> I learnt in my big but poor family that everyone had to work to make money. I faced oppression by myself. I had a lot of struggle both financially and in terms of social and national repression. This taught me and still encourages me to raise awareness in others to liberate them from the chains of oppression and control.

Therefore, he emphasized his values and collective commitment for the poor students despite the institutional and political barriers, as he thinks education is the only opportunity for them:

A Comparison of Social Justice Leadership Meaning and Praxis ▪ **163**

I am motivated by equality and respect. I have to make an impact on their lives as a change agent. Education is their only exit from oppression and poverty. I don't want them to accept this severe reality of discrimination. The obstacle is the lack of belief to engender justice, the strict institutional policy deteriorating the intellectual capital, a shallow pedagogy and lack of leadership, and the oppression of talents and abilities in the Palestinian society.

He associated his SJ perception with opportunity, equality, liberation, and the establishment of equal educational arenas for every religious group, probably because he lives in a diverse community under occupation and control while struggling with low-resources and discrimination. SJ for him is about recognition, access, and successful experiences for the Palestinian population in Jerusalem:

The occupation of East Jerusalem in 1967 forced the inhabitants to become embroiled in a national, geographic, and demographic struggle. We already live in a violent state under strain. I try to ease or at least not multiply our harsh reality, I am leading an organization to create a new social, national, and cultural reality, to attain distributive justice, to promote education for a true awareness for our national struggle, and to promote gender equality in our traditional society.

As the school is reached through the separation fence and security checkpoints, Khalil felt the urge to care:

Frequently, there is a roadblock with soldiers and police, adjacent to the school, causing tensions between the students and the police or soldiers. We have to protect the students, we do not allow them to leave the premises and risk their lives. Tear gas is sometimes used at the checkpoints, the girls are choked, there is panic, shouting, etcetera. Our routine is disrupted. The girls and the female teachers living outside the neighborhood are continually in friction with the police and soldiers. It's a reality of violence, that keeps me in constant human dilemmas. I accompany them through the fence and ensure their safety.

Khalil also raised his students' awareness of inequality and concepts of SJ, drawing on his personal heritage:

I come from this place, I know the community, their pain, and I encountered the oppression myself. I think that a bourgeois person cannot do what I manage to do.

Khalil was trapped at the crossroads of clashing intentions and policies and forced to cope with a policy of accelerated Israelization and education for dual-identities. He stated that he is formally accountable to the

164 ▪ K. ARAR, D. ÖRÜCÜ, and J. MAHFOUZ

Jerusalem municipality, the occupying administration, but he also followed the Palestinian curriculum as expected by the Arab authorities, deconstructing the Israeli curriculum where possible, seeking harmony with all parties, while trying to allocate resources from the two sides to empower his underprivileged students. He was expected to maintain the Palestinian identity and culture, in the face of the Jerusalem municipality's recent dictation to transfer to the Israeli learning program. He had to master his role as a mediator between the two sides, while trying to provide culturally relevant education and defend the right of the Palestinian students to maintain their national identity.

Finally, he highlighted the inner drive for SJ:

> I have done all that I dreamt about and I'm satisfied. It was hard to obtain resources but we managed to overcome the difficulties. We are guided by internal decisions, not dependent on others, not focusing on the mantra of oppression ... We have small circles of supporters increasing. We present the results to them. This gives them faith and hope and they continue to support us. We have also the alumni volunteering for different activities, we are building circles of trust, especially as we are transparent to all our partners.

Khalil's perception of SJ is woven into both his context and commitment to his people. He understands his duty and mission to liberate the future generation from the oppression they face as Palestinians.

Lebanese School and the School Principal, Fadia

Lebanese school (LS) is a Christian school, founded in 1882 as a missionary school, in a poor rural area in the North of Lebanon. The area is dominated by a strict Muslim faith with a political dominance in the government. It accommodates 1,054 students in total, 92% of whom are Muslims, and 8% of whom are Christians. The principles lie in Greek Catholic Christian faith, and French is the first language. Muslim parents send their children to this school as they believe it provides better quality education, despite the clashes between their understanding and the school's mission over the religion-based education.

The principal, Fadia, is a resilient religious woman, a nun with strong faith in Christian beliefs with 8 years of experience as a principal. She has awareness of the school's position and mission, of the community's cultural and societal realities, and of the religious political influence and dominance and a resultant awareness that she needs to be cautious as she makes her daily school-related decisions. She has passion for serving others, especially disempowered women. She considers school a space to cultivate love of one another, citizenship, and openness, and to break the social differences among all stakeholders.

This school's goal is to "harmoniously develop the physical, moral, and intellectual abilities of all learners, help them to gain a greater sense of responsibility, to act in solidarity and to be open to dialogue so that they can get involved in different acts of human community work." It was intentionally situated in the Beqaa area, characterized as a high-needs community. Considered a private school, students have to pay a tuition fee. More than half of the parents are of low SES and struggle with meeting these expenses. They can be considered as secluded marginalized communities trying to make a decent living to provide a route for their children to escape poverty and exclusion through education.

The Story of Fadia

Fadia emphasized that her SJ leadership stems from her core Christian beliefs based on openness, compassion, dialogue, and love. Her religious background shapes her beliefs and views; she explains, "I live by Jesus' way: Who is without a sin? And Augustine's love and do what you will." She describes herself as a resilient, determined believer. Her deep conviction is that one needs to have a mission and be passionate about addressing the struggles and injustices. She believes that one "has to live SJ in all aspects of life. You have to have compassion for everyone, even the ones who are not similar to you." She described an SJ leader as someone who is aware of the differences and prejudice in and outside school, is ready to address these injustices, and committed to embrace all students regardless of the differences. Based on her situated awareness, Fadia worked through three major SJ issues in terms of religious and political polarization, limited rural experiences, and poverty.

Despite the school's pride in Christian faith, Muslim parents seek to enroll their children in this school, known for its high-quality education. Nevertheless, the school needed to heed the dominant culture of the local community and had to include Islamic religious studies. Thus, students would experience some conflicting ideas related to religious practices:

> While at home they may be told that females need to wear a veil or they'd be considered sinners. I don't wear one. Also, Islam has the notion of martyrdom, so kids are taught certain religious beliefs conflicting with those of the school.

Since the school had students from various religious backgrounds and because Fadia was not happy with the idea that her students are attending

166 ▪ K. ARAR, D. ÖRÜCÜ, and J. MAHFOUZ

religious studies, she decided to omit these lessons altogether as a way to undercut the idea of religious differences for the sake of ensuring SJ. She narrated, "Islamic groups got upset. They fired 9 bullets on the school and threatened me. I didn't budge or give up."

She explained her strategy to keep peace projecting good intentions:

> I became more visible, active in the community—eventually the whole community supported me. I was everywhere, at funerals, weddings, events, socials. I was also respectful to their holidays such as Ramadan. I even requested to meet with the Sheikh to finalize an agreement. I set out my perspective and we agreed that we would no longer offer religious studies. I told them that I needed my space and autonomy if they wanted a quality education. I also invited them to be part of the school strategic plan.

In that sense, her SJ was enacted through inclusion and cultivation of religious openness, allowing a space for dialogue through acceptance of all students of various religious and political backgrounds and ensuring that all parties are heard. Her involvement with the community clarified her good intentions and willingness to accept all and basically "walk the talk."

Being in a rural school, the students felt inferior and uncared for due to their distance and exclusion from the resources and facilities of urban areas. Fadia tried to provide them with the learning experiences that they felt they were deprived of. She explained:

> I used to take my students to the cinema, taught them etiquette, had them experience new cultures by going on trips to urban cities. We raised money so that everybody could join these trips. I had my teachers attend professional development in Beirut. One teacher even mentioned that the students felt confident and that they were not backward in their skills and knowledge because I brought Beirut to them.

She even provided them with English classes in addition to French and Arabic to facilitate their application to prestigious universities in Beirut, which she thinks is part of her SJ initiatives. She had them visit these universities to make them feel they could achieve and be what they wanted. Fadia emphasized the importance of allowing students to express themselves and build their self-esteem, ready to be active citizens. She worked with her teachers and partnered with several NGOs creating spaces for learning, self-expression, and community service as part of her SJ leadership mission.

Fadia fought to ensure equity among all her students and staff, as she believed individuals need to sustain each other economically to thrive in a just society. As her students came from various SES levels, she was aware of the discrepancies:

A Comparison of Social Justice Leadership Meaning and Praxis ▪ **167**

Some come to school in private fancy cars; others in almost broken busses. Some wear brands—shoes evidently not less than $200 and others buy their outfits from thrift shops.

To address this issue, she urged all students to wear uniforms, even black shoes so they would not notice brands or worn out outfits. She believed that through such decisions as part of her continuous striving for SJ, students could develop a feeling of compassion toward one another, a feeling that they are all one.

CONCLUSION AND DISCUSSION

Recalling our aim, our findings indicate that national and ethnic cultures, organizational arrangements, intercultural interactions, and local educational ideologies lead to SJ challenges of these high-need schools in the ME, necessitating SJ leadership from the school principals *in this study* as detailed below.

Firstly, principals' SJ perceptions are shaped by their own values, which are the outcomes of their culture and circumstances they grew up in. Their belief in the power of education triggers their SJ endeavor. While Alp was driven by humanistic values and his strong belief in reducing inequalities, Fadia was driven by her faith, and Khalil was driven by diverse national agendas and related discrimination he experienced himself. In this respect, Fadia and Khalil are different from Alp in their struggle with the dominant groups in their community. Alp represents the majority in his context but he, similar to Khalil and Fadia, also works to address the diverse needs without discrimination. Khalil paints a more puritanical picture of school management overshadowed by a dire political reality, whereby he has to mediate between two conflicting and contested national projects.

Their determination and resilience to fix inequities through SJ (Marshall & Ward, 2004) and their concern for the common good, participation, justice, equity, and respect for the value and dignity of individuals and their cultural traditions (Murillo et al., 2010, p. 177) are evident within the harsh school contexts they operate in. This is most probably because of their inner motive and sensitivity towards different forms of inequalities they experienced and observed. Their conceptions of SJ influence their actions within their schools and beyond (Arar, Ogden, & Beycioglu, 2019). The impact of macro level politics and meso level dynamics on their SJ praxis (Angelle et al., 2015; Arar et al., 2017; Barnett & Stevenson, 2015) hinders their SJ leadership. For example, the community prejudice towards Syrian students and limited resources in the Turkish case, the marginalization and oppression in the Palestinian case, and religious and cultural clashes in the

168 ▪ K. ARAR, D. ÖRÜCÜ, and J. MAHFOUZ

Lebanese case, hinder the SJ efforts of the principals. Moreover, centralization and various forms of dilemmas are obstacles for SJ. Yet, their attempts to disrupt the long-standing systems of privilege in their school communities, promote change, and encourage compassion and reflection (Berkovich, 2014) is evident in their SJ implementations.

Secondly, concerning our question on SJ implementation at the school level, the three principals show similarities in this respect. Most frequently, in pursuit of promoting SJ, they take risks. Alp bargains with the wider community of rich people and confronts the Turkish parents and has to navigate through some policies cleverly, which is risky. In Fadia and Khalil's cases, they risk their lives regarding the religious and political conflicts in their contexts. All try to find and mobilize resources towards the good of their students and redistribute them. Moreover, their common tool for enacting SJ is their capacity of community engagement (DeMatthews, 2018). Regardless of the local adversities, they either utilize the power of the community or confront the community and change their perceptions . Whereas Alp fights with prejudice and facilitates his social network for resource making, Fadia struggles to consolidate different religions and Khalil safeguards his students from military tensions. Despite the different cultural and social contexts, all three have similar SJ visions and employ similar strategies to promote this vision such as role modeling, building communities both in the school and outside the school, and demonstrating an ethics of care and empathy for all students (Arar et al., 2019).

Finally, being at the intersection of multiple demands and diversity of contextual challenges, all three cases reflect the complex relationship between the leader and context (Gurr & Drysdale, 2018). Different forms of contested terrains and educational ideologies; wider political, social, and economic elements; and the evolution of the context shaped the work of the principals and furthered their SJ vision and implementations. To exemplify: Khalil had to resist and reconcile two different curriculums to help his students preserve their identities; Fadia had to reconcile Islam and Christianity through a holistic religious understanding; and Alp had to reconcile different expectations, work for the equal rights of his students, reduce prejudice and empower his students through negotiating with different external stakeholders. Their awareness of the realities, habits, characteristics, and dynamics of the society they live in (Klar & Brewer, 2013) led them to use their personal acumen effectively as they knew the inner dynamics of their communities. Thus, the three cases confirm Gurr and Drysdale's (2018) proposition that context shapes the leader's approach and the required leadership style to match the situation. If all three leaders failed to navigate the sociocultural elements effectively, they would have conflicts in their SJ pursuit.

This exploration of SJ leadership, from a non-Western perspective (Oplatka & Arar, 2016), reflects an agenda of inclusive and empowering education. Moreover, it helps us probe in detail how an educator working in a society dominated by inequitable practices can overcome political, economic, and cultural barriers and increase the potential for equity and SJ (Arar et al., 2019). This has implications in research and practice. We argue that principals' perceptions are shaped by sociocultural context and their personal acumen, but SJ leadership is not the automatic outcome of these two factors. Hence, development of SJ vision and enacting SJ leadership should be integral to leader preparation programs. Rather than focusing solely on effectiveness and efficiency, such programs should include issues such as cultural relevance, intercultural interactions, and mediating adverse local educational policies. The narratives of these school leaders are instructive and illuminating and those seeking to develop their practice as SJ leaders have a lot to learn from them for practice. Firstly, and most importantly, regardless of the context, a non-discriminatory approach with a humanistic stance is an asset of all three principals. Secondly, situated awareness and aligning practices based on the urgent needs is their common strategy. Thirdly, their moral compass; ethics of care and strong pursuit of SJ in terms of representation, redistribution, and recognition (Fraser, 2008) make their efforts remarkable. Fourthly, they exceeded their authority, autonomy, and official job descriptions such as mobilizing social networks, accompanying students through the checkpoints with soldiers, or battling with bullets of religious groups.

To sum up, what we, as researchers, learned from this crosscultural analysis is that SJ leadership is related to the value and belief systems of those who are concerned; yet an understanding of the contextual factors by school leaders is critical in meeting the realities of schools (Klar & Brewer, 2013). It is also about prioritizing the urgent contextual needs; navigating through diverse challenges and ideologies as well as maintaining care, dialogue, inclusion, and equity. Hence, contextual factors not only shape the perception but also the specific strategies of the school leaders.

REFERENCES

Angelle, P., Morrison, M., & Stevenson, H. (2015). 'Doing' social justice leadership: Connecting the macro and micro contexts of schooling. In J. Ryan & D. Armstrong (Eds.), *Working (with/out) the system: Educational leadership, micropolitics, and social justice* (pp. 95–118). Charlotte, NC: Information Age.

Angelle, P. S., & Torrance, D. (Eds.). (2019). *Cultures of social justice leadership*. Cham, Switzerland: Palgrave Macmillan.

Arar, K. (2012). Israeli Education Policy since 1948 and the state of Arab education in Israel. *Italian Journal of Sociology of Education, 4*(1), 113–145.

Arar, K., Beycioglu, K., & Oplatka, I. (2017). A cross-cultural analysis of educational leadership for social justice in Israel and Turkey: Meanings, actions and contexts. *Compare: A Journal of Comparative and International Education, 47*(2), 192–206.

Arar, K., Brooks, J. S., & Bogotch, I. (Eds.). (2019). *Education, immigration and migration: Policy, leadership and praxis for a changing world.* Bingley, England: Emerald.

Arar, K., Ogden, S., & Beycioglu, K. (2019). Social justice leadership, perceptions and praxis: A cross-cultural comparison of Palestinian, Haitian and Turkish principals. In *Cultures of social justice leadership* (pp. 43–66). Cham, Switzerland: Palgrave Macmillan.

Arar, K., Örücü, D., & Ak Küçükçayir, G. (2020). A holistic look at education of the Syrians under temporary protection in Turkey: Policy, leadership and practice. *International Journal of Leadership in Education, 23*(1), 7–23.

Bahous, R., & Nabhani, M. (2008). Improving schools for social justice in Lebanon. *Improving Schools, 11*(2), 127–141.

Banque Bemo. (2014). *Education in Lebanon.* Beirut, Lebanon: Author. Retrieved from https://www.bemobank.com/sites/default/files/annual_reports/Bemo%20AR%20-%20final%20low%20res.pdf

Baran, M. L., & Berry, J. R. (2015). *The International School Leadership Development Network's (ISLDN) high needs schools group research protocol and members' guide.* Washington, DC: British Educational Leadership, Management, and Administration and the University Council for Educational Administration.

Barnett, B., & Stevenson, H. (2015). International perspectives in urban educational leadership: Social justice leadership and high-need schools. In M. Khalifa, N. W. Arnold, A. F. Osanloo, & C. M. Grant (Eds.), *Handbook of urban school leadership* (pp. 518–531). Landham, MD: Rowman & Littlefield.

Berkovich, I. (2014). A socio-ecological framework of social justice leadership in education. *Journal of Educational Administration, 52*(3), 282–309.

Bogotch, I. E. (2002). Educational leadership and social justice: Practice into theory. *Journal of School Leadership, 12*(2), 138–156.

Bryant, M., Cheng, A., & Notman, R. (2014). Exploring high need and social justice leadership in schools around the globe. *Management in Education, 28*(3), 77–119.

Central Bureau of Statistics. (2019). *Israel in figures—Rosh Hashana selected annual data.* Jerusalem, Israel: Author. Retrieved from https://old.cbs.gov.il/reader/newhodaot/hodaa_template.html?hodaa=201911304

DeMatthews, D. E. (2018). *Community engaged leadership for social justice: A critical approach in urban schools.* New York, NY: Routledge.

Dimmock, C., & Walker, A. (2010). Developing comparative and international educational leadership and management: A cross-cultural model. *School Leadership and Management, 20*(2), 143–160.

Education Reform Initiative. (2018). *Education monitor report.* Retrieved from http://www.egitimreformugirisimi.org/wpcontent/uploads/2017/03/EIR_2017_2018_29.11.18.pdf

Fraser, N. (2008). *Scales of justice: Reimagining political space in a globalizing world* (Vol. 31). New York, NY: Columbia University Press.

Gibton, D. (2011). Post-2000 law-based educational governance in Israel: From equality to diversity. *Educational Management, Administration and Leadership, 39*(4), 434–454.

Greenfield, W., & Akkary, R. (1998 April). *Leadership and work context of public and private secondary schools in the Republic of Lebanon.* [Paper presention]. The Annual Meeting of American Educational Research Association, San Diego, CA, United States.

Gurr, D., & Drysdale, L. (2018). Leading high-need schools: Findings from the International School Leadership Development Network. *International Studies in Educational Administration, 46*(1), 147–156.

Gurr, D., Drysdale, L., Clarke, S., & Wildy, H. (2014). High-need schools in Australia: The leadership of two principals. *Management in Education, 28*(3), 86–90.

Harris, E. (2014). A grid and group explanation of social justice: An example of why frameworks are helpful in social justice discourse. In I. Bogotch & C. Shields (Eds.), *International handbook of educational leadership and social[in] justice.* London, England: Springer.

Jean-Marie, G., Normore, A. H., & Brooks, J. (2009). Leadership for social justice: Preparing 21st century school leaders for new social order. *Journal of Research on Leadership Education, 4*(1), 1–31.

Klar, H. W., & Brewer, C. A. (2013). Successful leadership in high-needs schools: An examination of core leadership practices enacted in challenging contexts. *Educational Administration Quarterly, 49*(5), 768–808.

Koren, D. (2017). Eastern Jerusalem: End of an intermediate era. *The Jerusalem Institute for Strategic Studies.* Retrieved from https://jiss.org.il/en/eastern-jerusalem/

Mahfouz, J., El-Mehtar, N., Osman, E., & Kotok, S. (2019). Challenges and agency: Principals responding to the Syrian refugee crisis in Lebanese public schools. *International Journal of Leadership in Education, 23*(1), 24–40.

Marshall, C., & Rossman, G. (2012). *Designing qualitative research* (2nd ed.). Thousand Oaks, CA: SAGE.

Marshall, C., & Ward, M. (2004). "Yes, but...": Education leaders discuss social justice. *Journal of School Leadership, 14*(5), 530–563.

MEHE. (2011). *The Ministry of Education and Higher Education: Achievements 2010.* Retrieved from http://www.databank.com.lb/docs/MEHE-Progress%20Report_of_Ministry%20of_Education_18_5_2011_(Repaired).pdf

Ministry of National Education. (2018). *National education statistics formal education 2017–2018.* Retrieved from https://sgb.meb.gov.tr/ mcb_iys_dosyalar/2018_09/06123056_

Morrison, M. (2017). *Conceiving context: The origins and development of the conceptual framework. In P. S. Angelle (Ed.), A global perspective of social justice leadership for school principals.* Charlotte, NC: Information Age.

Morrison, M., McNae, R., & Branson, C. M. (2015). Multiple hues: New Zealand school leaders' perceptions of social justice. *Journal of Educational Leadership, Policy and Practice, 30*(1), 4–16.

Murakami, E. T., Kearney, W. S., Scott, L., & Alfaro, P. (2018). Leadership for the improvement of a high poverty/high minority school. *ISEA, 46*(1), 2–21.

172 ▪ K. ARAR, D. ÖRÜCÜ, and J. MAHFOUZ

Murillo, J., Krichesky, G., Castro, A., & Hernández, R. (2010). Liderazgo para la inclusión escolar y la justicia social. Aportaciones de la investigación [Leadership for school inclusion and social justice. Contributions of research]. *Revista Latinoamericana de Inclusión Educativa, 4*(1), 169–186.

Ogden, S. B. (2017). Becoming an educational leader for social justice: A micro/meso/macro examination of a southern U.S. principal. *Research in Educational Administration & Leadership, 2*(1), 54–76.

Oplatka, I., & Arar, K. H. (2016). Leadership for social justice and the characteristics of traditional societies: Ponderings on the application of western-grounded models. *International Journal of Leadership in Education, 19*(3), 352–369.

Strauss, A. L., & Corbin, J. (1998). *Basics of qualitative research: Techniques and procedures for developing grounded theory* (2nd ed.). Thousand Oaks, CA: SAGE.

Sun, J., & Leithwood, K. (2017). Calculating the power of alternative choices by school leaders for improving student achievement. *School Leadership & Management, 37*(2), 80–93.

The Association for Civil Rights in Israel. (2017). *East Jerusalem facts and figures, 2017.* Retrieved from http://www.acri.org.il/en/wp-content/uploads/2017/05/Facts-and-Figures-2017.pdf

Theoharis, G. (2007). Social justice educational leaders and resistance: Toward a theory of social justice leadership. *Educational Administration Quarterly, 43*(2), 221–258.

Weldon, F. D. (2012). *Evaluating leadership styles of high-performing versus low-performing at risk schools* (Unpublished Doctoral Thesis). University of Phoenix, Phoenix, Arizona.

CHAPTER 10

ECONOMIC, CULTURAL, ASSOCIATIONAL, AND CRITICAL JUSTICE IN SCHOOLS IN CATALONIA, SPAIN AND BAJA CALIFORNIA, MEXICO

A Pilot Study

Brian Corrales-Maytorena
Benemérita Escuela Normal Estatal "Profr. Jesús Prado Luna"

Claudia Navarro-Corona
Technologic of Monterrey

Charles Slater
California State University Long Beach

Patricia Silva
University of Lleida

Serafin Antúnez
University of Barcelona

Michael E. Lopez
California State University Long Beach

Educational Leadership for Social Justice and Improving High-Needs Schools, pages 173–199
Copyright © 2021 by Information Age Publishing
All rights of reproduction in any form reserved.

174 ■ B. CORRALES-MAYTORENA et al.

There is increasing attention to social justice in education around the world (Bogotch & Shields, 2014). Schools can perpetuate the status quo, or they can be an instrument to overcome inequities and change society. This study is part of the ongoing International Study of Leadership Development Network (ISLDN) sponsored by British Educational Leadership Management and Administration Society (BELMAS) and the University Council for Educational Administration (UCEA) to examine social justice leadership of school directors in countries around the world. The network is made up of researchers who have completed qualitative studies of school directors who were identified as social justice leaders in high-needs schools (Gurr, Drysdale, & Good, 2019; Gurr, Drysdale, Longmuir, & McCrohan, 2019). It is connected to a study by the high-needs strand of ISLDN (Torres-Arcadia, Murakami, & Moral, 2019).

Much of the ISLDN research has been grounded in the views of social justice presented by Cribb and Gewirtz (2003, 2005). They developed this theory while working in schools in London, primarily serving African Caribbean students. They described three types of social justice: economic justice, cultural justice, and associational justice. Economic justice assures equal opportunity as well as a minimum standard of living; cultural justice includes recognition of a person individually and as a member of an ethnic group; associational justice refers to encouraging the participation of all. Woods (2005) has added developmental justice, which refers to educating every student to the highest potential.

We have added another type of social justice called *critical examination of society*. It is based on Shields' (2010, 2016) concept of transformative leadership. Shields proposed that transformational leadership should be extended to include a social justice perspective called transformative leadership. She studied the pedagogical conceptions of principals in relation to social justice and concluded that transformative leadership takes into account how inequalities in the outside world affect the results of what happens inside educational organizations.

This study reports on social justice leadership in schools in Mexico and Spain. There is a need to broaden the perspective from English speaking countries to include understandings of social justice in Latin America. The purpose of this study is to know to what extent the directors of schools in Catalonia, Spain and Baja California, Mexico perceive that their schools are socially just and to analyze the barriers that hinder the promotion of impartiality, respect, participation, and critical reflection on society.

The literature review addresses the historical development of the concept of social justice in Latin America. Cribb and Gewirtz's concepts of economic, cultural, and associative justice are very similar to those used in Latin America and serve as a guide for this review. First, we review the study of the term educational justice in the literature in Latin American

Economic, Cultural, Associational, and Critical Justice ▪ **175**

and connect it to the work of Cribb and Gewirtz (2003), Shields (2010), and Woods (2005). Then we adopt the term educational justice to describe issues of equality, equity, and inclusion in schools, and we look at the role of school directors and teachers in promoting educational justice. Following the literature review, we outline the methodology used to conduct a pilot study with a social justice questionnaire. The discussion section examines the views of school directors about parent involvement and the way they see social justice in the broader society.

THE STUDY OF SOCIAL JUSTICE IN LATIN AMERICA

Addressing the concept of social justice in education that operates in Latin America requires examination of different terms that refer to the rights of groups that have been systematically disadvantaged by social policies (Peña, 2012). This section reviews different works obtained from a literature review of the concept of social justice in Scopus, and open search engines such as Redalyc and Google Scholar. Search results yielded 32 studies from Argentina, Brazil, Venezuela, Chile, Costa Rica, Peru, Mexico, and Colombia.

Social justice, in a broad framework, refers to the conditions of access and participation of different groups in society to primary rights such as health care, equal treatment under the law, and access to job opportunities and education, especially for groups that have been systematically or historically excluded, in relation to the conditions of the dominant groups (Aguilar, 2016; Jiménez, Lalueza, & Fardela, 2017; León, 2005). Social justice disrupts education and influences both access and results. The present review covers associated concepts such as equity, equality, and inclusion as conceptual tools that help in the discussion about the ways in which education is offered as a right for all.

BASIC NOTIONS OF THE STUDY OF JUSTICE
IN THE EDUCATIONAL FIELD

Authors such as Latapí (1993) and Málaga (2016) in Mexico have reviewed the genealogy of the concept of justice. Málaga identified four groups of conceptualizations that allow us to account for the progression of the understanding of justice. A first group composed of Plato, Aristotle, and Thomas Aquinas, associate justice with laws of the state and natural laws. A second group of concepts based on Hobbes, Locke, Kant, and Rousseau expresses social justice in terms of democratic forms and the rights of individuals. A third group, which integrates the contributions of Smith, Mill, Hume, Spencer, Marx, Kropotkin, Rawls, and Habermas, refers to justice

176 ▪ B. CORRALES-MAYTORENA et al.

associated with the free market, private property, equality, ethics, and moral principles. Contemporary authors such as Anderson (1999) and Alexander (2008) form a fourth group that refers to justice as empowerment, especially of those who have been marginalized.

In a similar way, Latapí (1993) discusses the concept of distributive justice in which each person is treated according to what he or she merits; that is, "give to each his own." From this classical view, the concept of equality prevails. Latapí discusses two currents of equality. The first is to seek happiness and well-being for the greatest number of people, and the second is that social values such as freedom, opportunity, income, and wealth must be distributed equally.

The contributions made by Murillo and Hernández (2011) in Spain are the foundation for different Latin American authors. They identify the existence of three basic currents of social justice: distribution, recognition, and participation, which mirror those of Cribb and Gewirtz (2003). The Colombian De la Cruz (2016) describes each of these currents. The first current, distributive, refers to the distribution of rights such as freedom, wealth, opportunities, access, and income. These primary goods must be distributed according to principles of equality, equity, and merit. A second current refers to justice as recognition. From this position, the focus is on those who are historically or systematically excluded. Inclusion and openness to diverse groups as well as attention to excluded segments of society, are the basic orientation of justice. The third current refers to participation. Justice is addressed in terms of collaboration and decision-making and in the acquisition of active positions by those who have not had prior access and have been marginalized or excluded. Thus, justice can be understood as inclusion of disadvantaged groups (Chavez, 2013), access to resources, and the right to compensation for losses due to inequality (Fernández, 2013). These notions can be transferred to the ways in which educational policy and schools address diversity.

EDUCATIONAL JUSTICE IN LATIN AMERICA

The term social justice has not been used widely in Latin America, but the term educational justice has a history in the literature. The Latin American origins of the configuration of the concept of educational justice go back to studies of Pablo Latapí (1964a, 1964b). Educational justice is defined in distributive and remedial terms; educational policy establishes the right to education for all members of society including marginalized groups. Latapí insists that justice based on distribution is insufficient because other notions of justice are required in addition to distributive. For example, remedial justice is necessary to address past inequities.

Economic, Cultural, Associational, and Critical Justice ▪ **177**

In the sixties, the concept of educational justice served as a tool to enunciate inequalities and exclusion of students in the Mexican educational system (Latapí, 1993). Aguilar (2017) developed a concept of educational justice in Mexico, Argentina, and Spain that became a critical tool to advocate for students' right to an education, especially in the face of published reports that only reported positive developments in education. Thus, in its beginnings, educational justice referred to inequalities in schools propitiated by educational policy and the need for compensation for inequalities among students.

Schmelkes (2011) in Mexico, Peña (2012) and Martínez and Soler (2015) in Colombia, León (2005) in Venezuela, and Tedesco (2012) in Argentina, reported works that synthesized the injustices of educational systems and revealed structures that excluded and denied access and participation to certain groups (Martínez & Soler, 2015). Disproportionate increase in educational enrollment operated without an increase of the gross domestic product (GDP) in education (Peña, 2012). The process of selecting students in schools privileged the hegemonic culture (Di Piero, 2015; Jiménez et al., 2017) and politicians showed disinterest in addressing inequalities reported by Latin American researchers (Muñoz, 2016).

During the 1980s, equality, inclusion, and equity emerged as central concepts of educational policy (Martínez, 2016; Novaro, 2012). Equality was conceptualized as opportunities that were consistent in offering positions based on meritocratic principles and not associated with people's origin (Di Franco, 2016). In this sense, part of the struggle for equality is the fight against discrimination that does not allow marginalized groups the opportunities that members of hegemonic groups have.

Equity, in addition to access of opportunities, takes into account inequalities in order to compensate for disparities. In this sense, while equality favors access, equity recognizes differences and seeks to compensate them (De la Cruz, 2016). These concepts are not only discussed in terms of their development, but also in terms of their antithesis: inequality and inequity, which are used as descriptors of the social status and origin of students. Inclusion and exclusion are associated with discrimination of affected groups (Martínez & Soler, 2015); however, in education, exclusion is not limited to the deprivation of access to this right; but also by discrimination and segregation of those within the educational system because of their ethnicity, sexual orientation, origin, or other personal characteristics (Blanco, 2009).

The 1990s saw renewed emphasis on the concept of educational justice. Aguilar (2016, 2017) argues that this new discussion of the concept derived from the inadequacy of the concepts of equality, inclusion, and equity to deal with social complexity. Examples include the work on inclusion of the migrant community in Argentina, carried out by Martínez (2016); studies on equality between women and men in the university context in Brazil and

178 ■ B. CORRALES-MAYTORENA et al.

Spain (Montané & Pessoa, 2012); and the exclusion of women and members of indigenous communities from "prestigious" professions such as science, engineering, technology, or mathematics (STEM; Montané & Pessoa, 2012). In Mexico, Ordorika (2015) also analyzed the differences in access to education between men and women; the author points out that this disparity is not only among students, but also among academic personnel who participate in collegiate bodies or positions of authority at the university.

A separate line of work analyzes programs and curriculum. For example, Martínez and Soler (2015) discuss the tensions and challenges presented by the curriculum for teacher training. They favor incorporation of diverse curricula in education in a way that contributes to the balance between equal opportunities and knowledge differences. Also, Málaga (2016) made contributions on curricular justice and analyzed the basic education curricula in Mexico to determine the concept of justice in operation. The author concluded that there are at least two curricula: in preschool education, the classic concept of justice, according to Plato, Aristotle, and Thomas Aquinas, applies; that is, it is based on a review and understanding of the laws of the State. On the other hand, in primary and secondary education, the concept is more democratic and attached to ideas of equality, ethics, and moral principles.

EDUCATIONAL JUSTICE IN SCHOOL SYSTEMS

Education is the fundamental axis for the construction of a more democratic and open society (Peña, 2012), even as the field struggles against discrimination that prevents some from reaching the possibilities that others have (Di Franco, 2016). Education contributes to social mobility and to the understanding of cultures (Blanco, 2006), and is a tool for the construction and stabilization of a social order (Bianchetti, 2005). However, the school is far from able to respond to all social needs (Guarro, 2002).

Blanco (2006) points out the existence of three strategies carried out by countries to move towards a fairer condition regarding the right to education. The first strategy is to grant the right to education to people who historically have not had access, have had obstacles or are still excluded. The second is the adaptation of schooling to groups according to their mother tongue, their cultural, social, gender, and physical capacity. The third strategy is the adaptation of teaching to learning capacities and their referents; in this sense, it is no longer the communities that have to adapt to the system, but vice versa (Blanco, 2006).

However, in general, educational research presents a marked critical tendency toward educational policies aimed at incorporating market logic. Neoliberalism and globalization deepen differences and inequality in Latin

America. Efficiency is opposed to the cultures of equity and equality included in the political discourse itself (Fernández, 2013). Policies outside of the school are dominated by logics away from the context and experience of those in the school and as a result, the participants in the school become invisible. This installation of a dominant culture favors the processes of exclusion in which the minority cultures present in society are ignored (Martínez & Soler, 2015). Educational research exposes the need to permanently question how development and global economic growth can contribute to the reduction of inequalities. Given official discourses of politics, there are silences with respect to certain groups and how they will benefit (Peña, 2012).

In this framework, the concepts of equity and inclusion are once again established as useful tools for analyzing social justice. De la Cruz (2016) argues the need for educational policy to establish advantageous conditions for the most disadvantaged and encourages constant questioning on how to improve the condition of the worse off. Therefore, when studying educational policy proposals, the recipients, and those responsible for organizing support, the definition of disciplinary contents and teaching strategies should be considered (Bianchetti, 2005).

Despite the efforts being made by countries in education and the discussion of the tensions from educational research, authors such as Castillo-Cedeño (2015) contend that it is necessary to have legislative and regulatory frameworks that require the identification and inclusion of the diversity of groups and cultures, in addition to the educational philosophies that guide practices, curricular plans, and projects. Too often, the school is not managing to contribute to equal opportunities nor is it being an instrument of social mobility, but, on the contrary, continues to reproduce and accentuate inequalities of student origin (Bianchetti, 2005).

EDUCATIONAL JUSTICE IN SCHOOLS

Teachers and administrators are in direct contact with marginalized, segregated, or excluded social groups. An idea that basically serves as a starting point is that students arrive at the educational institution with unequal conditions originated in their social capital, the income of the parents, the social capital of their families (Blanco, 2006), levels of security, housing conditions, and even labor exploitation (Martínez, 2016); and these differences can be accentuated by thoughtless actions that arise in educational policy and the school.

The difficulties traversed by students from less favored contexts are not due exclusively to their personal characteristics. Complications arise that originate in the operation of the school, in the school culture, and in the

180 ■ B. CORRALES-MAYTORENA et al.

actions of those who participate in it. The installation of these obstacles can happen implicitly to the school or explicitly (Jiménez et al., 2017). When this occurs, new forms of exclusion are presented. Blanco (2009), for example, describes the "exclusive inclusion" that affects the school population by keeping students segregated by race, gender, or other characteristics.

Torres (2010) points out that in order to achieve a "multivocality" in education it is necessary to include all groups. The author argues that it is desirable to increase the inclusion of different groups in university education, such as the poor, the underemployed, the unemployed, and indigenous people; in this way the university will fully comply with offering education to society. The author, referring to university education, points out that the degree to which different groups are included, such as the poor, underemployed, unemployed, and indigenous, is the degree to which greater "brightness and luster" will be achieved. Education for justice requires (Castillo-Cedeño, 2015) explicit intentions to put into force provisions that allow access, participation, and equality for all (Di Franco, 2016).

Thus, the role of the school is described as the responsibility of offering equal opportunities of access and permanence, but also to promote the analysis of the social structures that generate oppression and to elaborate lines of action that increase the probabilities of resistance and transformation of the realities of marginalization (Di Franco, 2016). Fernández (2013) points out that justice is not obtained by the school alone, but produced in combination with the family, social environment, and individual characteristics (Fernández, 2013). The role of the school is to provide a diversity of management strategies.

MANAGING DIVERSITY EDUCATIONAL JUSTICE

Jiménez and Montecinos (2018) identify five ways in which teachers manage diversity in the classroom:

1. Make pedagogical adaptations to teach students from different cultures and students with special needs and overcome achievement gaps among students.
2. Promote harmonious human relations among students and place special emphasis on classroom climate to develop relationships. Diversity is conceptualized as an opportunity for individual and social skills.
3. Recognize the needs of groups that are not members of the dominant culture. Focus on historical and contemporary conditions of oppression to address inequalities.

Economic, Cultural, Associational, and Critical Justice ▪ **181**

4. Multicultural education calls for a reformulation of equitable educational approaches for all groups present in the school to address themes of power and privilege within the classroom and alters the hegemonic view.
5. Multicultural education along with social reconstruction transcends traditional schooling to help students become committed to social change. Students reflect on ways to change the structures that allow inequality, discrimination, and oppression.

Each of these ways of managing diversity requires leadership. The change does not occur without an explicit purpose or by accident; it requires vision and provision on the part of educators for the execution of practices that are developed in educational justice frameworks and for social justice. According to León (2005),

> We do not share those criteria that agree with the fact that the role of teachers is reduced to imposing an official truth, directed by a regime that analyzes, executes, makes decisions, and manages citizens as puppets, according to their political, economic, or ideological convenience. (p. 19)

School directors and teachers are the ones who must translate the guidelines of educational and curricular policy into concrete actions, appropriate to the context and its diverse groups. This action entails responding to extreme but not infrequent possibilities of providing access to education to those who have been disadvantaged, but also to students with extraordinary abilities, while at the same time attending to the external demands of the school (Fernández, 2013). Therefore, education for social justice requires competent educators whose training includes a clear understanding of the sense of justice that we wish to transmit to future generations (Sanz & Serrano, 2016). If the heritage to be communicated is full of concepts and contents of dominant cultures, it can detract from teaching that seeks to erode fundamental pillars of society that are socially unjust (Tedesco, 2012).

METHODOLOGY

The ISLDN project is now entering a quantitative phase to build knowledge across samples, and a number of questionnaires have been developed. The one most relevant to social justice was a pioneering work with a small sample in Canada. Zhang, Goddard, and Jakubiec (2018) found a relationship between school leadership and community context. These two variables played a prominent role as will be seen in the results section of this quantitative study. We decided to include these variables from Zhang et al.

182 ▪ B. CORRALES-MAYTORENA et al.

as well as others in a new questionnaire for this study that was connected to the theoretical framework of Cribb and Gewirtz (2003).

The project includes the development of a questionnaire that addresses the factors that help and hinder social justice leadership. Pam Angelle identified factors from the qualitative data: school culture, teacher characteristics, resources, teacher–student communication, policy, politics, community involvement, and principal behaviors (P. Angelle, personal communication, July 10, 2017). These factors formed the basis for the first draft of the questionnaire developed in this study.

An earlier questionnaire based on Angelle's factors was administered in Scotland in 2017 and plans are underway to administer another version in the United States. The purpose of this study was to develop and administer a questionnaire in Spanish speaking countries for the first time.

The Instrument

This study began with Angelle's factors mentioned above (school culture, teacher characteristics, resources, teacher–student communication, policy, politics, community involvement, and principal behaviors). The questionnaire focused on four types of social justice: economic justice or fairness of distribution; cultural justice or respect and recognition; associational justice or inclusion; and critical justice or transformative understandings. School directors were asked to rate the extent to which each social justice item described their school. The items were arranged in a Likert scale from one to five: 1 was *totally disagree,* 2 was *disagree,* 3 was *neither agree nor disagree,* 4 was *agree,* fi5ve was *totally agree.* Figure 10.1 shows the relationship between the dimensions of social justice and the questionnaire items that were perceived as supports and barriers. A copy of the questionnaire is in the Appendix.

The Sites

Baja California, Mexico and Catalonia, Spain were selected for several reasons. Baja California and Catalonia have been involved in previous ISLDN studies and local researchers conducted the study. The schools had experienced an increase in migration and were attempting to serve populations of students from poor families. These areas also represent Spanish speaking regions that complement other ISLDN sites where English or other languages are spoken.

This study was intended to complement the study done by our colleagues in the High-Needs Strand of ISLDN (Torres-Arcadia, Murakami, & Moral,

Economic, Cultural, Associational, and Critical Justice ▪ **183**

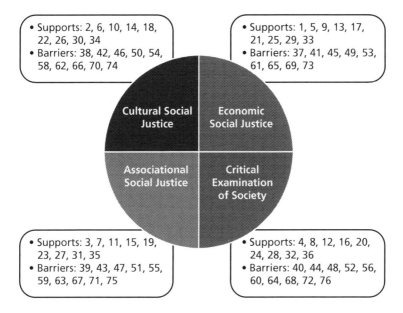

Figure 10.1 Relationship between the dimensions of social justice and the questionnaire items that were perceived as supports and barriers.

2019), who completed cases in Mexico, Spain and the United States. The sample in Mexico came from the south, where there were 30,000 inhabitants, half of whom spoke indigenous languages, such as, Maya or Nahuatl. They were mostly farmers with a low level of literacy. Most students worked during the day to provide income for their families and most did not perform well on standardized tests (ENLACE, 2013; PLANEA, 2015). Their sample in Spain came from Granada, with a population of 18,392, including many immigrants from low socioeconomic backgrounds, who were illiterate and unemployed.

Our samples came from multiple schools. In Mexico, school directors came from Baja California in the north of the country. Much of the population migrated from the south, spoke indigenous languages, and worked in agriculture. The overall area, however, also included students from middle class families who performed well on standardized tests. Our sample in Spain came from Catalonia, an area wealthier than Granada, but one that has experienced an increase in immigration from non-native speaking families who suffer from unemployment and poverty. This sample also included school directors who served middle class families.

Catalonia is an autonomous community within Spain, located northeast of the Iberian Peninsula. It has a population of 7.5 million inhabitants, which represents 16.1% of the total 46.5 million Spanish population (INE,

184 ■ B. CORRALES-MAYTORENA et al.

2017). It is a country that has always received a large migrant population from other regions of Spain. A new phenomenon between 2000 and 2010 was that Catalonia became a destination for preferential emigration in Southern Europe. For the first time, many communities and schools were experiencing an influx of migrants who spoke neither Catalan or Spanish.

Baja California is a Mexican state that is located in the northeast of the country. It is bordered on the north by California. It has a population of 3,315,766 inhabitants, which represents approximately 2.8% of the country's total population (INEGI, 2017). It has five autochthonous indigenous communities and 41,000 indigenous language speakers of various ethnicities. In the area of population flow, Baja California is a federated entity of a "high attraction of migrants," people who come from states located in central and southern Mexico (Corona, 2000; Viramontes, Vázquez, & Ramírez, 2013). In the same way, it is a recipient of migrants from Central American countries such as Haiti, Guatemala, El Salvador, and Honduras (COPLADE, 2016).

Sample

Researchers contacted educational authorities to obtain a list of elementary school directors in Baja California and in Catalonia. Questionnaires were emailed to 50 directors in the Fall of 2019 and responses were received from 22 directors in Baja California and 8 directors in Catalonia. The schools ranged in size from about 150–300 students and 18 teachers in Baja California and from about 350–400 students and 44 teachers in Catalonia.

Research Questions and Design

The purpose of this study was to determine the perceptions of school directors about social justice in their schools. There were four research questions that asked school directors about social justice in their schools:

What do school directors perceive as the factors that support social justice?

What do school directors perceive as factors that are barriers to social justice?

How do school directors perceive the dimensions [in Figure 10.1] when they are supportive of social justice?

How do school directors perceive the dimensions [in Figure 10.1] when they are barriers to social justice?

The research questions were tied to specific items on the questionnaire and were reported in tables for each question. A group of colleagues from Mexico, Spain, and the United States translated the questionnaire from English to Spanish.

ANALYSIS

The data were entered into SPSS and a code book developed to classify the factors examined and the dimensions of social justice leadership. There were composite variables for each of the nine factors for supports, 10 factors for barriers, four positive dimensions, and four negative dimensions. These composite variables are the mean scores, which were included in an SPSS file. Because of the small sample size, it was decided to report descriptive statistics only. Results are reported according to the research questions.

Supports for Social Justice

The first question was what do school directors perceive as the factors that support social justice within their school? The participants from Catalonia rated the items slightly lower than the participants from Baja California. Table 10.1 shows that both Baja California and Catalonia rated highly on most factors that supported social justice. They were all above four on a five point scale with the exception of two factors in Baja California (regulations and school policies) and three factors in Catalonia (resources, "outside of school" policies, and societal perspectives).

TABLE 10.1 Average Rating for Barriers to Social Justice

Supports	Baja, California; Mexico	Catalonia; Spain
School Culture	4.6591	4.5313
Teacher Characteristics	4.4809	4.1875
Resources	4.1591	3.8750
Students	4.6932	4.1250
School Education Policy	4.4091	4.2813
Regulations and Policies Outside of School	3.8182	3.0938
Family Participation	4.5909	4.1563
Management Practices	4.6818	4.1250
Societal Perspective	3.1932	2.3437

186 ▪ B. CORRALES-MAYTORENA et al.

Barriers to Social Justice

The second research question was what do school directors perceive as factors that are barriers to social justice? For most factors, neither sample agreed that there were barriers. However, Table 10.2 shows that both samples tended to agree that family context was a barrier, and Catalonia rated resources as the highest barrier with societal perspectives second.

These societal perspectives are outside of the control of the school, and only to a limited extent can the school advocate for more resources from central authorities by making the case for additional funds or solicit resources from other sources. Family context is also beyond the control of the school except insofar as the school can adopt an attitude of respect and inclusion versus a deficit approach.

Positive Dimensions of Social Justice

The third research question was how do school directors perceive the supports overall relating to each dimension of social justice? Table 10.3

TABLE 10.2 Average Rating for Barriers to Social Justice		
Barriers	Baja California, Mexico	Catalonia, Spain
School Culture	1.7841	1.6250
Teacher Characteristics	2.3674	2.5000
Resources	2.4091	3.5938
Students	1.4881	1.6563
School Education Policy	2.1932	3.0000
Regulations and Policies Outside of School	2.3409	3.0938
Family Context	2.7386	3.2188
Family Participation	2.6818	2.7500
Management Practices	1.7614	2.2812
Societal Perspectives	2.3636	3.3125

TABLE 10.3 Positive Dimensions of Social Justice		
Positive Dimensions	Baja California, Mexico	Catalonia, Spain
Economic Justice	4.2879	4.0156
Cultural Justice	4.4306	4.2778
Associational Justice	4.2304	3.5476
Critical	4.2626	3.5833

shows the average ratings for Baja California, Mexico and Catalonia, Spain. The dimensions of justice correspond to the items listed in Figure 10.1. For example, the rating of 4.2879 for economic social justice in Baja California, Mexico is the average of the responses to statements 1, 5, 9, 13, 17, 21, 25, 29, and 33. These are the items relating to supports for economic justice in Figure 10.1.

Baja California, Mexico had a high rating for each dimension of social justice, while Catalonia, Spain rated associational justice and critical justice somewhat lower. The higher ratings in Mexico may reflect recent changes in national politics, which seek an inclusive education that promotes social justice in every way, where teachers, in a professional community, constantly value their practices to recognize how they contribute to reducing actions that marginalize, discriminate against, or keep isolated the less favored. This idea allows us to assume that the manager, as a figure of leadership in the school, adopts the political-educational discourse and appropriates it in his practice.

Negative Dimensions of Social Justice

The fourth question was how do school directors perceive the dimensions when they are barriers to social justice? These are averages that correspond to the negative dimensions of social justice for items listed in Figure 10.1. Table 10.4 shows that both Baja California and Catalonia tended to disagree that most dimensions of social justice were barriers. However, Catalonia rated economic justice more highly as a barrier.

DISCUSSION

Several statements can summarize the mostly positive perceptions of the directors regarding the supports and barriers for social justice. In terms of supports, directors saw fair treatment, respect, and inclusion as values in their schools. They indicated that teachers promoted all aspects of social

TABLE 10.4 Negative Dimensions of Social Justice		
Negative Dimensions	Baja California, Mexico	Catalonia, Spain
Economic Justice	2.2207	2.9268
Cultural Justice	2.1778	2.4714
Associational Justice	2.2667	2.7750
Critical	2.2409	2.6375

188 ▪ B. CORRALES-MAYTORENA et al.

justice. They perceived that students were treated fairly and that they had a sense of the broader societal forces that affect their education. Directors perceived that school policy was based on fairness and respect, that parents were treated with respect, and that management practices were characterized by fairness and respect.

The directors' perceptions of what happens in their schools could be overly positive. This study did not investigate the perceptions of teachers, students, and others who might have different views from those of the director. The directors seem to be seeing social justice problems as predominantly emanating from society and while there is evidence from the research literature to support this, there may be a critical viewpoint within their own schools.

We might also be missing a critical perspective from the directors themselves. They did not report problems within their own schools, but recent interviews with experts in social justice leadership in Spain indicated that many school directors did not have a critical perspective, and that they needed more formation in social justice leadership (Slater, Silva, & Antúnez, 2019).

In Baja California, informal conversations with school directors have indicated that the work carried out inside the schools does go against broader social phenomena. It is common to hear that the schools teach and practice values that are hindered by societal practices against these values. Many of the problems that are experienced in the field of social justice, come from inequality, injustice, and discrimination in the community and the broader society.

In terms of barriers to social justice, directors did not see culture as a barrier to just treatment, respect, and participation. They did not see resistance of teachers as a barrier, nor did they see management practices as a barrier.

There were, however, several areas of concern that deserve additional discussion. Directors did not see financial, material, and human resources as a barrier in Baja California, but there was a tendency to see them as inadequate in Catalonia. According to Cribb and Gewirtz (2003, 2005), economic justice guarantees equal opportunities and a minimum standard of living. In schools, the purpose of financial resources not only implies the optimal and efficient operation and maintenance of schools, but also the creation of environments that favor the improvement of the students' learning and their integral formation.

In 2009, the state government of Baja California set a precedent to provide financial resources to educational centers. It outlined the self-management of resources and created the School Council of Social Participation made up of students, parents, teachers, union representatives, community members, and managers who are responsible for the planning, execution, and supervision of the assigned resources. These actions are likely related to the directors' opinion about fair use of resources.

The directors did not feel that fairness, respect, inclusion, and critical perspectives were prominent in society. Cultural justice includes the recognition of a person as an individual and as a member of a social group (Cribb & Gewirtz, 2003). In Mexico, and particularly in Baja California, the societal environment is characterized by economic crisis, insecurity, and political and cultural changes. This complex situation permeates the schools because "the school is clearly a sensitive crossroads of the problems that disturb contemporary society" (Ferreyro & Stramiello, 2007, p. 1) and the meeting point of multiple cultures.

In practice, school directors recognize a disruption between what is taught and promoted from school, and what occurs outside of it. According to the study participants, justice, inclusion, and critical perspectives are poorly identified in society outside the school boundaries.

Social problems become a school matter because they influence what goes on in schools. This is why Ferreyro and Stramiello (2007) state that social dynamics must be analyzed to understand what is happening in school, and schools must assume responsibility for how society is influencing practice.

Directors did not see policies within the school as barriers, but they did see barriers coming from regulations and policies outside of the school. The directors participating in the survey expressed that within their schools there are policies that favor social justice, which contrasts with those that come from regulations and policies outside of school. From their perspective, the latter can become a barrier to the delivery of justice.

From this perspective, educational policies make it difficult to create fair spaces, due to overuse of slogans related to resource management, the requirements of highly structured study programs loaded with content, and bureaucratic demands. For example, Zorrilla (2006) refers to the implementation of management improvement programs in Mexico since the 1990s, such as "La gestión en la escuela primaria" which was in effect between 1997 and 2000, and then the Programa Escueas de Calidad, which was launched in 2001 and is still in operation. According to the authors, these programs brought about changes in the way schools relate to the Mexican national education system by considerably increasing the demand on schools for verification of expenditures and bureaucratic procedures for approving school improvements and access to resources. Ibarrola (2012), Martínez (2016), and Martínez and Soler (2015) argue that these pre-established policies outside the educational establishments limit the autonomy of schools and exclude minority cultures.

Directors saw family context as a barrier to the participation of parents, and in some cases, they saw resistance of families to school initiatives. Shields (2010, 2016) recognizes that inequalities in the outside world affect what happens within educational organizations. The social reality of Mexico in recent times is abruptly different from what was known decades ago. Social transformations

190 ▪ B. CORRALES-MAYTORENA et al.

have changed the size, structure, and distribution of the population. This has gone from large traditional families to families of diverse form. A predominantly rural population is now concentrated in cities, with increased migration in border areas, and there are increasing numbers of women in the labor field. These transformations have impacted the economy, health services, education, and social development (Gutiérrez, Díaz, & Román, 2016).

Parents are exhausted from long working hours. Poverty, marginalization, insecurity, addiction, and crime are on the rise. Hence, the participating directors conceived of the family context as a barrier to parental involvement (Ordorica & Prud'homme, 2012).

School directors saw prejudice against marginalized groups as a problem in the school. Their view is consistent with Cordera, Ramírez, and Ziccardi (2008) who see social problems related to poverty and crime as part of Mexico's history. Discriminatory practices affect children because of race, gender, sexual orientation, religious beliefs, disabilities, and poverty.

CONCLUSION

These results are consistent with other ISLDN studies of social justice and high-needs schools, and they support the results of two studies in particular. The first study was conducted by Zhang, Goddard, and Jakubiec (2018) who highlighted the importance of leadership and community context in their study of school directors in Prince Edward Island, Canada. Like our study, they used a questionnaire to examine social justice, and they found a correlation between school leadership and community context. In the same way, school directors in our study reported concerns about the community and the larger society that impinged on their efforts to develop a more just community within the school.

The second ISLDN study by Torres-Arcadia et al. (2019) was a qualitative study that, apart from the United States, included two of the same countries that we studied: Mexico and Spain. The directors had to make adaptations to address their context. In Spain, the national curriculum was found to be inadequate to address the needs of poor and diverse immigrant populations. The director in Spain developed a shared leadership style to address diversity needs. In Mexico, the director focused on self-esteem and a sense of belonging for students and developed ways to involve parents. Torres-Arcadia et al. (2019) concluded:

> Common to all three schools was the importance of considering the context in which the students were immersed...We confirmed that principles and policies guiding fairness are dependent on each country's definition at a societal scale and consequently in their expectations of schooling. (p. 163)

Our study, and the work of ISLDN more generally, points to the interconnectedness of schools with their communities and communities with the larger society. School directors are concerned about these inter-relationships, and they may sense that they are being called upon to become aware of larger societal forces, and to make connections with their communities.

APPENDIX
Social Justice in the Schools of Catalonia and Baja California Questionnaire

Rating Scale

Strongly disagree, disagree, neither agree nor disagree, agree, strongly agree

BLOCK I

This block focuses on the support available to people who hold managerial positions to advance Social Justice

SCOPE: School Culture
1. Fair treatment is part of the school culture.
2. Respect for all people is part of the school culture.
3. The inclusion of all people is a value of the school.
4. The critical analysis of society is a value that is promoted in the school.

SCOPE: Teachers
5. Teachers treat students in their class fairly.
6. Teachers respect students in their class.
7. Teachers include all students in their class.
8. Teachers promote the critical analysis of society in their classes.

SCOPE: Resources
9. Resources (financial, material, human) are distributed fairly.
10. Resources (financial, material, human) are used to support those in the educational community who need it.
11. The School Board / Faculty Council participates in decisions on the use of resources.
12. There is a sensitivity about the influence of the social dimension in the distribution of school resources.

192 ▪ B. CORRALES-MAYTORENA et al.

SCOPE: Students

13. Students are treated fairly.
14. Students are respected.
15. Students are included.
16. Social factors influence the education of students in the school.

SCOPE: School Education Policy

17. The implementation of school policies promotes the fair treatment of all.
18. The implementation of school policies is based on respect for all.
19. The implementation of school policies is developed with contributions from members of the school community.
20. The implementation of school policies takes into account social dimensions.

SCOPE: Regulations and educational policies outside the school.

21. Educational regulations and policies outside the school promote fair treatment for all people.
22. Educational regulations and policies outside the school are based on respect for all people.
23. Regulations and educational policies outside the school are developed with contributions from the school community.
24. Educational regulations and policies outside the school consider social dimensions.

SCOPE: Families

25. Families are treated fairly.
26. Families are treated with respect.
27. Families are included in school activities.
28. The social dimension of families is taken into account in the development of school activities.

SCOPE: Management practices

29. The director treats all people fairly.
30. The director treats all people with respect.
31. The director includes all people in the educational community in decision making.
32. The director promotes reflection on the social dimension and its impact on school dynamics.

SCOPE: Social perspective

33. Society, in general, treats all people fairly.

Economic, Cultural, Associational, and Critical Justice ▪ **193**

34. Society, in general, treats all people with respect.
35. Society, in general, includes people from vulnerable groups.
36. Society, in general, maintains a critical perspective on social phenomena.

BLOCK II

This block focuses on the barriers that are presented to people who hold managerial positions to advance Social Justice

SCOPE: School culture
37. The culture of this school is a barrier to providing fair treatment to people.
38. The culture of this school is a barrier to respect for people.
39. The culture of this school is a barrier for the participation of all people.
40. The culture of this school is a barrier to critical reflection on society.

SCOPE: Teachers
41. Teacher resistance is a barrier to providing fair treatment to people.
42. The resistance of teachers is a barrier to the promotion of respect for people.
43. Teacher resistance is a barrier to the participation of all people.
44. Teacher resistance is a barrier to critical reflection on society.

SCOPE: Resources
45. Financial, material and human resources are a barrier to providing fair treatment.
46. Financial, material and human resources are a barrier to respect.
47. Financial, material and human resources are a barrier to the participation of all people.
48. Financial, material and human resources are a barrier to critical reflection on society.

SCOPE: Students
49. Students are treated unfairly.
50. Students are not respected.
51. Students are excluded.
52. Social factors do not influence the education of people studying at school.

194 ▪ B. CORRALES-MAYTORENA et al.

SCOPE: School Education Policy

53. The policies implemented by the educational authorities are a barrier to providing fair treatment to students.
54. The policies implemented by the educational authorities are a barrier to respect.
55. The policies implemented by the educational authorities are a barrier to the participation of the educational community.
56. The policies implemented by the educational authorities are a barrier to critical reflection on society.

SCOPE: Regulations and educational policies outside the school

57. Educational regulations and policies outside the school are a barrier to providing fair treatment for all people.
58. Educational regulations and policies outside the school are a barrier to respect for all people.
59. Regulations and educational policies outside the school are a barrier to the participation of the school community.
60. Educational regulations and policies outside the school are a barrier to critical reflection on society.

SCOPE: Family Context

61. The family context of the student body is a barrier to providing fair treatment.
62. The family context of the student body is a barrier to respect.
63. The family context of the student body is a barrier for the participation of all.
64. The family context of the student body is a barrier to critical reflection on society.

SCOPE: Families

65. Resistance of families to school initiatives is a barrier to providing fair treatment.
66. Resistance of families to school initiatives is a barrier to respect.
67. The resistance of families to school initiatives is a barrier to the participation of all.
68. The resistance of families to school initiatives is a barrier to critical reflection on society.

SCOPE: Management practices

69. Leadership at school is a barrier to providing fair treatment.
70. The leadership in the school is a barrier to the respect of all people.

Economic, Cultural, Associational, and Critical Justice ▪ **195**

71. Leadership in the school is a barrier to the participation of the entire educational community.
72. Leadership in school is a barrier to critical reflection on society.

SCOPE: Social perspective

73. Prejudices about people from vulnerable groups at school are a barrier to providing fair treatment.
74. Prejudices about people from vulnerable groups at school are a barrier to favoring respect.
75. Prejudices about people from vulnerable groups at school are a barrier to the participation of all people in the community.
76. Prejudices about people from vulnerable groups in school are a barrier to critical reflection on society.

REFERENCES

Aguilar, J. (2016). Hacia una historia conceptual de la justicia educativa en Iberoamérica. Sinéctica [Toward a conceptual history of educational justice in Iberoamerica: Synectic]. *Revista Electrónica de Educación, núm, 46,* 1–14.

Aguilar, J. (2017). Justicia educativa: Itinerario de su historia conceptual en México [Educational justice: Itinerary of its conceptual history in Mexico]. *Revista Electrónica de Investigación Educativa, 19*(2), 1–11.

Alexander, J. (2008). Towards a capability theory of justice. In A. Sen & M. Nussbaum (Eds.), *The political philosophy of capabilities and social justice* (pp. 53–77). Farnham, England: ASHGATE.

Anderson, E. (1999). What is the point of equality? *Ethics, 109*(2), 287–337.

Bianchetti, R. G. (2005). Las propuestas de transformación de la educación en los 90: Las paradojas (perversas) de hacer equilibrio entre la "lógica de mercado" y la "justicia social." El caso de Salta Espacios en Blanco [Proposals to transform education in the 90s: The paradoxes (perverse) of making equilibrium between the "logic of the market" and "social justice. The case of Salta Espacios en Blanco]. *Revista de Educación, núm, 15,* 89–114.

Blanco, R. (2006). La inclusión en educación: Una cuestión de justicia y de igualdad [Inclusive education: A question of justice and equality]. *Revista Electrónica Sinéctica, 29,* 19–27.

Blanco, R. (2009). El derecho a la educación de calidad para todos [The right to a quality education for all]. In *Organización de Estados Iberoamericanos, Experiencias educativas de segunda oportunidad* [Organization of Ibero-American States: Second opportunity experiences in education, Santiago, Chile]. Chile: SDL impresores.

Bogotch, I., & Shields, C. M. (Eds.). (2014). *International handbook of educational leadership and social (in) justice.* New York, NY: Springer.

196 ▪ B. CORRALES-MAYTORENA et al.

Castillo-Cedeño, I. (2015). Educar en la justicia social por ella y para esta: Una lucha ineludiblemente ética [To educate by and for social justice: An indubitably ethical fight]. *Revista Electrónica Educare, 19*(2) 467–478.

Chávez, J. (2013). Inclusión social y discriminación social [Social inclusion and social discrimination]. *Revista Lusófona de Educação, 24,* 135–150.

Comité de Planeación para el Desarrollo del Estado. (2016). *Estudio de situación socioeconómica de migrantes y extranjeros en Baja California* [Study of the socio-economic situation of migrants and foreigners in Baja California]. Baja California, Mexico: COPLADE.

Cordera, R., Ramírez, P., & Ziccardi, A. (Eds.). (2008). *Pobreza, desigualdad y exclusión social en la ciudad del siglo XXI* [Poverty, inequality and social exclusion in the city of the 21st century]. Mexico City, México: Siglo XXI: UNAM, Instituto de Investigaciones Sociales.

Corona Vázquez, R. (2000). *Migración interna/medición de la migración interestatal* [Internal migration: Measurement of interstate migration]. Demos, (013).

Cribb, A., & Gewirtz, S. (2003). Towards a sociology of just practices: An analysis of plural conceptions of justice. In C. Vincent (Ed.), *Social justice, education and identity* (pp. 15–30). Oxford, England: RoutledgeFalmer.

Cribb, A., & Gewirtz, S. (2005). Navigating justice in practice: An exercise in grounding ethical theory. *Theory and Research in Education, 3*(3), 327–342.

de Ibarrola Nicolín, M. (2012). Los grandes problemas del sistema educativo mexicano [The major problems of the Mexican educational system]. *Perfiles Educativos, 34*(SPE), 16–28.

De la Cruz, G. (2016). Justicia curricular: Significados e implicaciones. Sinéctica [Curricular justice: Significance and implications: Synectic]. *Revista Electrónica de Educación, 46,* 1–16.

Di Franco, M. G. (2016). Escuelas democráticas, justicia social y alteridad [Democratic schools, social justice and otherness]. *Praxis Educativa (Arg), 20*(1), 9–11.

Di Piero, M. E. (2015). ¿Mérito y azar? Nociones de justicia distributiva y selección soft: El caso de una escuela secundaria tradicional frente al mandato inclusor [Merit and chance? Notions of distributive justice and soft selection: The case of a traditional secondary school confronting a mandate for inclusion]. *Propuesta Educativa, núm, 43,* 152–154.

Evaluación Nacional de Logros Académicos en Centros Escolares. (2013). *Evaluación Escolar de Logro Académico en Centros Escolares* [Educational evaluation of academic achievement in schools]. Retrieved from https://mx.unoi.com/2013/09/17/publica-la-sep-los-resultados-de-la-ultima-prueba-enlace-2013/

Fernández, M. (2013). La igualdad, la equidad y otras complejidades de la justicia educativa [Equality and equity and other complexities of educational justice]. *Revista Portuguesa de Educação, 26*(2), 205–224.

Ferreyro, J., & Stramiello, C. (2007). Resignificar la escuela como escenario de participación [Redesigning the school as a scene of participation]. *Revista Iberoamericana de Educación, 42*(5), 1–7.

Guarro, A. (2002). *Currículum y democracia. Por un cambio de la cultura escolar* [Curriculum and democracy: For a change in school culture]. Barcelona, Spain: Octaedro.

Economic, Cultural, Associational, and Critical Justice ▪ **197**

Gurr, D., Drysdale, L., & Good, H. (2019). Global research on principal leadership. In R. Papa (Ed.), *Oxford encyclopedia of educational administration.* New York, NY: Oxford University Press.

Gurr, D., Drysdale, L., Longmuir, F., & McCrohan, K. (2019). Successful school leadership that is culturally sensitive but not context constrained. In *Educational leadership, culture, and success in high-need schools* (pp. 25–43). Charlotte, NC: Information Age.

Gutiérrez, R., Díaz, K., & Román, R. (2016). El concepto de familia en México: Una revisión desde la mirada antropológica y demográfica [The concept of family in Mexico: A review from an anthropological and demografic perspective]. *Ciencia Ergo Sum, 23*(3), 219–228.

Instituto Nacional de Estadística. (2017). *Informe Anual* [Annual Report]. Retrieved from https://www.ine.es/

Instituto Nacional de Estadística y Geografía. (2017). Anuario estadístico y geográfico de Baja California, México [Statistical and geographical yearbook of Baja California, Mexico]. Baja California, Mexico: State of Baja California.

Jiménez, F., Lalueza, J. L., & Fardella, C. (2017). Aprendizajes, inclusión y justicia social en entornos educativos multiculturales [Learning, inclusion and social justice in multi-cultural educational environments]. *Revista Electrónica de Investigación Educativa, 19*(3), 10–23.

Jiménez, F., & Montecinos, C. (2018). Diversidad, modelos de gestión y formación inicial docente: Desafíos formativos desde una perspectiva de justicia social [Diversity, models of management, and initial formation of teachers: Formative challenges from the perspective of social justice]. *Revista Brasileira de Educação, 23*, 1–21.

Latapí, P. (1964a). Educación y justicia social [Education and social justice]. *Excélsior, 22*(3), 13–44.

Latapí, P. (1964b). *Diagnóstico educativo nacional* [Diagnosis of National Education]. Mexico City, México: Textos universitarios.

Latapí, P. (1993). Reflexiones sobre la justicia en la educación [Reflections on social justice education]. *Revista latinoamericana de Estudios educativos, 23*(2), 9–41. Retrieved from http://www.cee.edu.mx/revista/r1991_2000/r_texto/t_1993_2_02.pdf

León, C. G. (2005). Política, ética y justicia social en la Educación Superior neoliberal [Politics, ethics, nad social justice in neoliberal higher education]. *Educere, 9*(29), 189–197.

Malaga, S. G. (2016). Significaciones de la justicia social: una mirada analítica a tres planes de estudio de educación básica Sinéctica [The signficance of social jsutice: An analytical perspective on three studies of elementary education plans]. *Revista Electrónica de Educación, 46*, 17.

Martínez, L. V. (2016). Niñez y migración: Concepciones sobre los derechos sociales en la escuela. ALTERIDAD [Conceptions about social rights in the school]. *Revista de Educación, 11*(1), 10–20.

Martínez, M. C. M., & Soler, C. S. (2015). Formación y acción pedagógica de los maestros: vínculos entre educación y justicia social [Formation and pedagogical action of teachers connected to education and social justice]. *Folios, 42*, 17–27.

198 ▪ B. CORRALES-MAYTORENA et al.

Montané, A., & Pessoa, M. E. (2012). Diálogo sobre género: justicia, equidad y políticas de igualdad en educación superior (Brasil y España) [Dialgoue about gender: Justice, equity, and policies of equality in higher education]. *Revista Lusófona de Educação, 21*, 97–120.

Muñoz, C. (2016). Relaciones entre educación y justicia [Relations between education and justice]. *Revista Latinoamericana de Estudios Educativos (México), 44*(4), 147–157.

Murillo, F., y Hernández, R. (2011). Trabajar por la justicia social desde la educación [Working for social justice in education]. *Revista Iberoamericana sobre Calidad, Eficacia y Cambio en Educación, 9*(4), 3–6. Retrieved from http://www. redalyc.org/pdf/551/55122156001.pdf

Novaro, G. (2012). Niños inmigrantes en Argentina: nacionalismo escolar, derechos educativos y experiencias de alteridad [Immigrant children in Argentina: Student nationalism, educational rights, and the experience of otherness]. *Revista Mexicana de Investigación Educativa, 17*(53), 459–483.

Ordorica, M., & Prud'homme, J. (2012). *Población* [Population]. Mexico City, México: El Colegio de México.

Ordorika, I. (2015). Equidad de género en la Educación Superior [Gender equity in higher education]. *Revista de la educación superior, 44*(174), 7–17.

Peña, F. (2012). La masificación de la educación y la búsqueda de igualdad, justicia y equidad sociales en Colombia [The mascification of education and the search for equality, justice and social equity in Columbia]. *Revista Folios, 36*, 189–200.

Plan Nacional para la Evaluación de los Aprendizajes. (2015). Plan Nacional para la Evaluación de los Aprendizajes [National plan for the evaluation of learning]. *Educación Basica*. Retrieved from http://www.planea.sep.gob.mx/

Sanz, J. R., & Serrano, Á. (2016). El desarrollo de capacidades en la educación. Una cuestión de justicia social. Sinéctica. [The development of capacity in education: A question of social justice] *Revista Electrónica de Educación, 46*, 1–16.

Schmelkes, S. (2011). Las grandes injusticias en el sistema educativo nacional. Conferencia Magistral presentada en el XI Congreso Nacional de Investigación Educativa, México, UNAM, 7-11 de noviembre [The great injustices of the national educational system].

Shields, C. M. (2010). Transformative leadership: Working for equity in diverse contexts. *Educational Administration Quarterly, 46*(4), 558–589.

Shields, C. (2016). *Transformative leadership primer*. New York, NY: Peter Lang.

Slater, C. L., Silva, P., & Antúnez, S. (2019). *Social justice leadership in Spanish schools: Researchers perspectives*. International Conference on Education, Research, and Innovation, Seville, Spain.

Tedesco, J. C. (2012). Educacion, tecnologia y justicia social en la sociedad del conocimiento [Education, technology, and social justice in the knowledge society]. *Revista e-Curriculum, 10*(3), 7–31.

Torres, C. A. (2010). La Educación Superior en Tiempos de la Globalización Neoliberal [Higher education in times of neoliberal globalization]. In A. Teodoro (Ed.), *Educação Superior no Espaço Iberoamericano. Do Elitismo à Transnacionalização* [Higher Education in Iberoamerican space. From Elitism to Transnationalization] (pp. 11–34). Lisboa, Portugal: Edições Universitarias Lusófona.

Torres-Arcadia, C., Murakami, M. T., & Moral, C. (2019). Leadership for social justice: Intercultural studies in Mexico, Spain, and the United States of America. In P. Angelle & D. Torrance (Eds.), *Cultures of justice: International studies of social justice enactment* (pp. 147–168). Basingstoke, England: Palgrave.

Viramontes, R. R., Vázquez, Y. T., & Ramírez, J. L. (2013). *Tendencias de la migración interna en México en el periodo reciente. La situación demográfica de México* [Recent internal migration tendencies in Mexico: The demographic situation in Mexico], 83-106.

Woods, P. A. (2005). *Democratic leadership in education.* London, England: SAGE.

Zhang, Y., Goddard, T. J., & Jakubiec, B. A. E. (2018). Social justice leadership in education: A suggested questionnaire. *Research in Educational Administration & Leadership, 3*(1), 53–86.

Zorrilla, M. J. P. (2006). Cómo se evalúa la comprensión lectora: descripción de dos evaluaciones concretas: Educación Primaria y Proyecto Pisa [How to evaluate reading comprehension: Description of two concrete evaluations from Primary Education Project Pisa]. In Leer con sentido o el sentido de leer: las bibliotecas y el desarrollo de competencias lectoras en los niños y jóvenes de hoy (pp. 65–90).

CHAPTER 11

SOCIAL JUSTICE LEADERSHIP IN HIGH-NEED CONTEXTS

Strategies From Principals in Spain, Mexico, and the United States

Cristina Moral
Universidad de Grenada, Spain

Elizabeth Murakami
University of North Texas

Celina Arcadia-Torres
Tecnológico de Monterrey, Mexico

Improving the quality of education in high-need contexts is currently a worldwide concern (Organization for Economic Cooperation and Development, 2012). When serving students in this context in public education, it is not enough to provide children with a right to education, it is also important to consider equitable opportunities. In this chapter, we focus on how school principals in high-need schools face challenging contexts in Spain, Mexico, and the United States, while successfully advocating for social justice.

Educational Leadership for Social Justice and Improving High-Needs Schools, pages 201–220
Copyright © 2021 by Information Age Publishing
All rights of reproduction in any form reserved.

The right to public education involves social justice, with the intent of providing opportunities for students regardless of their socioeconomic status, race, gender, ethnicity, ability, or religion (Angelle & Torrance, 2019; Chisolm, Waight, & Jacobson, 2019; Darling-Hammond, 1997; Jansen, 2006; Jean-Marie, 2008; Moral, Higueras, Martín, Martínez, & Morales, 2020; Prado de Oliveria & Paes de Carvalho, 2019; Theoharis, 2007). According to scholars examining social justice leaders, leadership is a key prerequisite in order to deliver equitable and fair education in disadvantaged neighborhoods and their schools (Pashiaridis, Brauckmann, & Kafa, 2018; Scheurich & Skrla, 2003; Theoharis, 2007). These scholars provide a rationale for our scholarly work, dedicated to Latinx/Hispanic principals in high-need contexts.

In this study, we describe the high-need contexts in which principals are observed, the framework we use, and a framework related to a principal's personal and professional identity impacting their leadership. Further, we describe the research methods used, including a description of the sample of principals in each of the three countries. A transnational and intersubjective analysis was used to examine social justice case studies in these high-need contexts. Later, our findings demonstrate commonalities across vulnerable populations in these countries, and social justice strategies offered by principals within their specific sociopolitical and economic contexts. These findings are applicable to a number of countries in similar conditions and brings attention to school principals facing similar vulnerability in their jobs, when leading high-need schools.

RATIONALE

In the past 10 years, we have been involved in the International School Leadership Development Network (ISLDN) to different degrees. ISLDN researchers from a number of countries have demonstrated a global need to improve equitable opportunities for students (Angelle & Torrance, 2019; Barnett & Stevenson, 2015; Murakami, Gurr, & Notman, 2019). ISLDN scholars examined the experiences of principals in high-need schools and those identified as social justice leaders. Concurrently, we have also contributed to the International Successful School Principal Project (ISSPP). This study, therefore, is based on case studies developed in the ISLDN and ISSPP projects, focusing on cases of successful principals demonstrating success in disadvantaged contexts (Day, 2007; Torres-Arcadia & Flores-Kastanis, 2014; Merchant, Garza, & Murakami, 2014; Moral et al., 2020).

Both projects overlap when identifying common features and strategies used by successful principals in different countries. Principals in these research projects not only focus on students' academic results, but also improve the well-being of families and communities, and the preparation of students for active and democratic citizenship. These studies exemplify how principals focus on the social inclusion of disadvantaged students, and the meaningful incorporation of these students into a current competitive world (Gurr, Drysdale, Longmuir, & McCrohan, 2018; Moral et al., 2020; Murakami & Torres-Arcadia, 2018; Torre-Arcadia, Murakami, & Moral, 2019; Ylimaki, Gurr, & Drysdale, 2011). We consider principals in this study as social justice leaders, who have high expectations for underserved students.

Even though aforementioned studies highlight features and strategies successful principals can use, we wanted to further examine *how* successful social justice school leaders confront dilemmas in countries where socio-political issues aggravate discriminatory experiences among historically/ socially excluded groups (i.e., generations of indigenous, migrant, or involuntary placed populations). We consider contingent and adaptive leadership models, where principals capitalize on their context to transform schools (Dimmock & Walker, 2000; Gurr et al., 2018; Hallinger, 2003, 2018). We considered this focus as further informing leadership knowledge, providing unique and effective personal and professional strategies. When advancing leadership knowledge towards understanding *how* principals serve these vulnerable populations, it was necessary to consider the principal's personal context, including attitudes, traits, and interpretation of reality as informing their professional identity (Crow, Day, & Moller, 2016; Crow & Moller, 2017; Hallinger, 2018; Moral, 2018). In the next section, we review the literature pertinent to this investigation.

LITERATURE REVIEW: SOCIAL JUSTICE AND PRINCIPALS IN SITUATED CONTEXTS

Leadership for social justice can be defined as leadership focusing on socio-political and transformative action on behalf of communities. Such leadership is perceived as addressing the context of oppression, exclusion, and marginalization (Angelle & Torrance, 2019; Kearney, Murakami, Bunch, Viamontes, & Campbell, 2018; Theoharis, 2007). Such leadership includes a socially just pedagogy (Furman, 2012; Jansen, 2006; Jean-Marie, 2008), one that considers disrupting a pervasive social circle of poverty experienced by parents, children, and communities. ISLDN researchers demonstrated that effective social justice leadership improves students' well-being concurrently with learning, especially when principals use strategies that include professional development of teachers, collaborative and participatory decision-making with authentic distribution of responsibilities, and increased support and success for historically disadvantaged families (Gurr & Drysdale, 2018; Murakami et al., 2019).

Personal Context and Identity in Leadership

Leadership is a variable that has been recognized as positively impacting school organizations and having direct and indirect effects on the social and academic development of students (Day, Gu, & Sammons, 2016). The principal's leadership is recognized to be a key factor in schools constrained by institutional, professional, political, and/or economic contexts (Clarke & O'Donoghue, 2017; Gurr et al., 2018; Hallinger, 2018). For example, when country, state, and local policies determine the education system's levels of centralization or decentralization, it impacts the degree of responsibilities and tasks leaders can perform. Principals may adapt their leadership style in face of these situated or contextual situations and carry out contingent strategies aimed at action for social change and societal improvement (Hallinger, 2003; Okilwa & Barnett, 2018).

Apart from the situational context, we consider the principals' personal context, which includes personal values, such as empathy, accessibility, responsibility, or commitment (Crow et al., 2016; Day et al., 2011; Gurr & Drysdale, 2018; Murakami, Kearney, Scott, & Alfaro, 2018). Such personal resources or competencies can be seen as a prism through which information, problems, opportunities, resources, and limitations are filtered and interpreted (Goldring, Huff, May, & Camburn, 2008; Kutz, 2008; Moral, 2018). Relevant to this study is Kutz's (2008) perspective of "contextual intelligence," or "the ability to assimilate cognitively and intuitively, past and current events in light of the preferred future" (p. 28). Moral (2018) considered the principals' interpretation of their current reality as being important, especially when dealing with limitations and constraints. Effective principals do not feel trapped by their disadvantaged context but are intentional and proactive when addressing social justice dilemmas (Moral, 2018).

Personal self-reflection and critical inquiry relate to leadership identity and involve reflection and action when observing their work (Brown, 2008; Crow & Møller, 2017; Robertson, 2017). Crow et al. (2016), for example, emphasized the importance of self-determination, as well as personal and professional experiences, as determining the school leader's commitment towards the development of students. Such characteristics help to further define social justice leadership and understand leadership pedagogies by applying strategies to modify, adapt, and generate relevant improvements in high-need schools.

METHODOLOGY

This study examines how school principals working in high-need schools cope with the challenging contexts in Spain, Mexico, and the United States, and successfully advocate for social justice. A case study design was

Social Justice Leadership in High-Need Contexts ▪ **205**

employed for this research, allowing for a holistic and real-world approach to explore schools in different countries (Yin, 2017). Case studies provide the opportunity for particularization, allowing for differences in contexts, meaning, and interpretation. These cases examine social justice action patterns in relation to how principals responded to country-specific situational contexts in high-need schools. Although qualitative case studies can be perceived as limited in creating generalized knowledge, their findings have been recognized as providing great conceptual validity (Denzin, 2011; Flyvbjerg, 2013). This validity is based on the thesis that the valid knowledge in social science research is knowledge obtained from specific cases and contexts and not general knowledge obtained outside of a specific context (Denzin, 2011).

Site and Participants

One principal from each country was selected from the ISLDN's corpus of data. The criteria used for the selection of principals included: (a) schools with a high percentage of communities with incomes below the poverty line; (b) schools with a high percentage of historically/socially excluded groups; (c) reduced access to basic physical infrastructures; and (d) demonstrated success of principals in these high-need schools and contexts. Neighborhoods surrounding the schools presented limited social and health services, limited educational degrees among the adults, and a large representation of historically underserved populations (i.e., indigenous groups in Mexico; immigrant, migrant, or ethnic groups in Spain; and immigrant/migrant including Latinx and involuntary or diasporic populations such as refugees or African Americans in the United States). Table 11.1 details the participants' background (pseudonyms were used to the extent possible to protect their identities).

Procedures

Data were collected through on-site visits and interviews with principals, teachers, students, parents, inspectors, and members of the community. Interviews were taped and transcribed. Contextual variables in this study related to principals and their interpretation of their contexts and the meaning and interpretation given to the data (Goldring et al., 2008; Kutz, 2008; Moral, 2018). Protocols included the ISSPP and ISLDN interview questions (Baran & Berry, 2015; Day, 2013). Table 11.2 shows the various areas covered in the interviews.

206 ▪ C. MORAL, E. MURAKAMI, and C. ARCADIA-TORRES

TABLE 11.1 Principals of High-Need Schools in Mexico, United States and Spain

Mr. Zapata: Mexico 9 years as principal at Mexican Elementary High-needs school in an urban area	He is in his 50s and has a graduate degree in education. He was a teacher for 13 years before being appointed to his first principalship. He has been a principal for 9 years, and this is the second school where he has been a principal. He received several awards for his professional career and particularly for promoting the community.
Mrs. Paz: United States 13 years as principal at Frank Orozco Elementary High-needs school in an urban area	She is in her 60s and she is an experienced educator and principal. She worked in private and public schools as a teacher, bilingual and early childhood specialist for more than 30 years. She has been the principal at Orozco for 13 years. She received the Life Changer award in recognition of promoting family education.
Mr. Ocaña: Spain 12 years as a principal at Secondary Vega School High-needs secondary school in a rural area	He is in his 50s and has been a principal for 12 years. He has extensive academic training because he has studies in teaching and psychology. He began as a primary school teacher at age 21 and went on to teach in secondary education and serving as a school counselor. He received several awards in recognition for his work in improving diversity.

TABLE 11.2 Spain, United States, and Mexico Principals' Interview Topics

1. Background: personal experiences
2. Early education and career choices
3. When, how, and why: decision to take on leadership roles
4. Social justice: presence, mission, commitment, and motivation
5. Factors helping or hindering social-justice leadership
6. High-need school characteristics: personal, teaching, leading experiences
7. Challenges developing a culture of learning
8. Major values motivating the career
9. Areas of major impact and contributions as a leader

Analysis

The analysis examined common practices addressing country-specific contextual challenges. In the analysis, context and societal culture (Dimmock & Walker, 2000) were observed and respected. A cross-comparison of principals in different countries was conducted, taking into account the following factors: (a) political power and government centralization, with the United States being a more decentralized system than Mexico and Spain and (b) all countries presented an increasingly individualistic societal

Social Justice Leadership in High-Need Contexts ▪ **207**

culture. We considered Dimmock and Walker's (2000) consideration of the degree to which societies manage uncertainty, as well as the observation of how principals followed country-specific prescribed rules and policies. We include a description of each societal culture and context prior to reporting about principals and their schools.

The analysis involved ethical considerations of intersubjectivity (Gillespie & Cornish, 2009) defined as the "variety of possible relations between people's perspectives" (p. 20). Intersubjectivity allowed for the ethical analysis of diverging and converging perspectives from both participants and ourselves, as researchers. Participants' responses from each country were initially analyzed based on the richness and limitations of each corresponding researcher's affiliated country in relation to the interpretation of data. Later, in the cross-country comparison, we describe the extent to which principals presented common high-need school experiences, with implications towards social justice issues. Patterns of actions/strategies were therefore considered within their social and situational contexts (institutional, communal, cultural, economic, and/or political). In the next section we share findings based on this analysis.

FINDINGS

The findings include the situational context corresponding to each country, followed by the personal context in which social justice leadership was exercised. Evidence of principals' social justice leadership was identified, reflecting their particular country's context. In general, all countries provide free public schooling (up to 16/19 years of age) and operate based on country/state guidelines. We begin with each country's situational context, followed by the principals' professional identity and social justice strategies.

Situational Context: Societal Culture and Schooling

Mexico

The country's population of 121 million inhabitants live in 2 million square kilometers (Instituto Nacional de Estadística y Geografía, 2015a; 2015b). Forty-six percent of Mexico's population lives in poverty and 34% are considered vulnerable due to a lack of access to social services or income below the poverty level (Consejo Nacional de Evaluación de la Política de Desarrollo Social, 2017). The Mexican government is responsible for providing free and basic schooling to the student population up to Grade 8. Around 55% of schools in the country serve low socioeconomic populations (Instituto Nacional para la Evaluación de la Educación, 2012) and

208 ▪ C. MORAL, E. MURAKAMI, and C. ARCADIA-TORRES

most of them can be defined as high-needs due to the shortage of qualified teachers, lack of books, and pedagogical materials (Martínez, 2012).

Revolución School is a high-need school situated in an urban area in one of the three biggest cities in the country. Mr. Zapata has been principal at Revolución for 9 years (pseudonyms were used). The school is an Escuela de Tiempo Completo (ETC) or a Full-Time School. ETCs are governmentally driven public schools serving vulnerable populations in social contexts of risk (Diario Oficial de la Federación, 2019). The ETC extends school hours from the usual 5 hours to 6–8 hours, offering additional services to address the needs of disadvantaged students. The additional hours support these students in academic or health issues, such as nutritious hot meals and complimentary workshops for parents. The high-need school reported in this study had 524 students, and 27 staff members (teachers and administrators).

Texas

United States public schools are organized under state and local district policies. Following national policies for educational administrators, principals are certified under the state of Texas. Texas' economy is currently the second largest in the country with $1.645 trillion in 2017 (businessintexas.com). The state's 267,000 square miles has a rich and diverse economy stemming from various industries, such as oil and natural gas, farming, steel, and banking. Despite the growing economy, there are geographical areas of extreme wealth and poverty. Almost 60% of students are economically disadvantaged, with more than 50% at risk of not graduating in 2018. In 2018, the Texas Education Agency (TEA, 2019a) reported 5,385,012 students attending public schools, and recognized that only 20% of seniors reached graduation in 2017.

Frank Orozco Elementary is one of 83 primary schools located in a high-need area of a large metropolitan city in Texas. Mrs. Paz is the principal of Frank Orozco Elementary School (pseudonyms used), serving 600 students in Grades 1–5. Ninety-eight percent of students are Latinx, 90% of which were identified as economically disadvantaged, and 95% at risk of not graduating (TEA, 2019b). Despite this context, students' academic performance is high.

Spain

According to UNICEF (2010), 2.3 million children are found at risk of poverty and social exclusion in Spain. Thirty percent of this population live in Andalusia, where Mr. Ocaña's school is located. The Spanish education system is decentralized and allows schools certain autonomy for decision-making. A national Curriculum Decree guides schools who are supervised through nationwide evaluations (Ministerio de Educación, Cultura, y Deporte, 2013). Local educational laws (MECD, 2013) recognize students in

Andalusia as in unfair and unequal conditions (Torres-Santomé, 2013). Vega Secondary School (pseudonym), located in the city of Granada, is housed by 800 students and 46 teachers. Despite being recognized as a high-need school, Vega is demonstrating excellence through innovative curricular projects focused on diversity, which are producing positive results for students both socially and academically (Agencia Andaluza de Evaluación Educativa, 2015). All three sites reflect low socioeconomic communities and high-need schools. Next, we share findings about the principals' social justice leadership.

Personal Contexts: Principals and Their Social Justice Leadership

Mexico

Mr. Zapata was educated in a private boarding school, where he learned about commitment, responsibility, and hard work. Living and studying in the same community allowed him to understand the students' struggles: "The teachers were committed, embracing additional responsibilities. I found them dedicated to teaching, beyond their duties." In his first post, Zapata was the only teacher in the community, so he was in charge of teaching all grades from first to sixth. Despite being on the payroll for morning duties only, he taught three lower grades in the morning and the higher grades in the afternoon. As a result, parents were grateful and dedicated to improving the school infrastructure (not often included in state budgets). Mr. Zapata shared:

> That's when I realized that I am the one who has to change first, in order to influence the community. The conscientious teacher is the one who has to change, in order to help others, because change only takes place when you recognize your own weaknesses and strengths, where he or she can decide the future according to the circumstances.

To make social justice visible and attainable, Mr. Zapata created mechanisms for adult and child engagement. Evidence of his social justice leadership included: (a) offering community meals to generate and provide parental support, (b) providing fine arts offerings to generate equity and opportunity, (c) being the role model as an example to transform lives, and (d) supporting activities to promote the participation of parents. His dedication to the community was evidenced through his actions in providing opportunities similar to those experienced by students in better socioeconomic conditions. Starting from modeling respect and encouraging participation in the fine arts, Mr. Zapata regained the interest of disadvantaged students who were then motivated to improve their academic achievement. He involved parents to be part of the school community to increase retention and provided support for the homes. Table 11.3 exemplifies his social justice leadership actions using his direct quotes.

210 ■ C. MORAL, E. MURAKAMI, and C. ARCADIA-TORRES

TABLE 11.3 Mexican Principal's Social Justice Leadership	
a. Providing community meals, and a space to learn and grow together	As teachers, we will accompany our children during meals. We will share a table with them, and we are able to teach table manners. We focus on formative interventions even at mealtime. While sharing our meals, we connect with them, teaching good manners, and dialoguing about their day, and academic issues.
b. Designing new offerings to compensate for inequities	With the teachers' and my abilities, we started thinking: "How can we get hands on?" We designed different educational offerings, and started workshops, where students were mixed in groups of first, second, and third to sixth grade. We started offering guitar, painting, jewelry, dance, and music. It was then that we realized that students needed to feel dignified and respected.
	With the teachers, I agreed that we have to care for the students as if they were our own children, because each of us also want a good teacher for our own child. That is why we included specialized offerings. Our students deserved no less than affluent students.
c. Teaching values and being the example to transform lives	When I talk about dignity, I mean that we are not dealing with objects. We deal with human beings—and every child. If you took off the eraser from a good pencil—would you fix it or throw it away? If a child says, "Teacher, I don't have a pencil," the child is learning a teacher's values from the way he or she responds, even if it is not an academic question like addition, subtraction, multiplication, or algebra. The students are learning how to be treated with dignity for life.
	Our work has to shine and, if our work shines, our students will shine. We will transcend and feel rewarded and worthy for having them under our care.
d. Designing recreational activities to promote the participation of parents	We have events where we invite parents. Parents have to see that their child is happy, attentive, and hard working. There is value in a child that shares about the beautiful experience of having their parents participate during events.

Texas

Mrs. Maria da Paz did not like to talk about herself, but her experience as a Bilingual teacher since 1996, and her number of licensures, specializations, and positions as coordinator and leader before becoming the principal at Orozco Elementary positioned her as a strong participant for this study. She recognized that faith was a personal motivator in her leadership serving teachers, students, and parents: "It is my life mission to educate parents and help them have a voice and become advocates for their children." She is dedicated to the school community needs, and she continuously worked to generate teacher, parent, and student engagement. Mrs. Paz is a

Social Justice Leadership in High-Need Contexts ▪ **211**

Latina like the majority of families in the neighborhood. The school name also honored a Latino community member.

Mrs. Paz's personal identity reflected her enthusiasm and commitment towards students at Orozco Elementary. She is seen as a collaborative leader, but in face of challenges, she does not hesitate to pull teachers and parents together to impact change. She believed that when adults are engaged in the academic lives of children, their future will most likely be successful. To make social justice visible and attainable, Mrs. Paz created mechanisms for adult and student engagement. Evidence of her social justice leadership included: (a) having a mailbox for students to write her letters of concern; (b) focusing on the students' achievement, cultural, opportunity, and knowledge gaps; (c) using metaphors to communicate behavioral expectations; (d) including adult males as role models for students; and (e) creating a Parent University. Her leadership was geared towards the students' and families' needs, and especially their social needs as demonstrated in Table 11.4.

TABLE 11.4 Texas Principal's Social Justice Leadership	
a. Having a mailbox where students can write letters and Mrs. Paz responds directly to them	My purpose is that when children step foot in here, they are transported to a world where learning is fun, where we sing and dance, where we laugh, where children are encouraged, where they have a voice and they can say, "I don't like that" or "I like this." They can write to me and they are heard and get a letter back from me.
	I want the students to know that every adult in this building works for *them* and that no matter how busy I am, if they need me, I will stop whatever I am doing to see about them, because I want to give them the confidence that their life is valued.
b. Focusing on student needs and opportunities	If we have a genius in school, the student cannot go untapped—we keep talking about closing the achievement gap, but you are never going to close the achievement gap, if you do not address the cultural gap, the opportunity gap, or the knowledge gap.
c. Using age-appropriate metaphors to communicate and convey behavioral expectations	I talk about a goose for its protective traits. I say: "The gift of the goose is that she looks for greatness in others and then she honks." The honks stand for noticing kindness. So, everyone in the school sends honks to those who should be recognized for their kindness.
	I also talk about how people need to have the spirit of a squirrel to fight, to survive. We must adopt the spirit of the squirrel, because when you are a student, every bit (*nut*) of information the teacher is giving you, is needed to survive in the future—or you will not make it. Now, the beaver has the best work ethic, because once they know what to do, they are not in anyone's business, they are about their own business.

(continued)

TABLE 1.4 Texas Principal's Social Justice Leadership (continued)	
d. Including adult males as role models for students	In the 6th week motivational morning events, I include police officers or fathers from the community. When I found that more than a third of the dads were incarcerated, I created the High FIVE (Fathers Imparting Value in Education) and invited men in their ties to be role models for the students. After the first year I did this, boys surpassed the girls in academic achievement by five points. The fathers also pick names from a box and give two bicycles out every 6 weeks.
	Also, if fifth grade students build a relationship with the police officers, next year when they move to secondary school, the officers will know their names. So, instead of students running away from the police, they are going to run towards them—and that might save their lives. In this community, police officers are often seen arresting family members. We must restore that bridge and stop hatred. Now the police visit all the time, parents talk to them, we love them. They help me deliver Christmas presents.
e. Creating a Parent University to generate parent support and pride.	As a school in high-need, Orozco Elementary is a Title Ia school. Since parenting classes are a requirement, with teacher volunteers, I have run what I call Parent University for the past 6 years. I named it Parent University because I wanted it to be something that has dignity. The classes include parenting courses, but also includes preparation for a high school diploma in partnership with a local college.
	After a 13-week bilingual program focused on raising highly capable children, parents wanted to continue learning. I designed the next 13-week course focusing on conflict resolution and communication, and a third series focused on parent leadership. The elementary students were so proud of their parents going to school at Parent University. It generated pride and stability for parents to move into college as well as supporting their children academically.

Note: Title I in the United States: Schools with high student concentrations of poverty can receive a Title I designation with supplemental federal funds to assist students to meet school educational goals (NCES, 2019).

Mrs. Paz's social justice lens related to her connection with the community and meeting the needs of students. She generated continuous activities that included adults to support students beyond the classroom. The academic success of students was evident through the students' excellent results in state test comparisons with other Texas school districts, in the state, despite high numbers of English language learners experiencing low socioeconomic conditions.

Spain

Mr. Ocaña was brought up in a family of merchants, and his parents had limited education and resources. He began teaching at 21 years old, and later became a secondary school counselor before serving as a curriculum

Social Justice Leadership in High-Need Contexts ▪ **213**

coordinator, and later as a principal. He was perceived by others as resilient, confident, optimistic, and empathetic in his leadership, having focused his entire educational career in disadvantaged schools. In his 12th year at Vega Secondary School, his focus has been on the academic and social improvement of students from different ethnicities and nationalities. In fact, he received the Vicente Ferrer National Development Education Award in 2015 from the Spanish Agency for International Development Cooperation (AECID) for his unique programs to fight for inclusive education. He established a center where the integration of families and students was a way to combat injustice, especially the eradication of poverty.

To make social justice visible and attainable, the school's situational context was not an impediment in the development of projects to bring attention to diversity and to improve student achievement. Mr. Ocaña demonstrated his social justice leadership through (a) providing a clear direction and identity for Vega, (b) being a leader who takes risks, (c) supporting schooling and its teachers, (d) incorporating families, and (e) developing an innovative curriculum based on students' interests. Table 11.5 summarizes Mr. Ocaña's social justice leadership strategies, using quotes from his interviews.

TABLE 11.5 Spanish Principal's Social Justice Leadership	
a. Establishing a clear direction to give identity to Vega School	To run Vega school, you have to navigate through problems and know that this process is slow . . . to navigate and navigate . . . opening doors and envisioning new paths. This direction where school is headed has been democratically constructed and gives identity to the Vega school.
	Teachers value the direction I am giving Vega. The greatest improvement has been to create a school identity . . . from a leadership that has a very clear vision.
b. Establishing leadership that takes risks and strives for improvement	If you are in the middle—seeing what is happening—this does not lead anywhere, you have to have an objective . . . that your school is the best, looking for excellence.
	There are principals who are not so enthusiastic . . . I am very committed and never manage from a place of uncertainty. "Do what I have to . . ." or by avoiding problems . . . I think about the cost and loss of not investing in students. At what cost can we not do anything to help students? We cannot afford to not do anything for students, parents, or teachers.
c. Supporting and caring for the ecology of schooling and its teachers	When I arrived at Vega, there was no interest by the staff in innovating. I managed to win them by acting in three fields: (a) from person to person, (b) by listening to them, and (c) by supporting their initiatives and projects.
	The important thing is to attend to teacher diversity. Children's diversity is important, but more so is teacher diversity . . . We have to stimulate people . . . our school is a living system, like a plant, you cannot disregard it, because it will dry out and die.

(continued)

TABLE 11.5 Spanish Principal's Social Justice Leadership (Continued)

d. Incorporating families	When I started working as principal here, I had 23 families participating at Parent Association. Now there are 200 families.
	We have a very troubled population … but we have a strong climate of collaboration. If this were not so, I can tell you that the school would be a "time bomb." The day-to-day running is very hard … when you have a school with 700 students and 700 families in front of you, it is a challenge!
e. Innovating curriculum and district requirements based on student interests	We are always looking for new ways to innovate. Now we are working on innovations proposed by the school district. We also have 19 ongoing projects. The purpose of this school is to design a curriculum connected to the problems and interests of the students, using a project methodology approach.

Mr. Ocaña strives to build the school's capacity for improvement. He perceived the school as being organic and alive, an organization in need of constant nurturing. Mr. Ocaña was not afraid to take risks on behalf of students. The 19 school projects Mr. Ocaña supported included environmental conservation efforts that linked families to their communities, such as the Vega-Educa project, Eco-school project, and Recapacicla, all of which connect academic activities with fine arts. Mr. Ocaña believed these projects provided students with a future in a globalized and competitive world.

DISCUSSION

We began the exploration of principals in high-need schools by considering their situational and personal contexts. The examination of high-need school cases in Mexico, Texas, and Spain showed unique strategies to level the playing field for underserved communities. The findings demonstrated how principals developed a professional identity to confront their situational contexts and generate strategies to address social justice issues. The principals presented strategies catered to students, teachers, and families in these high-need contexts.

The principals in each context focused on social justice beyond academics, while acknowledging the families and student needs. They understood the families' needs, generated support and motivation among teachers, educated parents, and provided students with role models and examples of ethics and dignity. They considered their own challenges as leaders in their high-need contexts, where sociopolitical support was lacking, and involved others in increasing awareness and participation. They connected the student needs with roles community members could take, in support of students (such as police officers, or parents to oversee facilities' and activities).

Social Justice Leadership in High-Need Contexts ▪ **215**

One of the principals (Mr. Ocaña from Spain) recognized the school as a living organism in which all stakeholders had a role and responsibility towards the students' futures.

A culture of learning was perceived as a base for innovative or imaginative strategies, which at first seemed indirectly related to academic disciplines, such as reading or math. Nonetheless, such a culture of support for families was a commonality in these high-need school environments. By focusing on enhancing community participation, emphasizing fine arts, educating students and teachers in acts of kindness, and demonstrating respect towards people, these principals transformed the students' experiences into successful academic achievement.

The principals' leadership in these settings was associated with their personal and professional identity, including their personal experiences and ways of interpreting their reality as leaders. For example, promoting values through role modeling, supporting teaching practices, and involving families in school activities were but a few of the strategies perceived as instrumental in addressing injustices experienced by families. This experience closely related to elements building a principal's professional identity (Crow et al., 2016; Crow & Moller, 2017; Moral, 2018; Hernandez & Murakami, 2016; Murakami, Hernandez, Mendez-Morse, & Byrne-Jimenez, 2016), and expanded the scope of our analysis of leadership required in support of high-need schools.

This study confirms earlier findings in ISSPP and ISLDN studies, showing that effective principals in high-need schools do not give in to the limitations of their challenging contexts (Angelle & Torrance, 2019; Barnett & Stevenson, 2015; Day & Leithwood, 2007; Murakami et al., 2019). Their strategies involved resistance and imagination. Their desire to challenge existing conditions did not prevent them from imagining new formulas to achieve social justice goals. These principals adapted to the children's needs, focused on supporting families, and prepared teachers to join in their mission. The only variable these principals could not change were the adverse economic, social, and political conditions families faced in their respective areas and countries. Social justice in these contexts related to a lack of public services. Despite the lack of resources, precarious facilities, limited curriculum, and socioeconomic difficulties, these principals endured in the development of strategies to address the needs of the students by using a fair and inclusive leadership pedagogy.

CONCLUSIONS

When considering the principals' professional identity to advance our understanding of social justice leadership in Mexico, the United States, and

Spain, we recognized the consequences experienced when principals fight for social justice. Especially in high-need schools, the work is far more demanding than in affluent schools. As Mrs. Paz said, "After 13 years, I am tired. Looking forward, who will support these children?" These principals not only recognized the complexity of their high-needs contexts, but also were very sensitive to their own capacity to serve as leaders. When analyzing social justice leadership, Kutz's (2008) contextual intelligence concepts resonated with us. High-need school principals demonstrated contextual intelligence capitalizing on those around them to build success for their students. Principals with contextual intelligence towards social justice seemed to move the "mosaic of their schools" (Gurr & Drysdale, 2018), with the purpose of achieving impactful improvement for their students. By establishing multiple, concurrent, and complex support strategies, they further developed their professional identity and established a culture of learning in their high-need schools.

For some school leaders, fighting for equity and excellence may be naïve or idealistic (Scheurich & Skrla, 2003). However, for principals in this study, fighting for equity and excellence was a mission essential to leading and learning. It was an instrument of social change and a way to guarantee lasting social justice efforts for their communities.

REFERENCES

Agencia Andaluza de Evaluación Educativa. (2015). *Indicadores homologados* [Official indicators]. Sevilla, Spain: Consejería-Educación.

Angelle, P. S., & Torrance, D. (2019). *Cultures of social justice leadership: An intercultural context of schools* (pp. 19–34). London, England: Palgrave McMillan.

Baran, M. L., & Berry, J. R. (2015). *The international school leadership development network (ISLDN) High needs schools group research protocol and members' guide.* Unpublished Guide.

Barnett, B., & Stevenson, H. (2015). International perspectives in urban educational leadership: Social justice leadership in high-need schools. In M. A. Khalifa, N. W. Arnold, A. F. Osanloo, & C. M. Grant (Eds.), *Handbook of urban educational leadership* (pp. 518–531). Lanham, MD: Rowman & Littlefield.

Brown, K. (2008). *Preparing future leaders for social justice, equity, and excellence.* Norwood, MA: Christopher-Gordon.

Chisolm, L., Waight, N., & Jacobson, S. (2019). School leadership for social justice and STEM: Findings from a high need secondary school in Belize. In E. Murakami, D. Gurr, & R. Notman (Eds.), *Educational leadership, culture, and success in high-need schools* (pp. 65–84). Charlotte, NC: Information Age.

Clarke, S., & O'Donoghue, T. (2017). Educational leadership and context. *British Journal of Educational Studies, 65*(2), 167–182.

Consejo Nacional de Evaluación de la Política de Desarrollo Social. (2017). Informe de Evaluación de la Política de Desarrollo Social 2016 México: CONEVAL

Social Justice Leadership in High-Need Contexts ▪ **217**

[Evaluation Report of the Social Development Policy 2016 Mexico: CONE-VAL]. Retrieved from http://www.coneval.org.mx/Evaluacion/IEPSM/Documents/IEPDS_2016.pdf

Crow, G., Day, C., & Møller, J. (2016). Framing research on school principals' identities. *International Journal of Leadership in Education, 20*(3), 1–13.

Crow, G., & Moller, J. (2017). Professional identities of school leaders across international contexts. *Educational Management, Administration & Leadership, 45*(5), 749–758.

Day, C. (2007). Sustaining success in challenging contexts: Leadership in English schools. In C. Day & K. Leithwood (Eds.), *Successful principal leadership in times of change.* New York, NY: Springer.

Day, C. (2013). *Conducting research on school principals: ISSPP members guide.* Nottingham, England: University of Nottingham.

Day, C., Gu, Q., & Sammons, P. (2016). The impact of leadership on student outcomes. *Educational Administration Quarterly, 52*(2), 221–258.

Day, C. & Leithwood, K. (2007). *Successful principal leadership in times of change.* New York, NY: Springer.

Day, C., Sammons, P., Leithwood, K., Hopkins, D., Gu, Q., Brown, E., & Ahtaridou, E. (2011). *Successful school leadership. Linking with learning and achievement.* London, England: McGraw Hill.

Darling-Hammond, L. (1997). *The right to learn.* San Francisco, CA: Jossey-Bass.

Denzin, N. (2011). The politics of evidence. In N. Denzin & Y. Lincoln (Eds.), *The SAGE handbook of qualitative research* (pp. 645–658). Thousand Oaks, CA: SAGE.

Diario Oficial de la Federación. (2019, December 3). Reglas de operación del programa de escuelas de tiempo completo para el año fiscal 2019 [Full-time schools program operating rules for fiscal year 2019]. Retrieved from https://dof.gob.mx/nota_detalle.php?codigo=5552556&fecha=12/03/2019

Dimmock, C., & Walker, A. (2000). Globalisation and societal culture. *Compare, 30*(3), 303–312.

Flyvbjerg, B. (2013). Case study. In N. Denzin & Y. Lincoln (Eds.), *Strategies of qualitative inquiry* (pp. 169–205). Thousand Oaks, CA: SAGE.

Furman, G. (2012). Social justice leadership as praxis. *Educational Administration Quarterly, 48*(2), 191–229.

Gillespie, A., & Cornish, F. (2009). Intersubjectivity: Towards a dialogical analysis. *Journal for the Theory of Social Behavior, 40*(1), 19–46.

Goldring, E., Huff, J., May, H., & Camburn, E. (2008). School context and individual characteristics: What influences principal practice? *Journal of Educational Administration 46*(3), 332–352.

Gurr, D., & Drysdale, L. (2018). Leading high needs schools: Findings from the international school leadership development network. *International Studies in Educational Administration, 46*(1), 147–165.

Gurr, D., Drysdale, L., Longmuir, F., & McCrohan, K. (2018). The leadership, culture and context nexus. *International Studies in Educational Administration, 46*(1), 22–44.

Hallinger, P. (2003). Leading educational change. *Canadian Journal of Education, 33*(3), 329–351.

218 ▪ C. MORAL, E. MURAKAMI, and C. ARCADIA-TORRES

Hallinger, P. (2018). Bringing context out of the shadows of leadership. *Educational Management, Administration & Leadership, 46*(1), 5–24.

Hernandez, F., & Murakami, E. (2016). *Brown-eyed leaders of the sun: A portrait of Latina/o educational leaders.* Charlotte, NC: Information Age.

Instituto Nacional de Estadística y Geografía (2015a). *Perfil sociodemográfico de la población que habla lengua indígena* [Sociodemographic profile of the population that speaks indigenous language]. Retrieved from http://internet .contenidos.inegi.org.mx/contenidos/Productos/prod_serv/contenidos/ espanol/bvinegi/productos/censos/poblacion/poblacion_indigena/leng _indi/PHLI.pdf

Instituto Nacional de Estadística y Geografía. (2015b). *Proyecciones de población a mitad de año* [Mid-year population projections]. Retrieved from https://www .inegi.org.mx/temas/estructura/

Instituto Nacional para la Evaluación de la Educación. (2012). *Estructura y dimensión del sistema educativo en México* [Structure and dimension of the educational system in Mexico]. Retrieved from http://www.inee.edu.mx/bie_wr/ mapa_indica/2012/PanoramaEducativoDeMexico/EstructuraYDimension/ Ciclo2011-2012/2012_Ciclo2011-2012__.pdf

Jansen, J. (2006). Leading against the grain. *Leadership and Policy in Schools, 5*(1), 37–51.

Jean-Marie, G. (2008). Leadership for social justice. *The Educational Forum, 72*(4), 340–354.

Kutz, R. (2008). Toward a conceptual model of contextual intelligence: A transferable leadership construct. *Leadership Review, 8,* 18–31.

Kearney, W. S., Murakami, E., Bunch, K., Viamontes, C., & Campbell, A. (2018). Leadership advocacy towards teacher and student success. *Rural Society, 27*(2), 143–156.

Martínez, F. (2012). Contextos vulnerables: Las aportaciones de la evaluación [Vulnerable contexts: the contributions of the evaluation]. *Bordón, 64*(2), 41–50.

Merchant, B., Garza, E., & Murakami, E. (2014). U.S.A.—Culturally responsive leadership. In C. Day & D. Gurr (Eds.), *Leading school successfully* (pp. 174–183). London, England: Routledge.

Ministerio de Educación, Cultura y Deporte. (2013). *Ley Orgánica de Mejora de la Calidad en la Educación* [Organic Law for the improvement of quality in education (LOMCE)]. Madrid, Spain: Ministerio de Educación, Cultura y Deporte.

Moral, C. (2018). A comparative study of the professional identity of two secondary school principals in disadvantaged contexts. *Leadership and Policy in Schools, 19*(2), 145–170. Retrieved from https://doi.org/10.1080/15700763.2018.15 13152

Moral, C., Higueras, L., Martín, A., Martínez, E., & Morales, M. (2020). Effective practices in leadership for social justice. Evolution of successful secondary school principalship in disadvantaged contexts. *International Journal of Leadership in Education, 23*(2), 105–130.

Murakami, E., Gurr, D., & Notman, R. (Eds.). (2019). *Educational leadership, culture, and success in high-need schools.* Charlotte, NC: Information Age.

Murakami, E., Hernandez, F., Mendez-Morse, S., & Byrne-Jimenez, M. (2016). Latina/o school principals: Identity, leadership, and advocacy. *International*

Journal of Leadership in Education, 19(3), 280–299. https://doi.org/10.1080/1 3603124.2015.1025854

Murakami, E., Kearney, W. S., Scott, L., & Alfaro, P. (2018). Leadership for the improvement of a high poverty/high minority school. *International Studies in Educational Administration, 46*(1), 3–22.

Murakami, E., & Torres Arcadia, C. C. (2018). A cross-national framework for the study of Latina/o school leaders in Mexico and Texas-United States. In E. Murakami & H. J. Mackey (Eds.), *Beyond marginality: Understanding the intersection of race, ethnicity, gender and difference in educational leadership research* (pp. 147–166). Charlotte, NC: Information Age.

Okilwa, N., & Barnett, B. (2018). Four successive school leaders' response to a high needs urban elementary school context. *International Studies in Educational Administration, 46*(1), 45–84.

Organization for Economic Co-operation and Development. (2012). *Equity and quality in education: Supporting disadvantaged students and schools.* Paris, France: Author. Retrieved from https://www.oecd.org/education/school/50293148 .pdf

Pashiaridis, P., Brauckmann, S., & Kafa, A. (2018). Leading low performing schools in Cyprus: Finding pathways through internal and external challenges. *Leading & Managing, 24*(2), 14–27.

Prado de Oliveira, A. C., & Paes de Carvalho, C. (2019). Principals' work in high-need schools: Findings from Rio de Janeiro. In E. Murakami, D. Gurr, & R. Notman (Eds.), *Educational leadership, culture, and success in high-need schools* (pp. 45–64). Charlotte, NC: Information Age.

Robertson, S. (2017). Transformation of professional identity in an experience. *Educational Management, Administration & Leadership, 45*(5), 774–789.

Scheurich, J., & Skrla, L. (2003). *Leadership for equity and excellence.* Thousand Oaks, CA: Corwin Press.

Texas Education Agency. (2019a). *Campus comparison group.* Retrieved from https:// rptsvr1.tea.texas.gov/perfreport/account/2019/group.srch.html

Texas Education Agency. (2019b). *Public education information management system (PEIMS).* Retrieved from https://tea.texas.gov/reports-and-data/data -submission/peims-0

Theoharis, G. (2007). Social justice educational leaders and resistance. *Educational Administration Quarterly, 43*(2), 221–258.

Torres-Arcadia, C., & Flores-Kastanis, E. (2014). Mexico—From fragmentation to community: A journey of change. In C. Day & D. Gurr (Eds.), *Leading school successfully* (pp. 31–43). London, England: Routledge.

Torres-Arcadia, C. C., & Murakami, E., & Moral, C. (2019). Leadership for social justice: Intercultural studies in Mexico, United States of America and Spain. In P. S. Angelle & D. Torrance (Eds.), *Cultures of social justice leadership: An intercultural context of schools* (pp. 19–34). London, England: Palgrave McMillan.

Torres-Santomé, J. (2013). *12 razones para decir no a la LOMCE* [12 reasons to say no to the LOMCE law]. Retrieved from https://www.yoestudieenlapublica.org/ descargas/16articulo12RazonesLeyLOMCE.pdf

UNICEF. (2010). *Annual reports.* New York, NY: Author.

Yin, R. K. (2017). *Case study research and applications: Design and methods.* Thousand Oaks, CA: SAGE.

Ylimaki, R., Gurr, D., & Drysdale, L. (2011). Sustainable improvement and leadership in challenging schools. In L. Moos, O. Johansson, & C. Day (Eds.), *How school principals sustain success over time* (pp. 151–167). Dordrecht, The Netherlands: Springer.

CHAPTER 12

LEADERSHIP FOR SUSTAINED SCHOOL IMPROVEMENT IN A HIGH-NEED SCHOOL IN NEPAL AND IN SOUTHERN CALIFORNIA

Vital Practices and Processes in Fostering Learning

Chetanath Gautam
Delaware State University

Rosario Ambriz
California Polytechnic State University

Betty Alford
California Polytechnic State University

Educational Leadership for Social Justice and Improving High-Needs Schools, pages 221–239
Copyright © 2021 by Information Age Publishing
All rights of reproduction in any form reserved.

222 ▪ C. GAUTAM, R. AMBRIZ, and B. ALFORD

Researchers have sought to understand ways that successful school leaders in high-need schools foster learning and organizational improvement (Barnett & Stevenson, 2016; Day & Gurr, 2014; Day & Leithwood, 2007; Klar & Brewer, 2013; Murakami, Gurr, & Notman, 2019; Ylimaki & Jacobson, 2007). This chapter adds to the research on educational leadership in high-need schools that results in increased academic achievement by illuminating the actions and beliefs that fostered learning in highly diverse high-need settings of a rural school in Nepal and an urban school in Southern California. Each of these schools predominately serve students from low-income families, and for many students in these schools, the language for instruction is not their first language. Although their contexts appear to be vastly different, similarities in ways that both leaders fostered learning and school improvement were identified.

The first section describes the external context of the two schools, which are identified by pseudonyms, followed by an examination of important processes of school leadership for improvement. Then, leaders' actions and beliefs that influenced positive results in each context will be discussed for each case followed by a cross-case comparison and concluding statements.

CONTEXTUAL INFORMATION

Nepal and Southern California differ in many ways such as demographics and school governance. However, although the contexts differ markedly, school leaders in both contexts are working purposefully to address educational challenges.

Demographics

Both Pragati School in Nepal and Mateo School in Southern California are within high-need contexts. Nepal has about 28 million people, and the life expectancy for adults is 70 years of age. About 25% of the Nepalese people live under the poverty line. The average annual income is $960 per person, and the major income source of the country is tourism (World Bank, 2019). Nepal is a multi-ethnic society with 125 caste/ethnic groups reported in the 2011 national census (Central Bureau of Statistics, 2012). Similarly, 123 languages are reported as the "mother tongue." Nepali is the official language of Nepal, which is spoken by almost half of Nepalese as a "mother tongue" (44.6%). Throughout the country, the Nepali language is spoken either as a first language or the second one while English is used in some government and business venues. In schools, English is taught as a second language. The right to a basic education in the student's "mother tongue" has made Nepalese schools a tri-lingual learning zone.

In contrast, there are 6.2 million public school students in California; 54.6% are Latino, 22.9% are White, 9.3% are Asian, and 5.4% are African American (California Department of Education, 2019). There are approximately 151,807 residents in the city where Mateo Elementary School is located (U.S. Census Bureau, 2017). According to the U.S. Census Bureau (2017), the city's demographics between 2012 and 2016 were: Hispanic/Latino (70.3%), Asian (9%), Black (6.7%), and White, not Hispanic (11.8%). In 2016, 68.2% of the residents age 25 and older had a high school diploma and 17.3% received a bachelor's degree or higher. The median household income for residents in 2016 was $50,360, which is still below the California median of $67,739. The percent of people living in poverty is 21.5%, which is higher than the California median of 13.3%. Contrasts between school governance in Pragati School and Mateo Elementary School will be discussed next.

School Governance

The 2015 Constitution of Nepal lists basic education, up to eighth grade, as a fundamental right of the people. As provided by the Constitution, public education up to the secondary level is free for all citizens whereas in the United States, a free, public education is provided through Grade 12. The public schools in Nepal are funded by taxpayers, international grants/loans, and local or community resources whereas in the United States, funding is received from state, federal, and local revenues. The federal government, states, and the local units share the responsibility of the education sector in Nepal whereas in the United States, local control is emphasized with the state and local units serving as the primary influences on school policies and state Departments of Education determining accreditation processes. Operation and management of public P-8 schools is the function of local units in Nepal, which are referred to as village development committees or municipalities. In the United States, locally elected school boards serve as the governing body with schools organized into districts with a superintendent as the leader of the district. The educational administrator who leads the school campus in Nepal is referred to as the head teacher, while in the United States, the campus administrator is referred to as the principal.

Educational Challenges

Both Pragati School in Nepal and Mateo School in Southern California constitute high-need contexts. Although the national and local contexts

224 ■ C. GAUTAM, R. AMBRIZ, and B. ALFORD

differ markedly between these two schools, improving the educational achievement of all students is a goal shared by school leaders in both Pragati School and Mateo School. In a recent update on the Nepalese context of education by UNICEF (2019), characteristics of Nepalese education were provided. The authors stated:

> The net enrollment rate in primary schools has risen to 97 percent. However, the country still has many challenges to tackle. Issues that persist in education include poor quality and inequity in access, geographical remoteness, and gender, socioeconomic, and ethnic differences. (para. 2)

Only half of Grades 3, 5, and 8 meet the academic achievement criteria for the Nepali language and mathematics, only a few schools meet the child-friendly school standards, and only about one in ten school buildings are earthquake resistant (UNICEF, 2019). These factors pose both internal and external constraints.

In the United States, disparities in educational achievement by students from different ethnic groups and socioeconomic groups persist (National Center for Education Statistics, 2017; O'Day & Smith, 2016). According to Education Trust-West (2018), in the United States, while Black–White and Latino–White educational gaps have narrowed over time, disparities in academic performance of students in these ethnic groups remain. Disparities also persist in the educational performance of students in schools serving high numbers of students from low-income families contrasted with schools serving a high percentage of students from high income families (National Assessment of Educational Progress, 2018). As Murakami and Kearney (2019) point out concerning the U.S. national educational context, "Even though a large number of public schools around the nation are preparing students well, there is increased awareness of the effects of poverty" (p. 5). In order to address challenges of low-performing schools in the United States, multiple reforms designed to turn around schools have been proposed including a federal grant competition for persistently low performing schools (U.S. Department of Education, 2009).

CONCEPTUAL FRAMEWORK

Turnaround schools is a phrase associated with "improving school conditions and teacher-related outcomes, which resulted in significant gains in student outcomes defined in various ways" (Sun, Mendiola, Sun, & Zhang, 2018, p. 209). In addressing the multifaceted challenges in low-performing schools, successful school leadership is context specific and multidimensional (Duke, 2006; Ylimaki & Jacobson, 2007). Toward reaching the goal of increased student learning, principal leadership is vital in establishing the conditions to support learning in the ongoing process of school improvement (Leithwood, Louis, Anderson, & Wahlstrom, 2004). The context and needs of the school influence a principal's actions in the complex work of school improvement, and simplistic, incoherent approaches do not produce lasting improvements (Fullan & Quinn, 2016). For example, in 2009, the U.S. Department of Education provided a grant competition designed to provide funding for turning around lowest achievement schools and required one of four models of a turnaround model, a restart model, school closure, or a transformation model (U.S. Department of Education, 2009, 2016). These highly prescriptive approaches, which included actions, such as replacing the principal or requiring the faculty to reapply, were largely ineffective in achieving sustained school improvement in schools that received the grants (Meyers & Darwin, 2017). In subsequent stages of funding, increased freedom in the selection of school improvement practices resulted (Meyers & Darwin, 2017).

Murphy and Seashore Louis (2018) remind us, "School leadership is, above all, a moral and ethical task: The lives of children and their families draw us to the work and sustain us when there are excruciating challenges" (p. 3). In their framework of positive school leadership, they propose that trust is the *glue* that sustains school improvement. Context and trust serve as the boundaries of their framework with trust as the foundation. They argue that an educational leader's orientation must include knowledge that context matters in the school improvement process since "context continually shapes how action unfolds" (p. 10). Additionally, the "development and deepening of interpersonal trust is central in positive school leadership" (p. 10). Educational leaders must recognize the unique strengths and challenges present within their context and work in concert with the community and all stakeholders in seeking to meet student needs. Achieving school improvement is not an individual endeavor accomplished by a sole educational leader. Instead, when collective responsibility is fostered and evidenced, strong gains in school improvement can be achieved (Murphy & Seashore Louis, 2018).

Greater understanding of ways that educational leaders foster a positive school culture with sustained, increased learning opportunities for all students is needed (Murphy & Seashore Louis, 2018). While Tschannen-Moran (2019) points out that in the school improvement process, fostering trust is vital, she adds that "despite recognition of the importance of a school culture that supports trust, evidence of how trust is cultivated remains understudied. We need greater clarity to understand the dynamics that foster trust" (p. 371). Gurr, Drysdale, Longmuir, and McCrohan (2019) point out, "Contexts do matter but not so much in terms of the core leadership practices that lead to success, but rather in the way these practices are

226 ▪ C. GAUTAM, R. AMBRIZ, and B. ALFORD

employed" (p. 40). Additional research is needed in "understanding the relationship of leadership and school success" (Gurr, Drysdale, Longmuir, & McCrohan, 2019, p. 41). This study provides deeper insights on the need identified by these authors.

METHODOLOGY

Purpose and Research Question

The purpose of this study was to identify the key practices and processes that a successful head teacher in Nepal and a successful school principal in Southern California implemented to promote strong cultures of learning and school improvement in these high-need settings and turnaround of these schools. The protocol of the International School Leadership Development Network (ISLDN) was used as a basis for data collection and analysis from these two diverse high-need schools (Baran & Berry, 2015). The protocol focuses on the areas of learning, leadership, and context through three research questions. Specifically, the research question examined for this chapter was:

> *What were key factors in fostering student learning in high-need schools that serve large numbers of students from low-income homes?*

This chapter illuminates ways that these two school leaders fostered learning and contributed to organizational changes that influenced school improvement.

Data Sources

Interviews served as the primary data sources for the study of Pragati School and Mateo School. Field notes, as a second data source, provided the opportunity for reflexivity in discerning key themes.

Interview Data in Nepal

The 15 participants who were interviewed at Pragati School were selected using purposeful sampling. Participants included three parent volunteers, five senior teacher leaders, six teachers, and the head teacher who had served in this role for more than 30 years. The five senior teacher leaders had more than ten years of experience in teaching and were in the school site for more than five years. The additional six teachers who were interviewed through a focus group were both new and veteran teachers

Leadership for Sustained School Improvement in a High-Need School ▪ **227**

having a range of experience from one to 20 years, and their involvement in the school varied. Among the three parents, two had their children in the school for at least three years. One parent went to this school, and now his two children were attending the school.

The researcher translated the protocol questions from English to Nepali. Both English and the Nepali language were used during the interviews. One of the researchers received the support of the school principal in translating the essence of the protocol for the interview of one of the parents who spoke only the local ethnic language.

Interview Data in California

In Mateo Elementary School, 18 individuals participated in the study. Individual interviews were conducted with the principal who had served in this role for 7 years and the assistant principal, two academic coaches, a district administrator, and the school principal's coach who each had been working with the school for 3 years. Three focus group interviews were conducted with four participants in each focus group. The support staff focus group participants included: the school counselor, the school family community facilitator, the school resource teacher, and a special education instructional aide from the school who had a range of experience in education from 15–25 years and who had worked at the school from three to 25 years. A focus group with four parents who had been involved with the school from three to 20 years and a focus group with four teachers, having a range of experience from three to 35 years at the school, were also conducted. All interviews were conducted in English.

Field Notes in Nepal and California

The second major method of collecting data was through observations, which were captured through field notes. Creswell (2015) defined observation as "the process of gathering open-ended, firsthand information by observing people and places at a research site" (p. 211). Thus, the researcher's role was that of a participant observer, who took field notes. Descriptive field notes as well as reflective notes were collected at both sites.

Data Analysis

The transcribed interviews were analyzed and coded using open and axial coding (Glaser & Strauss, 2012; Saldana, 2015) to discern themes relative to each of the research questions. The researchers reflectively read and reread the data in identifying the primary themes of the interviews and field notes. The process of coding was a recursive process until saturation of the key themes was obtained in reference to the research question (Denzin

228 ▪ C. GAUTAM, R. AMBRIZ, and B. ALFORD

& Lincoln, 2008). A cross-case comparison was attained through a constant comparative method of analysis.

Trustworthiness

Trustworthiness in the research process was achieved through triangulation of the key themes that were identified from the interview data and field notes (Merriam & Tisdell, 2016). Member checks with the participants to verify transcriptions of interviews were also conducted. An audit trail of the research methodology and transcriptions of interview data were maintained in a secure location. Names were removed from interview data to ensure confidentiality, and pseudonyms were provided for participants.

FINDINGS

In sharing each case, the internal context of each school will be described first, followed by key themes that were emergent in both contexts. Then, a discussion of the cross-case comparison will be provided.

What Fostered Learning in the High Need School in Nepal?

Pragati School is located in a rural, remote area and was recognized by the regional educational administrative agency of the Nepal government as an exemplary public school. Although this high-need school was located in a small community and local residents attended the school, students from surrounding communities as far as 10 hours from the school attended this residential school. These students lived at the school because the distance to their home was too far to commute daily. Although an examination was required for students from other communities to enroll in the school, the examination score was only used as a diagnostic tool instead of preventing any student from attending the school. In fostering learning at Pragati School, three themes emerged: identification of a sustained focus, collaboration, and an emphasis on meeting the needs of each child.

Identification of a Sustained Focus

The head teacher, Mr. Singh, described his outreach to the community in identifying the school's focus:

I asked the villagers, the local community people, what they wanted for their children from the school. I said, "What do you want me to teach to your children?" They said that since many tourists pass by the village and their major occupation after agriculture was a porter, they wanted their children to learn English. That was the local voice and the local need. We became a tri-lingual school.

The focus on preparing students to learn English required hiring teachers fluent in English as well as helping veteran teachers to learn English. Mr. Singh explained that very few of the teachers were fluent in English when the secondary school was established. When the school became an English medium school, course materials in English were acquired. Mr. Singh pointed out that he never forced the teachers to learn English for instruction. He explained the reason they supported changing to English as the language of instruction for the school was that they saw this as a way of preparing the students for career opportunities since tourism was the main economy of the region.

The community is proud of their school, which serves as the major community center for the entire village. Mr. Singh added:

> If we do not respect the voice and interest of the local people, we will break the trust, which we have gained in the last 35 years. We would not be the same school if that happened. It is the trust our parents have given us that has made us who we are today. We cannot simply overlook their voices.

Mr. Singh proudly explained, "They wanted an English medium education for their children, and we delivered. This is a tourist destination, and the English language helped us to connect to the world."

Collaboration and Community Engagement

The school's success also depended on how closely the educators were connected to the community that they served and the trust they had earned. The head teacher discussed his first step in engaging more fully with the community by explaining, "I learned the local language. Whatever we achieved here, we achieved by winning the trust of the community." The school's focus on the community partnership as a central value of the school was highlighted by Mr. Gurung, the teacher leader next to the head teacher, who stressed:

> Here, the local community and the school mean the same. We are such a part of the community, that now, we really do not know if we are within the village or if we are the village itself. If a small thing happens, if somebody falls ill in the village, or if anything goes right or wrong, the school supports or stands by the needs of the community.

Collaboration between the school and the community was further emphasized as a member of the focus group related the story of the earthquake of April 2015, "The earthquake happened. No buildings of the school remained usable; all the villagers lost their homes, too. They came even before starting to build their homes to volunteer to build the school."

Collaboration also characterized the head teacher's work with the teachers and the teachers' engagement with the community. When asked if the success would sustain if he were to retire, Mr. Singh answered quickly, "I am not overly confident, but I am confident enough that the teachers I have will take the lead. They have already taken the lead." Mr. Singh further explained:

> None of our decisions are my solo decisions. We decide together. The school itself has become a true sense of community. In another way, we are doers together. We teach, not only the text, but also through the life in our school. We also take our students from the school for community service. All of my teachers are assimilated within the community.

When the researcher asked the teachers whether the positive results would still be achieved when the current head teacher retired, Mr. Gurung, a teacher leader, emphatically replied, "We can never be him, but with his guidance, and support we are becoming closer and closer to the community."

Responding to the Needs of Each Child
The parents, Mr. Sharma and Ms. Tamang, painted a detailed picture of the school's learning culture. Mr. Sharma who was with his youngest son traveling with others, hiking up the hill, started to tell the story of how hard the school tries to teach the children:

> This school does not teach only reading and writing. This school teaches life skills through a culture of working together and taking responsibilities. On the content side, they are the best. For the last 10 years, they have remained the best in the entire region.

In terms of life skills, the first day of the fall semester, the students, teachers, and the principal all participated in a community service project. They collected plastics, cans, and other garbage as they cleaned up the walkways in cooperation with the community. Ms. Tamang, who was traveling with the researcher on the same bus, had two of her sons with her. She pointed to her elder son and described the school's academic focus:

> My elder son was not doing well in a big-name school in the city. I brought him here, and he is making progress. I decided to bring my youngest son here also. It is hard to be 10 hours away from your young children, but I am proud of what they do here. The educators become parents for my children. They love them, but at the same time, they help them to learn.

Leadership for Sustained School Improvement in a High-Need School ■ **231**

Ms. Limbu, a senior teacher in the focus group discussion emphasized aspects of the learning environment. "I do not think math, Nepali, English, or science are the problems of our children." She paused and stressed, "Here it is simple. We do not approach learning as something to memorize, but students develop habits of learning."

As in other parts of the world, the schools in Nepal are also ranked based upon the students' academic performance on national tests. The educators in this school are proud of the school's ranking in the regional and national chart of academic achievement, but they displayed more excitement when describing ways that the students are connected to the world and how they, as educators, see and explore the unseen potential of each child.

Concerning the focus of the school on the development of the whole child, Mr. Panta, a teacher, stated a commonly expressed viewpoint of the educators at this school:

> It is our moral duty to accept the child as he or she is and help him or her find out what they can do. We never tell them they cannot do something. Some students who fail in all the subjects have come here and stayed here for a few years and have graduated with distinction. We are proud of that. It is not easy for the new students in the beginning, but gradually, they start to put more effort into learning. We have proven that every child can, in fact, learn, no matter where they come from.

Clearly, the school is achieving powerful results, and the leader's actions and beliefs are influential in the school improvement process.

What Fostered Learning in the High-Need School in California?

Mateo Elementary School is one of 27 elementary schools within a K–12 unified school district and is characterized as a high-need school with 93% of the total enrollment from low-income homes. The English Learner student group is 30% of the total enrollment and the Students with Disabilities student group is 8% of the total enrollment. Two years prior to the principal's leadership of school reform, less than 20% of the students were reading at grade level whereas after a sustained focus on literacy for 2 years, 90% of the first-grade students were at grade level.

The three key practices identified for the high-need school in Nepal were also evident in the case study of a high-need California elementary school. These practices included a sustained focus, collaboration, and an emphasis on meeting each child's needs.

232 ■ C. GAUTAM, R. AMBRIZ, and B. ALFORD

Sustained Focus on Literacy

Identifying and sustaining a focus on literacy was pivotal in fostering student learning in this California elementary school. The administrative team was focused on reading. The principal explained the turnaround goal of the school:

> We wanted to show our district what it takes to transform a low achieving school's reading achievement. Our goal was to stay focused on what the research has been saying for 30 years. The teaching of reading is to teach comprehension, phonics, phonemic awareness, vocabulary, and fluency, and it was important to teach all these components to the students every day.

Mr. Bauer, an external school partner who served as the principal's coach in the improvement process described the sustained focus:

> If I had to pick one thing, I would say in this school, it's a singular focus on one thing for two years, not just having a workshop and then we talk about it for a week, and then we go to another workshop. That coherence by the leadership has been the one thing that's kept the eyes on the prize.

The sustained focus was readily apparent to parents as well as teachers. As Mrs. Piccirillo, a parent from Mateo, shared:

> Well, the school's goal, first of all, is to involve the students in reading, so that they will have a wide reading ability so that they can understand math problems and the rest of the subjects the school has, but the first thing is reading.

Mr. Martinez, a district administrator, described his viewpoint of the role of the principal in the success of this school in sustaining a primary focus for school improvement:

> From my vantage point, I think it always starts with leadership, and I think that at all levels, there has to be a vision. Leaders have to know where they want to go, and Principal Aguila has been consistent about where she wants to go, and that hasn't wavered. That's very helpful. She has high expectations, and that hasn't wavered. I think because of that and focusing on a few things has allowed the school faculty to go deeper in their own learning.

Mrs. Hill, a support staff from Mateo shared, "The thing that has been instrumental in achieving change is the leadership, and it starts at the top and trickles down. We have a phenomenal leader here, our Principal Aguila." Mr. Jordan, an academic instructional coach, further explained, "Principal Aguila is part of the process and anticipates what the challenges might be and provides direction and inspiration along the path to success."

Leadership for Sustained School Improvement in a High-Need School ■ 233

Teacher's pedagogy in the use of multiple instructional strategies and their skills in teaching the reading process were areas of weakness for the teaching staff at Mateo Elementary School. Principal Aguila shared, "In order to transform the teaching and learning, we needed to focus on the building teacher's knowledge." From attending additional professional development, Mr. Puente, a teacher from Mateo, shared:

> I didn't think at my age or at this stage in my career I could learn more, but I can. I'm much more focused with what I teach and how I plan lessons, as well. Everything is relevant, and I focus a lot on literacy.

Professional development was instrumental in building the capacity of the teachers to become better teachers of reading.

According to the administrative team, the focus for the first year was developing teacher's pedagogy. At the beginning of the second year, the administrative team wanted to ensure that the teaching and learning was, in fact, improving. Thus, the team chose several literacy assessments that all teachers administered to measure progress.

The sustained focus on the improvement of literacy resulted in students being more engaged and interested in their learning. Teachers and parents shared multiple indicators of student improvement in reading. For example, Mrs. Madrid, a parent, stressed, "I see that my daughter is more motivated to read when she did not read enough before, and today she is more focused on what she is reading because the teachers have motivated her." An important step in achieving that goal was cultivating a collaborative culture within the school.

Cultivating a Collaborative Culture

Collaboration was a key process in the school improvement process. The principal stressed, "You have to create opportunities for teachers to collaborate, and once they experience it, they will want to continue working in that manner. It's about working smarter not harder." The principal described ways that the teachers were now working together in lesson planning and data analysis. A culture of ownership was fostered. As the principal emphasized, "Teachers stopped blaming the students and began to reflect on what they could have done differently."

The parent participants from Mateo Elementary spoke about the transparency the principal created at the school. Parents are well informed about the school's initiatives, the achievement data by grade level, and they participate in Parent Learning Walks, so they, too, can learn and see the progress of the teaching and learning at Mateo Elementary. Mrs. Denney, a parent from Mateo Elementary, described the value of knowing the students in kindergarten and first grade were now performing similarly to the

234 ■ C. GAUTAM, R. AMBRIZ, and B. ALFORD

highest performing school in the district stating, "We're up there high on the chart, and that means a lot to us!" "Teachers are providing a highly supportive environment for learning to meet the needs of every child" was also frequently expressed.

Meeting the Needs of Each Child

Providing a safe, positive, and supportive environment to meet the specific needs of each child was stated in five of the six individual interviews and in the focus group interviews. Principal Aguila explained:

> Schools that provide a comprehensive web of support for the whole child ensure that students become successful. Part of the improvement plan was that Mateo Elementary would have a full-time assistant principal and a counselor who would assist with the demands of the high-need school and engage staff in addressing any barriers that were impeding students' learning.

Mr. Martinez, a district administrator, described the benefits of the additional assistance of a counselor for the students noting, "I think that having the counselor was huge. Having her on board to help support the social emotional learning, including some of the day-to-day things that our students are dealing with that we need to support and handle, mattered." Mrs. Hamski, the assistant principal, echoed this sentiment about the counselor:

> We have a counselor who works in conjunction with the administrators to provide guidance to achieve behavior expectations and resources for students who need social emotional support. The school counselor also provides valuable lessons within the class to ensure students learn valuable social skills.

Principal Aguila added, "Addressing the needs of the whole child is important if you want to affect a student's academic progress." One parent, Mrs. Vasquez, described the climate of the school, "I feel that my children are very well taken care of here, not just by the principal, but by the rest of the staff. I don't have to worry at home. I have peace of mind." Parents also spoke about ways that the school feels like a home to many of these children. Mrs. Piccirillo, a parent from Mateo Elementary stated, "Some of the students feel more welcome here, unfortunately, than their own home. They feel safer here. They feel more cared for, even, I want to say loved. This is why they always want to be here."

Mateo Elementary has been implementing Positive Behavior Interventions and Supports (PBIS) for the last few years. This school year, the PBIS team decided to rebrand their behavioral expectations to coincide with the instructional initiatives being taught to the students. The principal shared, "Everything we do at Mateo Elementary needs to connect to each other, a coherent system." Mr. Bauer, an external coach for the principal, discussed the positive results of the school:

> I would definitely say without reservation that Mateo Elementary is a much different place 2 years down the road than it was 2 years ago, a much, much different place. There are many classrooms that I would give the highest compliment I can, and that is, "I would have my child in those classrooms without reservation."

Principal Aquila stressed:

> Although many things are going in the right direction, we still encounter bumps in the road, but I don't allow this to change my course. Equity and excellence for all students is what we are striving to achieve at Mateo.

DISCUSSION

This chapter illuminated principals' actions that fostered student success and increased learning in two vastly different contexts. Despite differences of location, resources, professional development opportunities, and support structures, each school was recognized for achieving improved results in student learning. What fostered learning in these two contexts included similarities in the leaders' approaches to school improvement in three primary ways of sustained focus, collaboration, and an emphasis on meeting the needs of the whole child.

Sustained Focus and Targeted Initiatives

In both contexts, the school leaders, in collaboration with stakeholders, identified a clear area for improvement and maintained a consistent focus on meeting this need. In Nepal, the head teacher recognized the need for the students to learn English since tourism was becoming the primary source of income and English was needed to work in tourism jobs. In the California school, literacy was selected as the primary need to address, and a consistent focus was maintained on meeting this need through changes in instructional strategies, ongoing monitoring of student achievement, professional development for teachers, and provision of instructional coaches.

Collaborative Planning and Community Engagement

Both school leaders fostered collaboration and recognized the importance of involving all stakeholders. Due to the size of the school in

236 ■ C. GAUTAM, R. AMBRIZ, and B. ALFORD

California, structures for collaboration were also established. At the onset of the school improvement process, parents, teachers, and administrators provided input regarding the needs of the school. Time was set aside during the school day for meetings to discuss instructional practices and curriculum alignment. The collaboration included involving the parents and community members in understanding student performance data. In Nepal, the involvement with the community was especially visible after Nepal experienced an earthquake, and the school was destroyed. Community members and faculty were also central in supporting the focus of the school as an English medium school.

Meeting the Needs of the Whole Child

In many varied contexts worldwide, schools are ranked by how well students perform on external state, national, or international examinations, such as, the Program for International Student Assessment (PISA; National Center for Education Statistics, 2018). However, addressing the socioemotional needs of students in addition to their academic needs is important to address the purpose of school that holds "the good of human beings within it as sacred" (Starratt, 2014, p. 56). For this study of a high-need school in Nepal and a high-need school in Southern California in the United States, school leaders demonstrated authentic caring through an emphasis on meeting students' socioemotional as well as academic needs.

The focus of the Nepalese head teacher was not just on academics, but on the development of the whole child. No set curriculum or programs provided guidelines for this emphasis. Instead, community engagement was fostered through community service and shared responsibilities at the school. In the California school, the principal led the faculty in the focus on socioemotional learning through implementation of the positive behavior intervention system (PBIS) and provision of professional development for this approach. In both the Nepalese setting and the California setting, an emphasis on meeting the needs of each child's socioemotional as well as academic needs was clearly evident.

CONCLUDING REMARKS

Both the head teacher in Nepal and the principal in California were highly visible in leading the school. Both leaders demonstrated trust and confidence in the faculty and students and communicated their high expectations for student success through words and actions. They demonstrated care through their positive interactions with teachers, students, and the

Leadership for Sustained School Improvement in a High-Need School ▪ **237**

community. Their actions in seeking to prepare each student to his or her highest potential supported their commitment to social justice. There was no evidence that either principal was seeking personal gain. Instead, the faculty and the community recognized that these leaders authentically cared about the students. Their actions were transparent, and they modeled their beliefs. Each principal was fully present in the life of the school, modeling teaching, interacting with students, and communicating the vision of equity and excellence.

Turning around the performance of these schools was not a quick fix or simplistic solution. Understanding the contexts, engaging with the community, and meeting identified needs within the context were important in each school's improvement process as other researchers have identified (Gurr et al., 2019; Hallinger, 2016; Klar & Brewer, 2013). Results identified that despite differences in contextual needs, the fundamental principles of trust, purpose, and positive actions of the leaders influenced sustained community engagement, collaboration, and increased student learning. Identifying and sustaining a clear focus on meeting identified needs, fostering collaboration in the school improvement process, and maintaining an emphasis on meeting the needs of the whole child in addressing socioemotional as well as academic needs were influential leadership practices in fostering increased student learning across both contexts. The study reinforced that principal leadership mattered in achieving school turnaround for increased student learning in these vastly different contexts. In both settings, successful school leaders' actions and beliefs transcended challenging contexts and contributed meaningfully to positive results.

REFERENCES

Baran, M. L., & Berry, J. R. (2015). High needs schools group research protocol and members' guide. *The International School Leadership Development Network.* Retrieved from https://isldn.weebly.com/

Barnett, B. G., & Stevenson, H. (2016). Leading high poverty urban schools. In S. Clarke & T. O'Donoque (Eds.), *School leadership in diverse contexts* (pp. 23–42). Oxfordshire, England: Taylor and Francis.

California Department of Education. (2019). *Fingertip facts on education in California-Cal Ed Facts.* Retrieved from https://www.cde.ca.gov/ds/sd/cb/ceffingertip facts.asp

Central Bureau of Statistics. (2012). *National population and housing census, 2011.* Kathmandu, Nepal: NPHC. Retrieved from https://unstats.un.org/unsd/demographic-social/census/documents/Nepal/Nepal-Census-2011-Vol1.pdf

Creswell, J. W. (2015). *Educational research: Planning, conducting, and evaluating quantitative and qualitative research* (5th ed.). Boston, MA: Pearson Education.

238 ▪ C. GAUTAM, R. AMBRIZ, and B. ALFORD

Day, C., & Gurr, D. (Eds.). (2014). *Leading schools successfully: Stories from the field.* London, England: Routledge.

Day, C., & Leithwood, K. A. (Eds.). (2007). *Successful principal leadership in times of change: An international perspective* (Vol. 5). Dordrecht, The Netherlands: Springer.

Denzin, N. K., & Lincoln, Y. S. (Eds.). (2008). *Collecting and interpreting qualitative materials* (Vol. 3; 3rd ed.). Thousand Oaks, CA: SAGE.

Duke, D. L. (2006). What we know and don't know about improving low-performing schools. *Phi Delta Kappan, 87*(10), 729–734.

Education Trust-West. (2018, April). *National assessment of educational progress (NAEP) 2017 results.* Retrieved from https://west.edtrust.org/resource/national -assessment-of-educational-progress-naep-2017-results/

Fullan, M., & Quinn, J. (2016). *Coherence: The right drivers on action for schools, districts, and systems.* Thousand Oaks, CA: Corwin.

Glaser, B. G., & Strauss, A. L. (2012). *The discovery of grounded theory: Strategies for qualitative research.* Piscataway, NJ: Aldine Transaction.

Gurr, D., Drysdale, L., Longmuir, F., & McCrohan, K. (2019). Successful school leadership that is culturally sensitive but not context constrained. In E. Murakami, D. Gurr, & R. Notman (Eds.), *Educational leadership, culture, and success in high-need schools* (pp. 25–44). Charlotte, NC: Information Age.

Hallinger, P. (2016). Bringing context out of the shadow. *Educational Management, Administration, and Leadership, 46*(1), 5–24. https://doi.org/10.1177/ 1741143216670652

Klar, H. W., & Brewer, C. A. (2013). Successful leadership in high-needs schools: An examination of core leadership practices enacted in challenging contexts. *Educational Administration Quarterly, 49*(5), 768–808.

Leithwood, K., Louis, K. S., Anderson, S., & Wahlstrom, K. (2004). *How leadership influences student learning.* New York, NY: The Wallace Foundation.

Merriam, S. B., & Tisdell, E. J. (2016). *Qualitative research: A guide to design and implementation* (4th ed.). San Francisco, CA: Jossey-Bass.

Meyers, C. V., & Darwin, M. J. (2017). *Enduring myths that inhibit school turnaround.* Charlotte, NC: Information Age.

Murakami, E., Gurr, D., & Notman, R (Eds.). (2019). *Educational leadership, culture, and success in high-need schools.* Charlotte, NC: Information Age.

Murakami, E., & Kearney, S. (2019). Principals in high-performing, high-poverty, minority-serving schools in Texas. In E. Murakami, D. Gurr, & R. Notman (Eds.), *Educational leadership, culture, and success in high-need schools* (pp. 25–44). Charlotte, NC: Information Age.

Murphy, J. F., & Seashore Louis, K. (2018). *Positive school leadership: Building capacity and strengthening relationships.* New York, NY: Teachers College Press.

National Assessment of Educational Progress. (2018). *The nation's report card.* Retrieved from https://www.nationsreportcard.gov

National Center for Education Statistics. (2017). *Digest of education statistics: 2017.* Retrieved from https://nces.ed.gov/programs/digest/d17/tables/dt17_104 .20.asp

Leadership for Sustained School Improvement in a High-Need School ▪ **239**

National Center for Education Statistics. (2018). *Program for international student assessment (PISA): Overview.* Retrieved from https://nces.ed.gov/surveys/pisa/index.asp

O'Day, J. A., & Smith, M. S. (2016). Equality and quality in U.S. education: Systemic problems, systemic solutions. *Education Policy Center at American Institutes for Research.* Retrieved from https://www.air.org/resource/equality-and-quality-u-s-education-systemic-problems-systemic-solutions

Saldana, J. (2015). *The coding manual for qualitative researchers* (3rd ed.). Thousand Oaks, CA: SAGE.

Starratt, R. J. (2014). The purpose of education. In C. M. Branson & S. J. Gross (Eds.), *Handbook of ethical leadership* (pp. 43–61). New York, NY: Routledge.

Sun, J., Mendiola, B., Sun, J., & Zhang, S. (2018). Understanding leadership to turn schools around: A review of research evidence. In C. V. Meyers & M. J. Darwin (Eds.), *International perspectives on leading low-performing schools* (pp. 289–318). Charlotte, NC: Information Age.

The World Bank. (2019). *Nepal.* Retrieved from https://data.worldbank.org/country/nepal

Tschannen-Moran, M. (2019). Organizing in schools: A matter of trust. In M. Connolly, D. H. Eddy-Spicer, C. James, & S. D. Kruse (Eds.), *The SAGE handbook of school organization* (pp. 361–375). Thousand Oaks, CA: SAGE.

UNICEF. (2019). *Education.* Retrieved from https://www.unicef.org/nepal/education

United States Census Bureau. (2017). *QuickFacts: Pomona city, California.* Retrieved from https://www.census.gov/quickfacts/pomonacitycalifornia

United States Department of Education. (2009). *Race to the Top program executive summary.* Retrieved from https://www2.ed.gov/programs/racetothetop/executive-summary.pdf

United States Department of Education. (2016). *School improvement grants (SIG).* Retrieved from https://www2.ed.gov/programs/sif/sigsea452016ppt.pdf

Ylimaki, R., & Jacobson, S. (2007). The international study of successful school principals. *International Studies in Educational Administration, 35*(3), 1–74.

CHAPTER 13

SOCIAL JUSTICE IMPERATIVES FOR LEADERS IN HIGH-NEEDS SCHOOLS

Research From ISLDN Studies and Issues for Future Consideration

Stephen Jacobson
University at Buffalo

Paul Miller
Educational Equity Services, England

INTRODUCTION AND OVERVIEW

In recognition of the 10th anniversary of the International School Leadership Development Network (ISLDN), the coauthors, both of whom have been engaged in ISLDN case study research since the network's inception, use this chapter as an opportunity in two ways: to revisit findings from our past ISLDN studies, as well as others we have conducted, and to collaboratively consider some practical implications for school leaders who hope to

---

Educational Leadership for Social Justice and Improving High-Needs Schools, pages 241–258
Copyright © 2021 by Information Age Publishing
All rights of reproduction in any form reserved.

241

242 ▪ S. JACOBSON and P. MILLER

promote social justice in high-needs schools, regardless of national context. Specifically, our collective findings lead us to identify four imperatives that require the immediate attention of social justice leaders, especially in high-needs schools and communities:

1. Improve the academic performance of all their school's children.
2. Reconnect the school with its students' parents and the larger school community.
3. Create future economic opportunities for students, parents, and the community.
4. Provide for succession planning and sustainability.

In order to frame how we envision these imperatives, we cite examples from research we conducted in high-needs schools spanning the years 2005–2019. The high-needs schools studied were situated in six very different national contexts: Belize, Jamaica, England, Mozambique, New Zealand, and the United States, with specific (although not exclusive) attention paid to those national studies we conducted as part of the ISLDN, which represent 8 of the 12 studies reported. The cases cited include Jacobson's examination of the practices of successful elementary principals in the United States and the consequences of those practices on the community (Jacobson & Szczesek, 2013; Jacobson, Brooks, Giles, Johnson, & Ylimaki, 2007; Jacobson, Johnson, Giles, & Ylimaki, 2005); leadership practices of headteachers in early childhood education (ECE) centers in New Zealand (Jacobson & Notman, 2018; Notman & Jacobson, 2018); and the work of two leaders who started the first secondary school on a small island off the coast of Belize (Chisolm, Waight, & Jacobson, 2019; Jacobson, 2019; Waight, Chisolm, & Jacobson, 2018). Miller's cases include his study of school leaders in Jamaica and England (Miller, 2016); his examination of school leaders in 16 education systems (Miller, 2018); a study of leaders in Jamaican primary schools (Miller, Gaynor, Powell, Powell, & Simpson, 2019); an examination of small/rural schools in England, Jamaica, and Spain (Miller, Roofe, & García-Carmona, 2019); and his study of school leaders in England proactively trying to tackle race inequality in staffing (Miller, 2019).

The schools in the six countries we focus on serve economically disadvantaged youngsters living in communities dealing with problems such as, to name just a few, families living in poverty, high rates of crime and/or substance abuse, historically/socially excluded or indigenous groups and/or students with learning differences, and in the most extreme cases, limited access to schooling itself.

The chapter begins with a discussion of leadership for social justice, a description of each of the four imperatives and how their interrelationships are critical to future student, family, and community success. Next, we provide

Social Justice Imperatives for Leaders in High-Needs Schools ▪ **243**

a very brief overview of the national and local educational contexts of the schools that were examined. Using findings from these case studies, we then offer specific examples of how school leaders attempted to implement each of these imperatives to address and correct the inequities they encountered. The chapter concludes with a summary of the four imperatives we have identified for social justice that the leaders in these high-needs schools employed, and then we make recommendations for future ISLDN research.

WHAT IS SOCIAL JUSTICE LEADERSHIP IN HIGH-NEEDS SCHOOLS?

Larson and Murtadha (2002) define social justice school leadership as a set of "theories and practices of leadership that are vital to creating greater freedom, opportunity, and justice for all citizens—citizens who, through public education, are better able to participate in and sustain a free, civil, multicultural, and democratic society" (p. 136). For Marshall and Ward (2004), social justice is a means of "fixing" inequities, which for Goldfarb and Grinberg (2002) can be imagined in schools as a leader "actively engaging in reclaiming, appropriating, sustaining, and advancing inherent human rights of equity, equality, and fairness in social, economic, educational, and personal dimensions" (p. 162). Put differently, "Social justice leadership is activist both in its intent and its approach, and social justice leaders understand the material, economic, cultural, social, and other differences between different groups and try to do something to ameliorate the impact of these differences" (Miller, Roofe, et al., 2019, p. 96). Thus, leadership for social justice is motivated by and requires the ability to change a school's culture (Larson & Murtadha, 2002), which is often a microcosm of larger societal injustices, whether in developed or developing nations.

At its core, social justice school leadership views providing *all* children with access to a quality education as a central principle, since access to a quality education is believed to be essential for creating equitable personal and collective opportunity. This idea and principle is foregrounded in evidence from a study of school leaders of small rural schools in Jamaica, Spain, and England by Miller, Roofe, et al. (2019) who concluded that "quite paradoxically, by the presence and/or absence of certain characteristics, these schools bespeak crucial aspects of 'social justice' itself (i.e., close relationship with families, learning activities adapted to each student, individualized attention due to the size of the classroom, activities that include all the educational community, addressing lack of diversity, etc.)" (p. 115). Notwithstanding schools themselves being characterized as "sites of social in/justice," in order to begin fixing inequities, and therefore realizing social justice, social justice leaders must first recognize systemic obstacles that create and reify existing disparities in access to a quality education: barriers in the allocation of available resources, discriminatory practices in daily operations, and institutional policies that marginalize segments of the population—most often based on race, gender, religion, poverty, socioeconomic status, and/or disability (Jost & Kay, 2010; Larson & Murtadha, 2002). It is perhaps this recognition that led Miller, Hill-Berry, Hylton-Fraser, and Powell (2019) to assert that social justice has three parameters: pedagogic activism, regulatory activism, and emancipatory activism. Crucially, they argue, "Social justice is not passive; rather, it is active, seeking not only to disrupt and to challenge, but also to break down and to build up. Social justice work therefore requires concerted and purposeful effort on the part of education professionals, whatever their position and/or status, and irrespective of the country in which they are located" (p. 17).

For the past 10 years, researchers in the ISLDN network have focused their work on what leaders in schools serving students in high-need communities around the world have done to disrupt these inequities in the status quo and transform their schools in order to provide more equitable opportunities for their students and communities. The findings suggest that the practices of these school leaders, whether in developed or developing parts of the world, do not vary as much as one might expect because across these differing contexts school leaders all confront discriminatory policies established by those with power (Chisolm, 2017). However, in some developing nations this problem may be even more challenging because of a lack of access to basic schooling itself, not just access to a quality education—as in the study from Belize, where secondary schools may simply be too far from the homes of some children for them to attend, or too expensive, too restrictive, or simply non-existent in more remote parts of the country.

So what are the four social justice imperatives that require school leaders' immediate attention if they are to begin fixing the inequities they confront? First and foremost, these leaders must improve the academic performance of all their school's children. By academic performance, we are referring not only to student scores on standardized exams, but also enabling youngsters to attain, at a minimum, basic literacy and numeracy skills as well as other non-cognitive, pro-social, civic skills necessary for children to become productive, contributing members of their society. This is a non-negotiable foundational level of achievement and not the ultimate goal, because without a firm foundation in these cognitive skills, reaching and exceeding national standards of school performance may prove to be unattainable.

Secondly, to facilitate and accelerate these higher levels of student achievement, school leaders must actively work to reconnect the school with its students' parents and the larger school community. And, as a growing body of empirical evidence from the United States suggests—particularly

Social Justice Imperatives for Leaders in High-Needs Schools ▪ **245**

findings from the Perry Preschool study (Schweinhart et al., 2005)—for children living in poverty stricken, high-needs communities, this work should begin with a "quality" early childhood education (Reardon, 2011).

In many national contexts, schools were once tightly engaged with their local communities. In fact, schools were often the symbolic heart of a community. But over time, especially in developed nations, schools became more hierarchal, transactional organizations, modeled on efficiency approaches typically found in the business sector (Jacobson, 2018). Cost efficiencies, such as school consolidation, often changed the relationship between schools, parents, and their communities and, over time, may have eroded public trust, leaving parents and other community members feeling increasingly marginalized and distant from the larger educational bureaucracies that were created (Jacobson, 2018). Since their parents (and to a lesser extent the community) are a child's first teachers, this marginalization reduced the potential contributions from what should be a school's most valuable allies. Recreating these partnerships increases the probability of changing the educational culture of a child's home and thus increases the probability of student success (Leithwood & Patrician, 2017), especially for children from economically disadvantaged families (Epstein, 2011).

A third way school leaders can reconnect their school to its community is by creating future economic opportunities for students, as well as their parents and their community. In order to promote their desire to forge lasting partnerships, school leaders need to incentivize these efforts with community members by developing programs that have the potential to create future job opportunities and other economic gains, not just for students, but for the local economy itself. As we shall see, these activities might include intensive job training internships for students, which can produce better prepared future workers for local businesses, the creation of new commercial enterprises from sources both within and outside of the local community, or even increased home equity as property values increase in response to improved school performance and an upturn in the local economy (Jacobson & Szczesek, 2013). And finally, to prevent possible academic and/or economic improvements from quickly dissipating, school leaders for social justice must provide for succession planning and sustainability because the on-going success of any gains made must not depend solely on the efforts of one or two people. Understanding that these improvements may be fragile as they first emerge, it is imperative the school leaders anticipate future staffing and resource changes (including their own career movement) and develop plans that address these concerns and build stability in school leadership and community relationships.

In order to get a better sense of how these imperatives are operationalized in the daily practice of high-needs school leaders, we offer examples

246 ▪ S. JACOBSON and P. MILLER

drawn from the national cases mentioned earlier, but first we provide a brief overview of the national and local educational contexts of the schools that were examined.

THE NATIONAL CONTEXTS OF OUR STUDIES

The six nations from which our findings are drawn—Belize, Jamaica, England, Mozambique, New Zealand, and the United States—can be clustered into two distinct groups as measured by wealth, specifically gross domestic product (GDP) per capita. In the first cluster, we have the three developed nations: the United States, England, and New Zealand. The United States, the world's largest economy and third largest population, had a GDP per capita of $60,000 in 2019, which was 350% greater than the world average (ranking it #13 out of 185 countries reported), while the United Kingdom'sand New Zealand's figures are $45,000 (263%, #26) and $41,000 (238%, #32), respectively (Worldometers, 2019). It is important to note that England makes up by far the largest portion of the GDP reported for the United Kingdom. At the other end of this wealth continuum are the three developing nations: Belize, Jamaica, and Mozambique. Using the same metrics, Worldometers (2019) reports Jamaica at $9,000 GDP per capita or 53% of the world average, coming in at #111, while Belize is at $8,500 (50%, #114), and Mozambique is at $1,250, which is just 7% of the world's average, ranking it #180 out of the 185 countries reported. Obviously, direct comparisons across nations with this level of wealth disparity should be made with great caution, but within each national context there are some communities and schools that have far greater resource inequities than others and can accurately be described as "high needs." For example, in the United States, the most affluent of our six nations, New York State has an index that divides a school's needs—measured by the percentage of children enrolled who are on free and/or reduced lunch, plus the percent of children identified as having a disability, divided by the amount of available fiscal resources—to determine the relative stress that school is under relative to other schools in the state (Jacobson et al., 2005). The higher the number, the greater a school's needs. Therefore, the cases reported in the United States include only those in the highest need category. In contrast, the school examined in Belize didn't even exist before the school leaders arrived and they would be thrilled to have the resources available to the highest needs school in New York. Nevertheless, examining the practices of the leaders in both the most advanced nation of the six, as well as those in some of the poorest, is instructive.

WHAT ARE THE SOCIAL JUSTICE LEADERSHIP IMPERATIVES FOR HIGH-NEEDS SCHOOLS?

Reanalyzing the findings from our past studies, the authors considered some practical implications for school leaders who hope to promote social justice in high-needs schools, regardless of national context. Specifically, we developed four imperatives for school leaders in these schools as shown in Table 13.1, indicating which studies were used to develop each of the

TABLE 13.1 Cases by Country Reporting Each of the Four Imperatives 2019

	Imperatives			
Case Studies by Country	1	2	3	4
United States				
Jacobson et al. (2005)	X	X	X	
Jacobson et al. (2007)	X	X	X	
Jacobson et al. (2009)	X	X	X	X
Jacobson & Szczesek (2013)		X	X	
New Zealand				
Jacobson & Notman (2018)		X	X	
Notman & Jacobson (2019)		X	X	
Belize				
Waight et al. (2018)	X	X	X	
Chisolm et al. (2019)		X	X	X
England				
Miller (2014)				X
Miller (2016)	X			X
Miller (2018)	X	X	X	X
Miller et al. (2019a)	X	X		
Miller (2019)				X
Jamaica				
Miller (2014)				X
Miller (2015)				X
Miller (2016)	X	X	X	
Miller (2018)	X	X	X	X
Miller et al. (2019a)	X	X		
Miller et al. (2019b)	X	X	X	X
Mozambique				
Miller (2018)	X	X		

248 ▪ S. JACOBSON and P. MILLER

imperatives. Please note that all four imperatives were not found in each case study.

Improving the Academic Performance of All Children

While improving the academic performance of all children was an imperative for all the school leaders we studied, it was explicitly the case in U.S. schools that faced sanctions due to years of under-performing. In New York State, where this study was conducted, English/language arts (ELA) and mathematics scores were used as the benchmarks of student performance, and schools that persistently scored below state standards on these tests were publicly sanctioned, which in the most extreme instances meant closure. The public reporting of annual test-score report cards put schools on notice of potential penalties to come. In some cases, especially high-needs schools that enrolled predominately children of color, a "blame the victim" deficit mentality can emerge by which some teachers, and even some parents, come to believe that their youngsters are not capable of achieving at expected levels. But in one school we studied over a 5 year period, the principal, an African American woman in a predominantly African American community, took a social justice stance that simply would not tolerate that type of deficit perspective and with time the students' improved test scores bore witness to her confidence and efforts (Minor-Ragan & Jacobson, 2014). Using potential school closure sanctions as leverage, she worked ceaselessly to address these biased perceptions and eventually was able to convince the naysayers on her staff and in the community that their children could meet New York State requirements. In fact, over the course of our study, Fraser Academy (the pseudonym we used for the school) made such dramatic improvements in student academic performance that it was recognized by the state for its successful turnaround. But these gains would not have been possible if the principal had not reached out to teachers, parents, and other members of the Fraser community to address and disrupt the race-based performance biases that some held.

In contrast to the high-need schools studied in the United States, many schools in Jamaica and in Mozambique lack basic infrastructure. Poverty is a dominant feature of everyday life for students, and for schools where staff and students alike are often engaged in a daily game of satisficing— making do with what little is available and/or lobbying the community for financial/material assistance. What is unmistakable, however, is that, at the heart of the lobbying by communities that goes on, is a commitment from their teachers and school leaders to provide their children with a qualitatively unique and better schooling experience (Miller, 2016). This need is underpinned by a strong social justice mantra, "Education is a ticket out of poverty," and a recognition that students should be afforded the best possible learning experiences and opportunities. In one school in a remote community in Clarendon, Jamaica, we see the principal lobbying past students living in Canada and the United States to raise funds for her to purchase computers for her students so they could, within their classrooms, experience a different "world" or the "world out there." This was crucial for her as, due to poverty, many of the students at her small, multi-grade primary school of 70 students, had not traveled to the nearby town, located only some 30 kilometres away. Similarly, we see the principal of a large oversubscribed primary school in Maputo, Mozambique (over 5,000 students), lobbying benefactors in the United Kingdom for financial assistance to purchase classroom furniture for her students who would otherwise sit on the dirt floor (Miller, 2018). These school leaders, located in rural and urban areas, in different countries, showed a similar passion, enthusiasm, and care towards students, and towards providing them with a learning experience that would broaden their horizons, and an overall schooling experience that was fit for purpose.

RECONNECTING THE SCHOOL WITH ITS STUDENTS' PARENTS AND THE LARGER SCHOOL COMMUNITY

While our findings from Fraser Academy are instructive about the importance of school–parent partnerships, what we learned from leaders in early childhood education (ECE) centers in New Zealand were the most revealing. For these ECE leaders, developing the parenting skills of their children's parents was absolutely central to their social justice ethic, especially for those families dealing with relocation caused by major life disruptions such as job loss or relocation caused by catastrophic upheavals like political unrest, war, and natural disasters like the 2011 earthquake in Christchurch. The magnitude of this problem cannot be overstated given that the number of international immigrants reached 232 million in 2013 and continues to grow (UNHCR, 2013). To put this figure in clearer perspective, the number of displaced people across the world in 2013 was actually greater than the population of Brazil, the world's fifth most populous nation (Goddard, 2015). For many of their center's parents, these disruptions and relocations meant separation from extended family and thus the loss of traditional childrearing support typically received from grandparents, siblings, aunts, and uncles. We found that many of these young parents now had to work and parent, but without the familial support they had anticipated. Especially for first-time parents, it was the leaders and teachers at the center who were teaching them how to deal with challenging childhood behaviors such as anxiety, tantrums, and/or physical

250 ▪ S. JACOBSON and P. MILLER

aggression. Parents began to trust and model the parenting skills of these experienced educational professionals (Jacobson & Notman, 2018), who quickly became surrogates for extended family members. Parents' newly learned after-school skills began to complement the faculty's in-school efforts, enabling what Epstein (2011) calls a "family-like school," which research suggests may be twice as predictive of student success than as family socioeconomic status considered alone (Bonci, Mottram, McCoy, & Cole, 2011) and as much as ten times greater than other relevant factors (Leithwood & Patrician, 2017). As Jeynes (2017) argues,

> When parents are both motivated and mobilized to become more active in their children's education, they can make a profound difference in their children's success at school. When school leaders identify features of parenting that matter and work to develop those features with their parent communities, the impact is likely to be as significant as most improvement efforts focused on the school organization itself. (p. 324)

Although perhaps not originally intended to connect and/or reconnect the school to students, parents, and the local community, the actions of the principals in Jamaica and Mozambique illustrate this re/connection rather powerfully. By reaching out to the local community for financial assistance, school leaders and teachers suggested they were challenging community members (local and international) and local business owners to "own" the school, and the students therein—since the students "come from" the community, they also "belong to" the community, and they "are for" the community. In both cases, the school was at the heart of the community. In the Jamaican school, aside from the church and a few corner shops, there were no other "social" spaces. Concomitantly, the school became the space of "coming together" and of "being" where events were organized and held several times during the year, and where the values of the community were affirmed and re-imagined across generations. For example, the importance of respect for the elderly, of being thrifty, of gaining an education were not only values held and shared at home, at church, and the corner shop, but quite commonly where and when members of the community got together. Furthermore, the school in Mozambique was bursting at its seams responding to the demands of providing "education for all." Accordingly, three shifts of students, of very different age groups, including adults, were accommodated each day. These examples underline the fact that the schools were at the heart of community life, but also that the community was also at the heart of the schools. The crucial symbiotic relationship between school and community (described by Miller, 2018, as school–community partnerships) is regarded by school leaders in the case study countries as foundational to the success of schools regardless of size, location, and/or country context. Although reconnecting the school to parents and their community

Social Justice Imperatives for Leaders in High-Needs Schools • **251**

is a critical key step in improving the lives and performance of students, it is imperative that leadership for social justice take the additional step of leveraging these school–community partnerships to create economic improvement and future opportunities for everyone.

Create Future Economic Opportunities for Students, Parents, and the Community

Education can create future economic opportunities, not only for students, but also for their families and communities. Although it is common practice for many schools in England to offer classes in English language and computing to parents, especially migrant parents, one principal saw this as sufficiently important to offer these opportunities to any parents who were interested. School X, a large secondary school, is located in a seaside town. Many parents were either unemployed, did not speak English, or did not hold "standard" qualifications. This was hugely problematic for the principal, Mr. X, who saw these factors as mitigating the impact and the efficacy of schooling received by students. In other words, if parents were able to understand what students were learning, they could better support and/ or challenge them. Importantly, if parents were able to gain a qualification, this could improve conditions for the family—all round. Accordingly, Mr. X joined forces with his teachers and launched a "community learning partnership." This partnership saw the school providing free tuition in English language and computing to parents. Many would later complete a full qualification which allowed them an opportunity to gain entry level employment to some organizations, including the school. Furthermore, the essential basic knowledge and skills picked up by parents meant they were better able to support their children's homework and educational journey. Teaching is an ethic of care (Owens & Ennis, 2005), and so is leadership. And this care does not stop with students. Rather, it extends to their families and communities as well (Miller, Roofe, et al., 2019). Accordingly, in this rather powerful example, we see a principal moving beyond the expected, by offering hope and essential life tools to families and their communities.

In a less developed country like Belize, there are far fewer economic opportunities for students and community members than in a developed nation like England, especially for those living in impoverished rural or remote areas. Furthermore, while primary education is available in most parts of the country, access to secondary schooling is often far more limited in Belize. Most of that nation's secondary schools are located in larger towns and cities, which means that students from rural areas hoping to get a secondary education are forced to travel or relocate. Coupled with the burden of travel and/or relocation, the cost of school tuition (which is not free in

Belize) often makes a secondary education out of the reach of youngsters coming from more remote, high-need communities.

To address this problem, Social Justice Academy (SJA) was founded in 2008 on a small island located about an hour away from the mainland by water taxi. Prior to SJA's establishment, there was no secondary school on the island. One of the espoused goals of the school's founders was to prepare students to contribute to the economic growth of their own community, which was beginning to emerge in the eco-tourism sector. The school's curriculum was intentionally designed to reflect the environmental/ecological context of the school's community, with coursework related to issues such as tourism, climate change, marine biology, and coral reef ecology, to name a few. The theory of action was that students would benefit from engaging in authentic inquiry that would allow them to be economically successful with a secondary education, without having to leave the island or necessarily go on to college. The goal was to help ensure that students and their parents understood the ecological value of their community and that, in turn, would encourage them to engage in an ecologically sustainable approach to tourism. The pedagogical approach employed involved both formal science content and informal experiential, applied learning. In addition to more traditional classroom instruction, students engage in "site-based learning" opportunities and internships with island businesses focused on tour guided activities, such as kayaking, fly-fishing, scuba diving, and biking. These opportunities provide pathways to some of the highest paid jobs on the island and many local entrepreneurs have opened their doors to these youngsters, because they have the potential to become the bedrock of a stable and sustainable workforce for the community's continued economic growth. By expanding their focus beyond the school's walls and immediate community of students and families, the social justice imperative of the leaders at SJA has also begun laying the groundwork for the future economic stability of the entire island. But preparing for school and community improvement and sustainability requires thoughtful consideration and careful planning in order to put the right people in place to make it happen, and very often the "right" people are already in place, particularly teachers, but existing biased practices impede their opportunities. Research by Miller, Gaynor, et al. (2019) on educational sustainability in Jamaica supports these observations through findings which call for transparent planning and practices in staffing to ensure the sustainability of school organizations (Miller, Gaynor, et al., 2019).

Provide for Succession Planning and Sustainability

Across very different sociocultural contexts, the experiences of teachers seeking progression opportunities highlights similarities and differences

Social Justice Imperatives for Leaders in High-Needs Schools ▪ **253**

(Miller, 2014). These similarities and differences point to how individual teachers see themselves within their education system, and to how they see the education system. For example, in England many teachers see the system that governs progression/promotion as racist and discriminatory (Miller, 2019), and in Jamaica, many teachers see the system governing progression/promotion as corrupt (Miller, 2013). Findings from these and other studies suggest school leaders, whether in Jamaica or England, are aware of the views and perceptions of teachers, as well as other evidence that supports the views of teachers. Accordingly, these leaders have tried to "do things differently" in order to respond directly to the concerns of teachers, and to acknowledge the role of institutions in creating/leading change. In Jamaica, there are several examples of school leaders vowing not to promote teachers based on "long service," "social connections," and/ or "political affiliation" (Miller, 2015), but rather on merit. One Jamaican principal, for example, challenged herself to no longer promote based on long service, since long service did not always mean you would be putting the best person in the right job. She also spoke of the demoralizing effect long-service promotion does have and can have on those teachers who believe in the meritocratic ideal; that having an education should open doors for everyone equally (Miller, 2016). We also see examples of four Jamaican principals ensuring teachers are given appropriate professional development in order to raise their level of awareness and understanding of school leadership. Furthermore, these principals argue that making schools sustainable through the recruitment of qualified and skilled individuals would augur well for leadership succession planning—something they were keen to ensure (Miller, Gaynor, et al., 2019). In England, some school leaders are standing up to, and pushing back against race discrimination in teacher progression. They have moved forward from, in some cases, turning a blind eye to the problem or, in other cases, sympathizing but doing nothing or very little to address the problem of race discrimination in teacher progression. We see examples of three principals moving beyond acknowledging the problem to inventing tactics and deploying strategies towards changing cultures, attitudes, and behaviors among staff, and to purposefully creating and leveraging developmental and growth opportunities for teachers of Black, Asian, and minority ethnic heritage (Miller, 2019).

Providing progression opportunities for Black, Asian, and minority ethnic staff is clearly only one important approach to successful succession planning and sustainability. Another significant approach is to make a conscious and concerted effort to anticipate leadership change and assure that there is the capacity for organizational self-renewal so that any gains made during one administration can be institutionalized, sustained, and even enhanced by the next (Jacobson, Johnson, Ylimaki, & Giles, 2009). To achieve this transition successfully requires a "goodness of fit" wherein

254 ▪ S. JACOBSON and P. MILLER

new leadership maintains the trust and partnerships with students, parents, and community engendered by their predecessor. With this imperative, we offer as an example its contrapositive, that is, a situation where succession planning was not thoughtfully undertaken and therefore sustainability was almost lost. For this we return to Fraser Academy in the United States— the school described earlier that experienced a marked improvement in student achievement under the leadership of a remarkable African American woman whose tenure as the school principal lasted 17 years. When she retired, she was succeeded by a relatively young White man from a different city in New York State. Although he had an impeccable resumé as an instructional leader, he simply did not "fit" the community and culture that had emerged at Fraser. Unfortunately, but not surprisingly, he did not last long at the school and sadly, over the past 6 years, Fraser Academy has had three different principals (all male). While Fraser remains a school in "good standing," meaning it is not currently under any state sanctions, its student achievement scores had declined so much that it had to be carefully reviewed by the New York State Education Department before its "good standing" rating could be reaffirmed. While there are no guarantees that this situation could have been averted had there been a more thoughtful effort at succession planning, anecdotal evidence suggests that there was a sense among some faculty and community members that bad decisions were made and that the school's decline in student performance could have been averted had a candidate been identified early in the process who was a better fit for the school. That said, these same individuals expressed a sincere hope that the current principal can return the school to the levels of success it had a decade earlier.

SUMMARY OF THE FOUR IMPERATIVES AND RECOMMENDATIONS FOR FUTURE ISLDN RESEARCH

In reviewing our past studies, we find that school leaders who hope to promote social justice in high-needs schools, regardless of national context, work to improve the life chances of all their students, not only while these youngsters are in school but also in providing them a future that has more opportunities. There is a logical sequence to the work these social justice leaders undertake, which is encapsulated in four imperatives:

1. First and foremost, they must focus on improving the academic and social skills of their students; then
2. they must engage parents as partners in their youngsters' development; whilst also

Social Justice Imperatives for Leaders in High-Needs Schools ▪ **255**

3. trying to connect to the larger school community in ways that might potentially improve the economic opportunities for all within the community; and

4. finally, they need to be very conscious in their efforts to develop their school's ability to self-renew through careful succession planning in order to sustain and advance the gains they have made, even well beyond their own time in the position.

Each of these steps can be fraught with obstacles as these leaders begin to tackle societal inequities that need to be identified and fixed. Oftentimes, fixing these inequities can mean confronting those in power who have been knowingly or unknowingly advantaged by past practices, and therefore reluctant to change. The four imperatives we have articulated seem necessary, but perhaps insufficient to produce the kind of just society these leaders would prefer.

So what ought to come next for ISLDN research? In his analysis of the country reports undertaken by the International Successful School Principalship Project (ISSPP), Leithwood (2005) noted "progress on a broken front" (p. 619), based on the growing number of school leadership cases that were "nibbling at the lower edges of external validity within countries" (p. 626). ISLDN should take heed and try to expand the number of countries involved and also the number of cases being studied within each country. Clearly, this latter recommendation is a shortcoming of the findings reported in this chapter, that is, while we have reported cases from six nations, in one (Belize), the analyses are based on only one school. In addition to expanding the number of country cases undertaken, future ISLDN researchers can also use these four imperatives as markers to better determine whether and how school leaders in high-needs schools have been able to promote social justice. Researchers should also return to these schools every few years, especially after there has been a change in leadership, in order to determine whether succession planning has been undertaken and where improvements have been sustained.

REFERENCES

Bonci, A., Mottram, E., McCoy, E., & Cole, J. (2011). *A research review: The importance of families and the home environment.* London, England: National Literacy Trust.

Chisolm, L. (2017). *Social justice leadership that matters: An evaluation of school leadership practices in a high-need secondary school in Central America-Belize* (Unpublished doctoral dissertation). State University of New York at Buffalo.

Chisolm, L., Waight, N., & Jacobson, S. (2019). School leadership for social justice and STEM: Findings from a high need secondary school in Belize. In E.

Murakami, D. Gurr, & R. Notman (Eds.), *Leadership, culture and school success in high-need schools* (pp. 65–83). Charlotte, NC: Information Age.

Epstein, J. (2011). *School, family, and community partnerships: Preparing educators and improving schools* (2nd ed.). Boulder, CO: Westview Press.

Goddard, J. T. (2015). A tangled path: Negotiating leadership for, in, of and with diverse communities. *Leadership and Policy in Schools, 14*(1), 1–11.

Goldfarb, K., & Grinberg, J. (2002). Leadership for social justice: Authentic participation in the case of a community center in Caracas, Venezuela. *Journal of School Leadership, 12*(2), 157–173.

Jacobson, S. (2018). Managing the school organization. In M. Connolly (Ed.), *The SAGE international handbook on school organization* (pp. 67–83). London, England: SAGE.

Jacobson, S. (2019). Social justice school leadership for academic, organizational and community sustainability. In P. Angelle & D. Torrance (Eds.), *Cultures of justice: Intercultural studies of social justice enactment* (pp. 21–42). London, England: Palgrave.

Jacobson, S., & Notman, R. (2018). Leadership in early childhood education (ECE): Implications for parental involvement from New Zealand. *International Studies in Educational Administration, 46*(1) 86–101.

Jacobson, S., & Szczesek, J. (2013). School improvement and urban renewal: The impact of a turn-around school's performance on real property values in its surrounding community. *Leadership and Policy in Schools, 12*(1), 1–11.

Jacobson, S., Brooks, S., Giles, C., Johnson, L., & Ylimaki, R. (2007). Successful leadership in three high poverty urban elementary schools. *Leadership and Policy in Schools, 6*(4), 1–27.

Jacobson, S., Johnson, L., Giles, C., & Ylimaki, R. (2005). Successful leadership in U.S. schools: Enabling principles, enabling schools. *Journal of Educational Administration, 43*(6), 607–618.

Jacobson, S., Johnson, L., Ylimaki, R., & Giles, C. (2009). Sustaining school success: A case for governance change. *Journal of Educational Administration, 47*(6), 753–764.

Jeynes, W. (2017). Effects of family educational cultures on student success at school: Directions for leadership. In K. Leithwood, J. Sun, & K. Pollock (Eds.), *How school leaders contribute to student success* (pp. 311–328). Dordrecht, The Netherlands: Springer.

Jost, J., & Kay, A. (2010). Social justice: History, theory, and research. In S. Fiske, D. Gilbert, & G. Lindzey (Eds.), *Handbook of social psychology* (pp. 1122–1165). Hoboken, NJ: Wiley.

Larson, C., & Murtadha, K. (2002). Leadership for social justice. *Yearbook of the National Society for the Study of Education, 101*, 134–161.

Leithwood, K. (2005). Understanding successful principal leadership: Progress on a broken front. *Journal of Educational Administration, 47*(6), 619–629.

Leithwood, K., & Patrician, P. (2017). Changing the educational culture of the home to increase student success at school. In K. Leithwood, J. Sun, & K. Pollock (Eds.), *How school leaders contribute to student success* (pp. 329–351). Dordrecht, The Netherlands: Springer.

Social Justice Imperatives for Leaders in High-Needs Schools ■ **257**

Marshall, C., & Ward, M. (2004). "Yes, but . . .": Education leaders discuss social justice. *Journal of School Leadership, 14*(5), 530–563.

Miller, P. (2013). *The politics of progression: Primary teachers' perceived barriers to gaining a principalship in Jamaica.* Kingston: University of Technology, Jamaica & the Institute for Educational Administration & Leadership–Jamaica.

Miller, P. (2014). Becoming a principal: Exploring perceived discriminatory practices in the appointment and selection of principals in Jamaica and England. In K. Beycioglu & P. Pashiardis (Eds.), *Multidimensional perspectives on principal leadership effectiveness, IGI Global.* https://www.igi-global.com/chapter/becoming-a-principal/121137

Miller, P. (2015). Politics, religion and social connections: Pillars for progression among primary teachers in Jamaica. *School Leadership & Management, 35*(3), 237–250.

Miller, P. (2016). *Exploring school leadership in England and the Caribbean: New insights from a comparative approach.* London, England: Bloomsbury.

Miller, P. (2018). *The nature of school leadership: Global practice perspectives.* London, England: Palgrave Macmillan.

Miller, P. (2019). 'Tackling' race inequality in school leadership: Positive actions in BAME teacher progression—Evidence from three English schools. *Educational Management Administration & Leadership, 48*(6), 986–1006.

Miller, P., Gaynor, V., Powell, C., Powell, S., & Simpson, E. (2019). Leadership as sustainability: context and primary school principals in Jamaica. *Journal of School Leadership, 29*(2), 130–149.

Miller, P., Hill-Berry, N., Hylton-Fraser., & Powell, S. (2019). Social justice work as activism: The work of education professionals in England and Jamaica. *International Studies in Educational Administration, 47*(1), 3–18.

Miller, P., Roofe, C., García-Carmona, M. (2019). School leadership, curriculum diversity, social justice and critical perspectives in education. In P. Angelle & D. Torrance (Eds.), *Cultures of social justice leadership: An intercultural context of schools* (pp. 21–42). London, England: Palgrave Macmillan.

Minor-Ragan, Y., & Jacobson, S. (2014). In her own words: Turning around an under-performing school. In C. Day & D. Gurr (Eds.), *Leading schools successfully: Stories from the field* (pp. 9–18). London, England: Routledge.

Notman, R., & Jacobson, S. (2019). School leadership practices in early childhood education: Three case studies from New Zealand. In E. Murakami, D. Gurr, & R. Notman (Eds.), *Leadership, culture and school success in high-need schools* (pp. 169–184). Charlotte, NC: Information Age.

Owens, L. M., & Ennis, C. D. (2005) The ethic of care in teaching: An overview of supportive literature. *Quest, 57*(4), 392–425. doi:10.1080/00336297.2005.10 491864

Reardon, S. (2011). The widening academic achievement gap between the rich and the poor: New evidence and possible explanations. In G. Duncan & R. Murnane (Eds.), *Whither opportunity: Rising inequality, schools, and children's life chances.* New York, NY: Russell Sage.

Schweinhart, L., Montie, J., Xiang, Z., Barnett, W., Belfield, C., & Nores, M. (2005). *Lifetime effects: The HighScope Perry Preschool study through age 40.* Ypsilanti, MI: HighScope Press.

258 ▪ S. JACOBSON and P. MILLER

United Nations High Commission for Refugees. (2013). *Mid-year trends, 2013.* Retrieved from https://www.unhcr.org/news/press/2013/12/52b30eba6/

Waight, N., Chisolm, L., & Jacobson, S. (2018). School leadership and STEM curriculum development and enactment in a high needs secondary school in Belize. *International Studies in Educational Administration, 46*(1), 102–122.

Worldometers. (2019). *Info 5, 2019.* Dover, DE: Worldometers.

CHAPTER 14

WHAT HAVE WE LEARNED ABOUT SOCIAL JUSTICE LEADERSHIP IN STRUGGLING AND UNDERSERVED SCHOOLS AND COMMUNITIES?

Philip A. Woods
University of Hertfordshire

Bruce G. Barnett
University of Texas at San Antonio

This book is the first comprehensive overview of the studies conducted by ISLDN members engaged in examining how social justice leaders and leaders of high-need schools strive to turn around the conditions, learning experiences, and performance of their students. In this final chapter, we analyze the authors' findings, ideas, and insights about effective social justice leadership in underserved and struggling schools and communities. Our

---

Educational Leadership for Social Justice and Improving High-Needs Schools, pages 259–282
Copyright © 2021 by Information Age Publishing
All rights of reproduction in any form reserved.

260 ■ P. A. WOODS and B. G. BARNETT

analysis begins with a description of two conceptual frameworks capturing the structural factors, personal beliefs and values, and contextualized change management strategies that shape school leaders' actions aimed at ensuring the best learning outcomes for their students. Next, we examine several promising possibilities for expanding the ISLDN research agenda to increase the visibility, scope, and impact of the project. Finally, we conclude by highlighting the authors' and our own perspectives on the factors inhibiting and fostering effective collaborative international research projects.

WHAT HAS BEEN LEARNED ABOUT SOCIAL JUSTICE LEADERS AND LEADERSHIP IN HIGH-NEED SCHOOLS

To better understand the major findings and conclusions from these research studies, we employ two conceptualizations. First, Woods' (2016) trialectic conceptual framework is used to examine how school leaders address the structural issues in their settings as well as the personal agency driving their decisions and practices. Second, applying the concepts of policy assemblages and change (Ureta, 2014), we explore how social justice leaders recontextualize their environments and reconfigure their organizations to better meet the needs of underprivileged children and communities. Numerous examples from the ISLDN are provided to illustrate how these concepts reflect the actions, beliefs, and values of school leaders committed to social justice.

Trialectic Framework

We wanted to use a framework to guide our reflections on the chapters in this volume. For this we drew upon the conception of social life as a trialectic process in which there is perpetual interplay between *structure* (comprising institutional, cultural, and social structures), *person*, and *practice* (Woods, 2016). Based on the distinction in analytical dualism between structure and agency (Archer, 1995), the trialectic process distinguishes analytically within agency between the person (their feelings, ideas, values, motivations, deliberations etc.) and practice (their actions and interactions).

Institutional, cultural, and social structures are the interacting conditions within which the agency of leaders and others in schools takes place. Empowering forms of these structures—enabling institutional structures, participatory culture, and open social environments—have been identified in work on democratic and collaborative leadership (Woods, 2020; Woods & Roberts, 2018). The framework and definitions are presented in Table 14.1. This framework offers an analytical format encompassing the

What Have We Learned About Social Justice Leadership ▪ **261**

TABLE 14.1 Structure and Agency Definitions

Structure	Definitions
Institutional	Procedures, roles, opportunities, resources and their allocation, meeting structures, and arrangements in the school; enabling institutional structures are the kind of mix of institutional features that help to facilitate democratic practice and enhance social justice.
Cultural	Shared bank or library of ideas, knowledge, and values that school stakeholders draw upon and engage with in their practice; participatory culture is the ideas, knowledge, and values that foster democratic practice and attention to social justice, and can include, for example, the valuing of critical enquiry, ethical aspirations, and development of awareness of social injustice issues.
Social	Patterns and quality of relationships; open social environments are characterized by relationships that cross status and other organizational boundaries, are not hidebound by hierarchy and inflexible roles and distinctions, and display a sense of collective identity and commitment to shared endeavor, open dialogue, and mutual respect.

Agency	Definitions
Person	The individual's capabilities, motivations, values, intentions, and inner deliberations interpreting structure and others' actions and communications.
Practice	Actions, individual and collective, utilizing, working within, and influencing structures, which respond to and affect others' actions.

"policies, rules, practices, organizational arrangement, roles, and relationships [and] . . . how they marginalize some groups" (Slater, 2017, p. 17), guiding the ISLDN research. Using the idea of cultural structure, the framework additionally brings to the fore the influence of words, ideas, and values that act as reference points in the school and its context.

Institutional

Studies in this volume highlight a range of institutional structures that are seen as affecting social justice in school education. The school's institutional structures are seen as significant. Those at the wider, macro-level loom large as perceived barriers or supports to social justice in education. As has been noted previously in the ISLDN project, the influence of schools' context is well-documented (Angelle, 2017b). The reviews of ISLDN work in this volume reinforce how the agency of school leaders is influenced by these structures. There is much in these studies that supports the view that schools "cannot overcome economic injustices directly when the generative site of those injustices is not located within the education system" (Lynch, 2019, p. 303).

At the school level, institutional structures include the resources available to the school, and their allocation, which school leaders sought to

262 ■ P. A. WOODS and B. G. BARNETT

increase, target, and redistribute as part of their strategies to enhance social justice (Chapters 2, 4). Beyond resources, institutional arrangements and opportunities are also important. For example, opportunities for professional development were highlighted. These can be supportive of social justice where they directly address social justice issues by enhancing professional learning about the wider policy context and issues of inequality and social justice (Chapter 4) and leveraging developmental and growth opportunities for minority teachers, such as those with Black, Asian, and minority ethnic heritage (Chapter 13).

The institutional structures—local and macro—in which schools are situated could be seen as supports or barriers to social justice depending on their specific nature (Chapter 4). In countries such as Jamaica and Mozambique, basic infrastructure is lacking and poverty is a dominant feature of everyday life (Chapter 13). Wider institutional structures include legislation and government policies on education and social policy, as noted in the review of findings from eight education systems reported in Chapter 4. Two school leaders in Sweden—part of the research reviewed in Chapter 4—stood out as perceiving no macro-level barriers on the grounds that policy documents support the work of social justice leaders. In other national contexts included in their review, perceived barriers included:

- legislation and policy that provide little opportunity and recognition for the significant issues of inequality and marginalization;
- a narrowing of the policy agenda, with increased focus on performance and attainment, and funding tied to specific initiatives and centrally dictated initiatives; and
- wider social issues such as poverty and marginalization of specific groups (Chapter 4).

School directors in Catalonia (Spain) and in Baja (Mexico) considered that social justice problems predominantly emanated from society, rather than their schools (Chapter 10). A more specific point is made in Chapter 7, concerning the influence of neo-liberalism. The authors argue that the logic of neo-liberalism can show itself in procedures adopted in schools. Instances cited were a school in Sweden where enhancement of social justice was reduced to theme days and surveys with important issues boiled down to a checklist, completed once a year, diminishing the professionalism of teachers. In the U.S. school in the study, the accountability movement impacted upon what was taught and how it was taught in classrooms, detracting from a focus on social-emotional learning. These observations concerning neo-liberalism are consistent with understanding it not as a singular phenomenon, but as an influencing factor on education that in practice manifests in different ways and in a multiplicity of forms (Wilkins, 2019).

What Have We Learned About Social Justice Leadership ▪ **263**

For some school leaders, the implication is that the wider structural context needs changing—for example, by increasing and redistributing resources (as noted above) or, more widely, actively creating future economic opportunities (Chapter 13). We discuss in more detail school leaders' actions for social justice in the practice section below.

Cultural

School leaders participating in the ISLDN research studies attach importance to the ideas and values that permeate the school's culture. This again is about altering an aspect of structure. At the level of the school, cultures and attitudes were perceived as in need of changing (Chapter 13). This might mean a specific need relating to the circumstances and context of the schools. In one school, for example, the principal cultivated religious openness, allowing a space for dialogue through acceptance of all students of various religious and political backgrounds and ensuring that all parties were heard (Chapter 9).

Another factor identified as important was the school being imbued by a sustained focus or vision. What was seen as essential was a school culture that clearly identified the school's most important priority. In some schools, the animating idea was the emphasis given to the child and learning, keeping at the forefront a focus on meeting the needs of each child (Chapters 3, 12). In other schools, the sustained focus was described as a culture of learning (Chapter 11), high expectations (Chapter 5), social justice vision (Chapter 9), collective responsibility (Chapter 5), or a school climate that values teamwork and kindness (Chapter 7).

The cultural structures in which schools are situated (such as the values, knowledge, and ideas circulating in communities and government policy discourses) are also significant. The factors generating inequalities in the communities that schools serve are not solely material and economic (concerned with institutional structures), but involve associated values and ideas that imbue social relationships. The most disadvantaged live in a context where those with higher socio-economic status tend to "define what is socially and culturally valuable" (Lynch, 2019, p. 204). Concern about the wider, macro level cultural structure is evident in accounts of social justice leadership in this volume. For example, school directors in Mexico cited prejudice against marginalized groups and some families' resistance to school initiatives (Chapter 10); school leaders in Jerusalem and Lebanon dealt with unavoidable political and religious differences affecting students and families (Chapter 9). Equally important, are the values and ideas that give a community meaning, which are not diminished by inequality but retained as a strength. In Chapter 3, for example, we learn of indigenous Tūhourangi Ngāti Wāhiao inhabitants of a Māori village in New Zealand

264 ▪ P. A. WOODS and B. G. BARNETT

whose awareness of their culture and history infused the daily activities of school students and staff.

Analytically, we can distinguish the culture of ideas and values, though in practice these are interconnected with the social relationships in the school. Ideas and values that form a participatory culture—such as ensuring social justice as a highly valued aim, valuing each and every child, encouraging religious openness, and showing high regard for collective endeavor and kindness—help to nurture particular kinds of social relationships, to which we turn next.

Social

The importance of relationships appears in many accounts in the studies in this volume as central to understanding social justice leaders and their work. Three themes were apparent concerning the nature and quality of relationships deemed important for social justice. These concerned relationships within the school and between the school and its community.

The first theme is a school community being caring, supportive, and safe. This was highlighted in Chapter 5. In the study reported in Chapter 12, the importance of providing a safe, positive, and supportive environment to meet the specific needs of each child came out strongly: a parent from a primary school in Southern California commented that "students feel more welcome here, unfortunately, than their own home. They feel safer here. They feel more cared for, even, I want to say loved. This is why they always want to be here."

The second theme is collaboration. This highlights the importance of community within and beyond the school being characterized by collaborative relationships. It includes collaborative community building, as well as distributed leadership (Chapter 5), and collaborative practices in the development of professional networks (Chapter 4). Integral to the community being collaborative and participative are the caring and supportive relationships highlighted in the first theme. Hence, strategies were seen as important that enhanced community participation, built a collaborative culture for learning and improvement, gathered the community together (through an emphasis on fine arts in one case), educated students and teachers in acts of kindness, and demonstrated respect towards people (Chapters 5, 12).

The third theme is engaging with the community. Connecting or reconnecting the school with its students' parents and the larger school community and earning trust was seen as important (Chapters 12, 13). For example, in Nepal (Chapter 12), a school leader described his outreach policy, asking people in the local community what they wanted for their children, and another, how their school was embedded in the village. He commented, "We really do not know if we are within the village or if we are the village itself. If a small thing happens, if somebody falls ill in the village, or if anything goes right or wrong, the school supports or stands by the needs of the community." This is reminiscent of the school in Belize (Chapter 5) where leaders extended their traditional role to serve the community through home visits and social welfare checks.

All of these themes help in forging an open social environment where there is a sense of collective identity and a commitment to shared endeavor, open dialogue, and mutual respect. It creates a different kind of social structure in which the agency of teachers, students, and others takes place; one that can have a positive influence on learning. Research suggests, for example, collaborative relationships between teachers tend to have a positive impact on teachers' pedagogical skills and students' learning (Day et al. 2009; Vangrieken, Dochy, Raes, & Kyndt, 2015). The features of relationships highlighted in this section—caring, supportive, safe, collaborative communities—can be seen as expressive of love as an integrative power which challenges "boundaries and hierarchies from the perspective of human interconnectedness, cultivating the resolution to challenge these where they chiefly serve the unfair accumulation of power and privileges" (Woods, 2019, p. 173).

Person

Here we turn to the inner resources that reflexive school leaders use as part of their agency. Several qualities are apparent when examining the capabilities, motivations, values, and intentions of school leaders that are identified in the studies reported in the chapters.

The first quality we discern from the studies is clarity of purpose (Chapter 8). In Chapter 12 it is expressed more specifically as school leaders never losing sight of addressing students' social-emotional needs, and in Chapter 2, as having a strong sense of mission and moral purpose. Additionally, the importance of sustaining purpose, taking the long view, exercising patience (Chapter 8), and demonstrating determination and resilience (Chapter 9) emerged from several studies.

The second quality we identify is possessing guiding values—for example, a concern for the common good, participation, justice, equity, respect for the value and dignity of individuals and their cultural traditions, and sensitivity towards different forms of inequalities they experienced and observed (Chapter 9). Self-awareness of values also was identified as important (Chapter 2).

The third comprises personal qualities that enable school leaders to engage and work with people. These are described in Chapter 2 as skill sets that helped school leaders deal with conflict, harness support and resources, align people with school directions, and develop and implement key improvement strategies.

266 ▪ P. A. WOODS and B. G. BARNETT

The fourth quality, which appears to be particularly significant and related to the third, consists of capabilities for engaging with communities. The exploration of the ISLDN project in Chapter 2 concludes that common to the studies is successful leaders possessing an understanding of the contexts of their schools. School leaders need contextual intelligence (Chapter 11) and to be capable of community engagement and developing an acumen for dealing with the inner dynamics of their communities (Chapter 9), as well as a professional identity that allows them to confront their situational contexts (Chapter 11).

The review of findings from eight education systems reported in Chapter 4 draws attention to the importance of the capabilities, motivations, values, and intentions of those in schools other than the principal leader. A significant positive factor is the skill and commitment of staff to further the aims of social justice. However, the attitudes and capabilities of teachers could be barriers where there are issues of morale, lack of commitment to meet the needs of all pupils, limited experience of marginalization in the communities the school serves, low aspirations for those communities, and lack of awareness of wider socio-political developments.

Practice

The qualities summarized in the previous section are suggestive of a broad conception of democratic consciousness

> which is characterized by a mindset that includes independent-mindedness and a co-operative disposition, values that encompass compassion and the values of democracy and social justice, and skills and capabilities that include criticality, mindful practice, skills for resource mobilization and creative visualization for change. (Woods, 2011, p. 102)

To take an example, Fadia, a school leader in Lebanon, sees her leadership as embedded in values of openness, compassion, dialogue, and love, with a capacity for community engagement (Chapter 9). Her description of part of her action for social justice leads us into this section on practice:

> I became more visible, active in the community—eventually the whole community supported me. I was everywhere, at funerals, weddings, events, socials. I was also respectful to their holidays such as Ramadan. I even requested to meet with the Sheikh to finalize an agreement. I set out my perspective and we agreed that we would no longer offer religious studies. I told them that I needed my space and autonomy if they wanted a quality education. I also invited them to be part of the school strategic plan. (Fadia, as quoted in Chapter 9, p. 166)

The framework of a trialectic process emphasizes that school leaders' agency is inevitably interrelated with the schools' structures and structural context. An overarching theme in many of the ISLDN studies is that school leaders adapted their interventions and practices to suit the context. School leaders' agency, however, is not solely determined by their structural context because they actively employ the human capacity to "develop and define their ultimate concerns" (the things of greatest importance to them and that they most value) and to work out reflexively how they can make some progress towards these within the structural context they inhabit (Archer, 2007, p. 7). School leaders, through their development as a person and their practice, act upon structure. They are doing what they can to change structural features that restrict opportunities for disadvantaged students, families, and communities and to make them more enabling, participatory, and open (Table 14.1).

Forms of activism are evident, taking on some of the structural factors that generate social injustices and that constrain attempts to deal with them. Like "critical democratic actors," the school leaders are applying and working through adaptive strategies that facilitate conceptual innovation (helping to reframe the way people think and feel) and experimental innovation (incremental practical change; Woods, 2011). Some, as we have seen, explain how they are active in increasing and redistributing resources, lobbying the community for financial and material assistance, or creating future economic opportunities (Chapter 13). Such action can involve confronting those in power (Chapter 13) and taking risks, including risking their lives (Chapter 9), as well as engaging their local school communities.

School leaders' strategies are also directed to the institutional, cultural, and social structures of the school. This includes using autonomy and creative approaches to be innovative and, in some cases, the deliberate cultivation of disruptive strategies to give momentum to change (Chapters 5, 8). Specific initiatives, as we have seen above, include building communities that are caring, supportive, safe, and collaborative, and creating an open social environment. Other examples found in the studies were school leaders concentrating on learning and teaching through leading learning (Chapter 8), identifying specific learning goals (learning English, literacy; Chapter 12), seeking to improve the academic performance of all their school's children (Chapter 13), and supporting teaching practices (Chapter 11). Change was activated by being persuasive, highly visible and influential, acting as role models (Chapters 2, 11), demonstrating an ethic of care and empathy for all students (Chapter 9), and showing trust and confidence in staff and students (Chapter 12). All these are visible practices displaying the ideas and values that are intended to characterize the cultural and social structures of the school.

Policy Assemblages and Change

The studies in this volume show how social justice leaders and leaders of high-need school settings are sensitive and responsive to their external and internal contexts. Many other scholars acknowledge the importance of understanding contextual factors affecting school leadership (e.g., Clarke & O'Donoghue, 2016; Lee & Hallinger, 2012; Walker, Hu, & Qian, 2012) and the "multi-layered" character of these contexts (Angelle, 2017b, p. 305), which is particularly important when conducting international comparative research. It is helpful to see each social justice leader as engaging in a process of assemblage as they act, utilize, and seek to change differing contexts and their complex layers, features, and interconnections. Thinking in terms of assemblage emphasizes how a project of change works with the array of elements that exist already—using, building upon, and recontextualizing them; interconnecting them in new ways; altering what can be changed and being prepared to compromise where needed; holding heterogeneous elements together in a direction of change that can be transforming; and managing instabilities that continually emerge (Ureta, 2014; Wilkins, 2019).

Considering the processes involved in assemblage is useful in making sense of what social justice leaders are doing within these diverse and complex contexts. Two processes are suggested here, informed by Ureta's (2014) analysis of policy assemblages. One is *problematization*—turning an issue into a matter of policy—which social justice leaders are doing when they sustain over time a clarity of purpose focused on tackling injustices in education. The second involves *reconfiguration* of the existing assemblage. Social justice leaders are reconfiguring when they strengthen or change aspects of the institutional, cultural, and social structures, and the practices and the subjective awareness and capabilities of themselves and others. They are engaging, from within the dialectical process, an ongoing redesign of elements within the existing assemblage that continually interact.

From the ISLDN studies, certain principles can be discerned as guides, which acquire a specific shape, character, and emphasis in the particular reconfigurations being pursued. Based on this analysis, our suggestions are indicative, not comprehensive. One principle that emerges is seeking change through collaboration. At the same time, there is a need to deal with inequalities of power (Angelle, 2017b). Thus, a second principle is to recognie the role of "politically adaptive" leadership, which is sensitive and responds to "the ubiquity of power issues and the need to navigate differences" (Woods, 2020, p. 13). A third is the development and deployment of contextual intelligence and an acumen for dealing with the inner dynamics of communities in and outside the school. A fourth is seeking change in institutional, cultural, and social structures external to the

What Have We Learned About Social Justice Leadership ▪ **269**

school that are most important to enabling structural change within the school. A fifth is building school communities that are caring, supportive, safe, and collaborative.

Given the scale of these challenges confronting school leaders, it is not surprising that the action and qualities summarized in the ISLDN studies could be read as affirming the importance of the heroic leader. A narrow focus on that one preeminent leader of change, to the detriment of considering other actors in and beyond the school and different perspectives on social justice, has been questioned. If the individual leader pursues a single-minded, individualistic approach that is deaf to others' views, it belies the imperative that there is not one single solution and that "all social justice/educational reform efforts must be deliberately and continuously reinvented and critiqued" (Bogotch, 2000, p. 154). The ISLDN study reported by McNae (2017) highlighted the strategy of a social justice leader for reconfiguring relationships in the school to be, in her words, "collaborative, problem-solving, problem talk, bringing everything into the open, professional expectations as opposed to a very top–down model with no consultation, no control..." (p. 262). One view is that change for social justice in schools requires a combination of the "superhero" and collaborative leadership (Capper & Young, 2014, p. 162). Taking the insights of distributed leadership and realizing their implications through democratic and collaborative values and practice, recognizes that non-positional and positional leaders—teachers, students, and others—play an ongoing, active role in leading change (Woods & Roberts, 2018).

Indicators of the importance of a more distributed view of leadership and developing leadership as a collaborative process can be seen in studies reported in this volume. The significance attached to a climate of relationships that are collaborative (the social element in Table 14.1), and school leaders devising collaborative strategies for teachers and parental engagement, are testament to this. The need to provide for succession planning and sustainability also implies enabling others in and around the school to nurture leadership capabilities. Taking action, developing qualities and capabilities, and challenging structural constraints in order to advance social justice derive power from collective effort. They also require building capacity for shared critical reflexivity to sustain problematization and reconfiguration for social justice in the complex settings and contexts of schools.

FUTURE RESEARCH

Besides capturing the range of findings emerging from various ISLDN studies conducted over the past decade, many authors indicate additional activities should be initiated to strengthen and improve our understanding of

270 ■ P. A. WOODS and B. G. BARNETT

social justice leaders and leaders of high-need schools. These suggestions include broadening the dissemination of our findings to increase the visibility of the project, expanding the research methods beyond qualitative interviews, incorporating studies from non-Anglophone countries, and augmenting the scope of our analyses and research focus.

Increase Publication Outlets and Visibility

Many of the project's findings have been disseminated in special issues of journals; international journals; and books published by Information Age Publishing, New Zealand Council for Educational Research Press, and Palgrave Macmillan and presented at a variety of professional conferences around the world (i.e., Canada, New Zealand, Spain, United Kingdom, United States). In comparing the productivity of the ISLDN and the International Study of Successful School Principals Program (ISSPP; Chapter 2), the authors note the ISLDN's contribution could be improved by setting publication targets, especially in highly reputable journals (e.g., *Educational Administration Quarterly, Journal of Educational Administration, Educational Management Administration and Leadership*). In addition, efforts can be made to obtain funding and to publish and present findings in practitioner venues to broaden our impact and visibility in the field (Chapter 5).

Expand Methodological Approaches

Semi-structured and focus group interviews with school-level leaders and teachers have been the primary data sources, resulting in a set of rich case studies of social justice leadership in high-need school settings around the world. Now, however, research team members believe it is important to utilize additional data collection methods. For instance, in Chapters 2 and 6, the authors encourage conducting large-scale quantitative studies as a way to expand our findings to improve our credibility with the academic community, universities, and policy makers. This expansion also can serve as a catalyst to secure external funding. The thoughtful development, pilot testing, and distribution of the Social Justice-Behaviors and Supports (SJ-BAS) instrument (Chapter 3) in various countries is a big step in this direction to employ quantitative surveys. Chapter 10 reports the results of the first distribution of the SJ-BAS with school directors in Mexico and Spain. In addition, other approaches should be considered, including mixed method and longitudinal designs, especially ones that compare the self-perceived effects and actions of leaders with others within and outside the school (teachers, parents, community leaders, policy makers; Chapter 6).

What Have We Learned About Social Justice Leadership ▪ **271**

Incorporate Non-Anglophone Countries

As noted in Chapter 1, studies of school leaders from 19 different countries are captured in this book; however, there tends to be an under representation of non-Anglophone countries as study sites. On one hand, many of the cases reflect Western societies and cultures, including Australia, England, New Zealand, the Republic of Ireland, and Scotland. On the other hand, only a handful of cases reflect leadership in non-Anglophone countries (e.g., Hong Kong, Spain, Sweden) and developing countries (e.g., Belize, Jamaica, Mozambique). Therefore, the project's members strongly recommend involving scholars from non-English speaking countries to mitigate the potential Eurocentric bias reflected in the current range of studies (Chapters 3, 5, 6, 13). Some movement in this direction has occurred based on professional networks ISLDN members have established with colleagues from Central and South America, Israel, Mexico, Nepal, and Spain. Clearly, more studies from the African continent should be pursued.

Broaden Analysis and Research Focus

The studies reported in Part II blend findings across the two research strands and provide important cross-country comparisons. This is our first attempt to conduct cross-strand analyses; however, as the project matures, increased attention should be devoted to utilizing more nuanced comparisons. Examples include conducting studies to examine the challenges mid-career school leaders face as change agents (Chapter 2); expanding study samples to include governing boards, parents, and community members (Chapter 6); and delving more deeply into the perspectives of students (Chapters 7, 12). The prospect of conducting these cross-case analyses and interpretations will present challenges due to the variety of national and international contexts where social justice school leaders are working (Chapter 2), a situation that will become even more complex as the project expands the countries participating in the network.

Several other promising expansions and comparisons have been recommended. First, to underscore the importance of the developmental aspects of leadership, future ISLDN studies should explore the personal and professional formation of leaders using life histories and narrative approaches (Chapter 8). This is particularly relevant given the importance social justice leaders place on their personal and professional experiences in shaping their values and perspectives (Chapters 4, 9, 11). Second, similar to what transpired in the ISSPP, researchers can re-examine previously studied schools to gain a longitudinal perspective of how one or more school leaders affect teaching and learning over time (Chapter 13). Several ISLDN

272 ▪ P. A. WOODS and B. G. BARNETT

studies have utilized this long-term approach to determine how successive principals have sustained school improvement efforts (e.g., Jacobson, 2019; Jacobson, Johnson, Ylimaki, & Giles, 2009; Okilwa & Barnett, 2018, 2019).

IMPLICATIONS FOR LEADERSHIP PREPARATION AND DEVELOPMENT

There are large differences in how different countries prepare aspirants for school leadership roles and improve the knowledge and skills of practicing administrators (Barnett & Okilwa, 2020). Developmental opportunities for aspiring and practicing principals "range from receiving little initial preparation and having induction/apprenticeship experiences post appointment to engaging in formal structured programs for preparation and development" (Clark & Wildy, 2013, p. 20). The lack of preparation resources and infrastructure is particularly evident for school leaders in many developing nations (e.g., Africa, Latin America, former Union of Soviet Socialist Republic countries), who have access to isolated, piecemeal, and random opportunities for growth and development. Subsequently, many school leaders around the world feel inadequately prepared to facilitate teaching improvements and manage financial or human resources (Schleicher, 2012). To address these shortcomings, the research on turnaround schools and the findings from the ISLDN studies offer promising approaches for preparing and developing school leaders for high-need schools.

Turnaround School Research

Professional learning opportunities have been created for aspiring and practicing school administrators working in high-need, low-performing, and underserved settings. A major catalyst for preparing educators responsible for turning around low-performing schools is the University of Virginia's School Turnaround Specialist Program (UVA-STSP) developed in the early part of this century (Duke, 2015; Duke, Tucker, Salmonowicz, & Levy, 2008). Practicing principals participate in a residential program at the University of Virginia and campus- and district-level leaders receive ongoing assistance and support, including retreats in participating districts, peer coaching, an online portal of resources, and teleconferences. Although research reveals that student performance improves in many schools when their leaders participate in school turnaround programs (Duke, Tucker, & Salmonowicz, 2014), many challenges remain, especially for turning around low-performing high schools (Duke & Jackson, 2011).

The UVA-STSP launched a number of other turnaround leadership preparation programs across the United States, including the Texas Turnaround Leadership Academy, the Florida Turnaround Leaders Program, and the South Carolina Turnaround Leaders Program. A variety of other school turnaround leadership programs in the United States have surfaced with the support of the federal government, universities, and state departments of education (e.g., Colorado Department of Education, 2020; Harvard University Principals' Center, n.d.; Texas Education Agency, n.d., United States Department of Education, n.d.). These programs recruit individual principals and school and district teams who develop and refine their school turnaround plans, receive training and ongoing professional development, and monitor their schools' turnaround progress.

ISLDN Research

Conceptual Framework

Our conceptual framework of the trialectic process reflects the fact that the structures and agency leaders attend to can shape the content and instructional processes driving leadership preparation and development. On one hand, socially just school leaders need to attend to these *structural* dimensions of their work: (a) the school's institutional procedures, roles, and resources that facilitate democratic practice and enhance social justice; (b) the shared cultural knowledge and values that foster critical inquiry, ethical aspirations, and development of understanding of social injustice issues; and (c) the social relationships that connect people, provide a sense of collective identity, and build a shared commitment to open dialogue and mutual respect. On the other hand, school leaders need to attend to the *agency* of their work by (a) understanding how their personal capabilities, motivations, values, and intentions influence their commitment to social justice and (b) consciously acting to confront the inequities, discrimination, and oppression facing students, families, and communities.

Interestingly, our framework is similar to the conceptualization developed by members of the International Study of the Preparation of Principals (ISPP; Chapter 2). Their conceptual framework suggests principal preparation and development should allow leaders to strengthen their knowledge and skills across five dimensions: (a) place—context, people, community, and culture; (b) people—interpersonal, ethical, and political dimensions of working with diverse constituent groups; (c) system—bureaucratic regulations, policies, and protocols; (d) self—personal values, beliefs, and attitudes; and (e) pedagogy—leadership actions focusing on teaching and learning (Clarke & Wildy, 2016; Slater, García Garduño, & Mentz, 2018; Webber, Mentz, Scott, Okoko, & Scott, 2014).

274 ■ P. A. WOODS and B. G. BARNETT

TABLE 14.2 ISLDN and ISPP Conceptual Frameworks for Leadership Preparation and Development

Dimension	ISLDN	ISPP
Structural (macro and meso contexts)	Cultural—Shared knowledge and values	Place—Context, community, culture
	Institutional—School procedures, roles, and resources	System—Regulations and policies
	Social—Relationships connecting people	People—Interpersonal, ethical, and political dimensions of working with others
Agency (micro context)	Personal—Capabilities, motivation, values	Self—Personal values, beliefs, attitudes
	Practice—Actions focusing on social justice	Pedagogy—Actions focusing on teaching and learning

Table 14.2 highlights the similarities between the ISLDN and ISPP conceptualizations. The structural dimension reflects both the macro context (cultural/place) and meso context (institutional/system, social/people), whereas the agency dimension captures the micro context (practice/pedagogy). As mentioned earlier, principals working in high-need school settings acknowledge how these cultural/place, institutional/system, and social/people factors support and hinder their ability to lead in socially just ways. They also are keenly aware of how their own values, beliefs, and attitudes (personal/self) influence how they strive to improve learning opportunities for students who have been discriminated against and oppressed (practice/pedagogy). Together, the ISLDN and ISPP frameworks paint a consistent picture of the contextual factors affecting school leaders' thoughts and actions, which reinforces other studies acknowledging the importance of leaders' contextual acumen (Angelle & Torrance, 2019; Clarke & O'Donoghue, 2016; Lee & Hallinger, 2012; Walker et al., 2012).

Instructional Practices

Several types of instructional activities and experiences would allow aspiring and practicing principals to use these conceptualizations to better understand effective leadership practices in schools and to clarify their own beliefs and values. First, Lochmiller and Chesnut's (2017) study of preparation experiences for developing turnaround school leaders for high-need urban schools reveals the importance of providing an ongoing apprentice experience. Their analysis suggests successful apprenticeships utilize these specific design features: (a) locate the apprenticeship experience in a turnaround school setting, (b) focus the apprenticeship on district structures and procedures, and (c) situate the apprentice's work

What Have We Learned About Social Justice Leadership ▪ **275**

within the district's approved school improvement process. When educators engage in apprenticeship experiences they can obtain a better sense of the various institutional and school-level contextual factors affecting change in high-need school settings.

Second, as part of their apprentice experiences, school leaders can design and implement action research projects. Typically, action research consists of individuals or groups of practitioners identifying a problem, determining an action plan, collecting and analyzing data, and using the results to shape future action (Caro-Bruce, 2000; Hines et al., 2020; Sagor, 2000). Action research is well suited to assist participants in university, government, or state department school turnaround leadership preparation programs to determine the effects of their school improvement strategies. Because action research focuses on social change, researchers make an "explicit ideological commitment to addressing social and political problems of education through participatory research" (Hollingsworth, 1997, p. 89). Therefore, action research experiences allow school leaders to use a social justice lens to examine the factors affecting the achievement of marginalized students, student participation and engagement in school- and community-based activities, school structures that segregate students, teachers' capacities to work successfully with at-risk learners, and the influence of school culture on disenfranchised groups and individuals (Caro-Bruce, 2000; Hollingsworth, 1997; Theoharis, 2007). Through action research, school leaders reveal how the institutional and school contexts affect policies, teachers, learners, and student performance. As Theoharis and O'Toole (2011) remind us, "Future and current leaders can benefit from this [social justice] lens; it positions issues of inclusion beyond classroom membership to valuing and involving all members of a school community" (p. 681).

Finally, when examining their personal beliefs and actions (the agency dimension), school leaders can develop their self-knowledge and critical consciousness about serving underprivileged students, families, and communities. Merchant and Garza (2015) describe how preparation programs can emphasize critical self-reflection by having school leaders develop three types of auto-ethnographies (personal, professional, and transformational), prepare video documentaries capturing their transformational journey as social justice leaders, and engage in community projects with parents and students from underserved communities. These consciousness-raising activities are similar to using life history and narrative approaches (Chapter 8) to assist leaders to critically reflect on the relationship between their personal and professional experiences and their social justice leadership practices.

276 ▪ P. A. WOODS and B. G. BARNETT

INSIGHTS ABOUT CONDUCTING COLLABORATIVE INTERNATIONAL RESEARCH

The studies, ideas, and insights presented in this book reveal how international collaborative research projects can add to the knowledge base of the ways effective school leaders make a difference for students and families in challenging circumstances. However, there is far more to the ISLDN story than conducting studies and sharing findings. These researchers' journeys reveal the obstacles to and benefits of engaging in these types of collaborative ventures. To conclude our discussion, we share these challenges as well as the factors facilitating the ISLDN research team members' engagement, growth, and development.

Challenges

ISLDN members identified several issues affecting the formation and evolution of an international research project (Chapters 2, 3). On one hand, logistical and practical issues must be acknowledged and resolved to ensure productive interactions occur. Examples include communicating digitally with colleagues living in different time zones, meeting infrequently with colleagues face-to-face, recruiting and involving new members, keeping members apprised of information and decisions, and communicating with members in different languages. On the other hand, substantive issues can hinder these international professional networks. Members must understand different governance structures, policies, and practices operating in various countries and educational systems; sustain the work with little or no funding; develop research protocols in different languages; compare results across different cultural contexts; and acknowledge their colleagues work in institutions with different teaching, scholarship, and service expectations.

Factors Affecting Engagement, Growth, and Development

Similar to other international research collaborations (e.g., ISSPP and ISPP, Chapter 2), the ISLDN has managed to engage research team members for a prolonged period of time. Social justice team members (Chapter 3) acknowledge the importance of sharing their positionality and identity to reveal their biases and worldviews, creating a clear eligibility criteria for researchers to participate, and hosting network meetings in different locations to equalize travel costs and conduct school visits to better understand different cultural contexts.

What Have We Learned About Social Justice Leadership ▪ **277**

High-need schools members (Chapter 5) recognize the network allowed them to build a collaborative, inclusive culture where experienced and novice scholars were accepted for their ideas and contributions. As a result, a *culture of learning* emerged, allowing members to authentically connect with scholars with similar interests, develop their research knowledge and skills, challenge their ethno-centric thinking, and expand their understanding of how context influences leadership practice. Similarly, social justice members (Chapter 3) echo the importance of the learning environment created by network organizers, indicating they developed a *community of practice* reflecting Wenger's (2010) dimensions: (a) domain—focusing on socially just leadership, (b) community—collaboratively investing in activities and thinking, (c) practice—engaging in discursive interactions and sharing resources, (d) convening—organizing and creating a communal working space.

Many of these features reinforce the underlying elements necessary for successful international research projects (Chapter 1), such as engaging a group of committed researchers, encouraging diversity of thoughts and actions, conducting events in different locations, and developing activities and products that allow all members to contribute (Walker & Townsend, 2010). In reflecting on their experiences, members realize a fluid, diverse, and geographically dispersed network requires investing in relationships, initiating strategic conversations, negotiating conflict, coordinating physical and virtual meetings, communicating decisions, and sharing research findings and products at international conferences and in professional publications (Chapter 3).

We believe several other factors have been significant in sustaining the project for a decade. First, support from the two sponsoring organizations, BELMAS and UCEA, was instrumental in launching and legitimizing the project. Under the direction of the BELMAS director of research and the UCEA associate director for international initiatives, members of their respective organizations were polled to determine their interest in creating an international research initiative. Once the research teams formed, BELMAS and UCEA leaders reserved meeting space for members to collaborate during their annual conferences; disseminated information about the project in their publications; and provided funds to support members' participation in the networking events in the United Kingdom, New Zealand, and the United States. Although there have been changes in the original leadership of the project, other members have stepped forward and taken on these roles.

Second, several ISSPP members from Australia, Mexico, New Zealand, Sweden, and the United States chose to participate in the ISLDN. Because these scholars understood the realities of conducting and sustaining an international research project, they were instrumental in establishing the initial agreements for the project and sharing important resources (e.g., research protocols, professional networks, previous studies). These

278 ▪ P. A. WOODS and B. G. BARNETT

colleagues' initiative and commitment not only guided and supported less experienced faculty, but also resulted in products that increased the visibility and expansion of the network. As experienced international scholars, they immediately conducted social justice or high-need school studies in their own countries, hosted network events in their countries (England and New Zealand), promoted the project during professional conferences (e.g., 2016 New Zealand Educational Administration and Leadership Society Conference), and oversaw the publication of books (e.g., Angelle, 2017a; Angelle & Torrance, 2019; Murakami, Gurr, & Notman, 2019) and special issues of journals (e.g., Bryant, Cheng, & Notman, 2014; Gurr & Drysdale, 2018) reporting the project's findings. These efforts allowed team members, especially less experienced researchers, to expand the outlets where their work was published and presented.

Finally, the social connections among ISLDN members were instrumental in fostering personal and social relationships. When members physically met to discuss ongoing research projects and future plans, they also spent time together outside of these meetings socializing and engaging in other professional activities. For example, the evening before the UCEA Conference, members congregate at a local restaurant; many people bring other colleagues or friends to these gatherings. In addition, during network meetings in England, New Zealand, and the United States, members visited local schools to learn more about the educational system, the community, and how teachers and principals were shaping the learning environment for their students and families.

As we complete the preparation of this book, societies around the world are experiencing the disorientation, trauma, and deadly results caused by the coronavirus pandemic. During this time of fear, confusion, and isolation, digital platforms are keeping many people connected with family, friends, and colleagues. However, many people yearn for the social connections and relationships they are missing due to sheltering in place, quarantines, and physical distancing. With schools closing for long periods of time, teachers are working tirelessly to prepare online lessons and learning experiences for their students. In addition to these digital connections, many individuals are finding other ways to stay connected with one another by placing messages and pictures in their windows for others to see as they drive or walk by, singing and playing music from balconies where others can hear these soothing sounds, and leading physical workouts in open spaces so others can participate from a distance. Many groups of teachers are caravaning through their schools' neighborhoods, honking horns, and displaying signs of support for the children and families in their communities.

Perhaps this is one of the major lessons our societies will learn from our temporary separation from others—human connection is vital and strengthens our resolve to persist in difficult circumstances. This, too, is an important revelation from the ISLDN experience—the social and professional relationships we create with people we trust and value are what ultimately allows international research networks to thrive. We believe if the suggestions for broadening and strengthening the visibility and impact of the project are followed, the next 10 years of the ISLDN will be an exciting, productive, and rewarding journey.

REFERENCES

Angelle, P. S. (Ed.). (2017a). *A global perspective of social justice leadership for school principals*. Charlotte, NC: Information Age.

Angelle P. S. (2017b). Moving forward. In P. S. Angelle (Ed.), *A global perspective of social justice leadership for school principals* (pp. 303–320). Charlotte, NC: Information Age.

Angelle, P. S., & Torrance, D. (Eds.). (2019). *Cultures of social justice leadership: An intercultural context of schools*. Cham, Switzerland: Palgrave Macmillan.

Archer, M. S. (1995). *Realist social theory: The morphogenetic approach*. Cambridge, England: Cambridge University Press.

Archer, M. S. (2007). *Making our way through the world: Human reflexivity and social mobility*. Cambridge, England: Cambridge University Press.

Barnett, B., & Okilwa, N. S. A. (2020). Preparation programs for school leaders. In *Oxford research encyclopedia of education*. Oxford University Press. doi: http://dx.doi.org/10.1093/acrefore/9780190264093.013.628

Bogotch, I. E. (2000). Educational leadership and social justice: Practice into theory. *Journal of School Leadership, 12*(2), 138–156.

Bryant, M., Cheng, A., & Notman. R. (Eds.). (2014). Exploring high need and social justice leadership in schools around the globe. *Management in Education, 28*(3), 77–119.

Capper, C. A., & Young, M. (2014). Ironies and limitations of educational leadership for social justice: A call to social justice educators. *Theory into Practice, 53*(2), 158–164.

Caro-Bruce, C. (2000). *Action research: Facilitator's handbook*. Oxford, OH: National Staff Development Council.

Clarke, S., & O'Donoghue, T. (Eds.). (2016). *School leadership in diverse contexts*. New York, NY: Routledge.

Clarke, S., & Wildy, H. (2013). Investigating preparation for the principalship: Deliberating on possibilities. In C. L. Slater & S. Nelson (Eds.), *Understanding the principalship: An international guide to principal preparation* (pp. 25–44). Bingley, England: Emerald.

Clarke, S., & Wildy, H. (2016). Australian and pacific perspectives. In P. Pashiardis & O. Johansson (Eds.), *Successful school leadership: International perspectives* (pp. 41–51). London, England: Bloomsbury.

Colorado Department of Education. (2020). *Turnaround leadership development program*. Retrieved from https://www.cde.state.co.us/accountability/2020_2021 provideroverview

Day, C., Sammons, P., Hopkins, D., Harris A., Leithwood, K., Gu, Q.,...Kington, A. (2009). *The impact of school leadership on pupil outcomes: Final report* (Research Report DCSF- RR108). London, England: Department for Children, Schools and Families.

Duke, D. L. (2015). *Leadership for low-performing schools.* Lanham, MD: Rowman & Littlefield.

Duke, D. L., & Jackson, M. (2011). Tackling the toughest turnaround—Low-performing high schools. *Phi Delta Kappan, 92*(5), 34–38.

Duke, D. L., Tucker, P. D., & Salmonowicz, M. J. (2014). *Teachers' guide to school turnarounds.* Lanham, MD: Rowman & Littlefield.

Duke, D., Tucker, P., Salmonowicz, M., & Levy, M. (2008). U turn required: How Virginia's first school turnaround specialists are meeting the challenges of improving low performing schools. In W. K Hoy & M. F. DiPaola (Eds.), *Improving schools: Studies in leadership and culture* (pp. 137–167). Charlotte, NC: Information Age.

Gurr, D., & Drysdale, L. (Eds.). (2018). Leading high needs schools: Findings from the international school leadership development network. *International Studies in Educational Administration, 46*(1), 147–156.

Harvard University Principals' Center. (n.d.). *School turnaround leaders.* Retrieved from https://www.gse.harvard.edu/ppe/program/school-turnaround-leaders

Hines, M. B., Armbruster, K., Henze, A., Lisak, M., Romero-Ivanova, C., Rowland, L., & Waggoner, L. (2020). Action research in education. *Oxford Bibliographies.* https://doi.org/10.1093/OBO/9780199756810-0140

Hollingsworth, S. (Ed.). (1997). *International action research: A casebook for educational reform.* London, England: Falmer Press.

Jacobson, S. (2019). Social justice school leadership for academic, organizational and community sustainability. In P. Angelle & D. Torrance (Eds.), *Cultures of social justice leadership: An intercultural context of schools* (pp. 21–42). Cham, Switzerland: Palgrave Macmillan.

Jacobson, S., Johnson, L., Ylimaki, R., & Giles, C. (2009). Sustaining school success: A case for governance change. *Journal of Educational Administration, 47*(6), 753–764.

Lee, M., & Hallinger, P. (2012). National contexts influencing principals' time use and allocation: Economic development, societal culture, and educational system. *School Effectiveness and School Improvement, 23*(4), 461–482.

Lochmiller, C. R., & Chesnut, C. E. (2017). Preparing turnaround leaders for high needs urban schools. *Journal of Educational Administration, 50*(1), 85–102.

Lynch, K. (2019). Inequality in education: What educators can and cannot change. In M. Connolly, D. H. Eddy Spicer, C. James, & S. Kruse (Eds.), *The international handbook on school organization* (pp. 301–317). London, England: SAGE.

McNae, R. (2017). School leaders making sense of the 'self' with[in] social justice: Embodied influences from lived experiences. In P. S. Angelle (Ed.), *A global perspective of social justice leadership for school principals* (pp. 251–270). Charlotte, NC: Information Age.

Merchant, B., & Garza, E. (2015). The urban school leaders collaborative: Twelve years of promoting leadership for social justice. *Journal of Research on Leadership Education, 10*(1), 39–62.

Murakami, E., Gurr, D., & Notman, R. (Eds.). (2019). *Educational leadership, culture and school success in high-need schools.* Charlotte, NC: Information Age.

Okilwa, N. S., & Barnett, B. G. (2018). Four successive school leaders' response to a high-needs urban elementary school context. *International Studies in Educational Administration, 46*(1), 45–85.

Okilwa, N. S., & Barnett, B. G. (2019). Sustaining a culture of academic success at a high-needs elementary school. In E. Murakami, D. Gurr, & R. Notman (Eds.), *Leadership, culture, and school success in high-need schools* (pp. 149–167). Charlotte, NC: Information Age.

Sagor, R. (2000). *Guiding school improvement with action research.* Alexandria, VA: Association for Supervision and Curriculum Development.

Schleicher, A. (Ed.). (2012). *Preparing teachers and developing school leaders for the 21st century: Lesson from around the world.* Paris, France: Organization for Economic Co-operation and Development.

Slater, C. L. (2017). Social justice beliefs and the positionality of researchers. In P. S. Angelle (Ed.), *A global perspective of social justice leadership for school principals* (pp. 3–20). Charlotte, NC: Information Age.

Slater, C. L., García Garduño, J. M., & Mentz, L. (2018). Frameworks for principal preparation and leadership development: Contributions of the International Study of Principal Preparation (ISPP). *Management in Education, 32*(3), 126–134.

Texas Education Agency. (n.d.). *Campus turnaround plan guidance and resources.* Retrieved from https://tea.texas.gov/student-assessment/monitoring-and -interventions/program-monitoring-and-interventions/campus-turnaround -plan-guidance-and-resources

Theoharis, G. (2007). Social justice educational leaders and resistance: Toward a theory of social justice leadership. *Educational Administration Quarterly, 43*(2), 221–258.

Theoharis, G., & O'Toole, J. (2011). Leading inclusive ELL: Social justice leadership for English Language Learners. *Educational Administration Quarterly, 47*(4), 646–688.

United States Department of Education. (n.d.). *Turnaround school leaders program.* Retrieved from https://www2.ed.gov/programs/turnaroundschlldr/eligibility .html

Ureta, S. (2014). Policy assemblages: proposing an alternative conceptual framework to study public action. *Policy Studies, 35*(3), 303–318.

Vangrieken, K., Dochy, F., Raes, E., & Kyndt, E. (2015). Teacher collaboration: A systematic review. *Educational Research Review, 15,* 17–40.

Walker, A., Hu, R., & Qian, H. Y. (2012). Principal leadership in China: An initial review. *School Effectiveness and School Improvement, 23*(4), 369–399.

Walker, A., & Townsend, A. (2010). On school management–International Council on School Effectiveness and Improvement, Commonwealth Council on Educational Administration and Management. In P. Peterson, E. Baker, & B. McGaw (Eds.), *International encyclopedia of education* (pp. 681–697). Oxford, England: Elsevier.

Webber, C. F., Mentz, K., Scott, S., Okoko, J. M., & Scott, D. (2014). Principal preparation in Kenya, South Africa, and Canada. *Journal of Organizational Change Management, 27*(3), 499–519.

Wenger, E. (2010). Communities of practice and social learning systems: The career of a concept. In C. Blackmore (Ed.), *Social learning systems and communities of practice* (pp. 179–198). London, England: Springer.

Wilkins, A. (2019). Assembling schools as organisations: On the limits and contradictions of neoliberalism. In M. Connolly, D. H. Eddy Spicer, C. James, & S. Kruse (Eds.), *The international handbook on school organization* (pp. 509–523). London, England: SAGE.

Woods, P. A. (2011). *Transforming education policy: Shaping a democratic future.* Bristol, England: Policy Press.

Woods, P. A. (2016). Democratic roots: Feeding the multiple dimensions of 'leadership-as- practice'. In J. Raelin (Ed.), *Leadership-as-practice: Theory and application* (pp. 70–87). London, England: Routledge.

Woods, P. A. (2019). School organisation: Authority, status and the role of love as an integrative power. In M. Connolly, D. H. Eddy Spicer, C. James, & S. Kruse (Eds.), *The international handbook on school organization* (pp. 156–176). London, England: SAGE.

Woods, P. A. (2020). Democratic leadership. In R. Papa (Ed.), *Oxford encyclopedia of educational administration* (pp. 1–24). New York, NY: Oxford University Press.

Woods, P. A., & Roberts, A. (2018). *Collaborative school leadership: A critical guide.* London, England: SAGE.

ABOUT THE EDITORS

Bruce Barnett is a professor emeritus in the Educational Leadership and Policy Studies Department at the University of Texas at San Antonio. Previously, he has worked at the Far West Laboratory, Indiana University, and the University of Northern Colorado. Besides developing and delivering master's, certification, and doctoral programs, his professional interests include: educational leadership preparation programs, particularly cohort-based learning and school–university partnerships; mentoring and coaching; reflective practice; leadership for school improvement; and realities of beginning principals and assistant principals.

Bruce's work in these areas appears in a variety of books, book chapters, and journals including *Educational Administration Quarterly, Journal of Educational Administration, International Journal of Urban Educational Leadership, Journal of Research on Leadership Education, Journal of School Leadership, Journal of Staff Development,* and *Leading and Managing.*

For the past 2 decades, he has become involved in international research and program development, coauthoring books on school improvement; researching mentoring and coaching programs operating around the world; and presenting workshops in Australia, New Zealand, England, Ireland, and Canada. From 2008–2013, he served as the associate director of international affairs for the University Council for Educational Administration, a role intended to increase international cooperation by developing partnerships and international research and learning opportunities. He is a founding member and codirector of the International School Leadership Development Network, a collaboration of colleagues around the world examining leadership preparation and development in different cultural contexts.

Educational Leadership for Social Justice and Improving High-Needs Schools, pages 283–284
Copyright © 2021 by Information Age Publishing
All rights of reproduction in any form reserved.

284 ■ About the Editors

Philip Woods is professor of educational policy, democracy, and leadership and director of the Centre for Educational Leadership at the University of Hertfordshire, United Kingdom, and a fellow of the Academy of Social Sciences. A former chair of the British Educational Leadership, Management and Administration Society (BELMAS), Philip is a recipient of a Distinguished Service Award from the Society. He has supported the work of the International School Leadership Development Network since its inception. Philip's work focuses principally on educational leadership and policy, with a special focus on distributed, collaborative and democratic leadership and change towards more democratic environments fostering collaborative and holistic learning. Recent work includes research and leading roles in the European Policy Network for School leadership (2011–2015) and the European Methodological Framework for Facilitating Collaborative Learning for Teachers (2015–2018). Current work includes leading the Erasmus+ funded European Arts-Based Development of Distributed Leadership and Innovation in Schools (ENABLES) project (2019–2021) and the BELMAS project, Educational Leadership, Management and Administration in the United Kingdom: A Comparative Review (2018–2020). Recent publications include: "Democratic Leadership" (coauthored with Joy Jarvis, Amanda Roberts, and Suzanne Culshaw) and "School Leadership Preparation and Development in England," both chapters in R. Papa (Ed.), *Oxford Encyclopedia of Educational Administration,* Oxford University Press (2020); "School Organisation: Authority Status and the Role of Love as an Integrative Power," in Connelly et al. (Eds.), *The iInternational Handbook on School Organization,* SAGE (2019); and (coauthored with Dr Amanda Roberts) *Collaborative School Leadership: A Critical Guide* published by SAGE (2018).